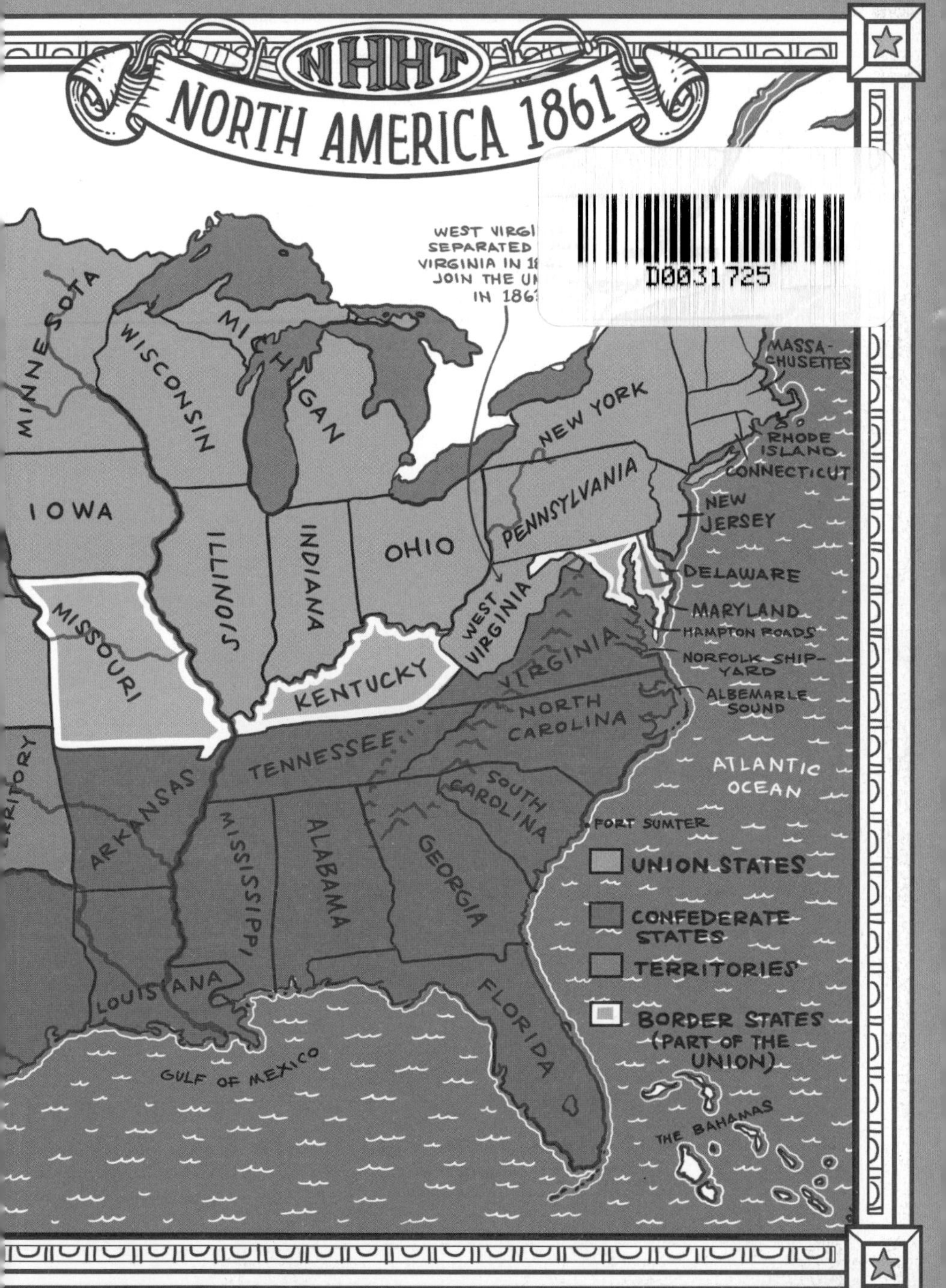
NHHT
NORTH AMERICA 1861
MINNESOTA
WISCONSIN
MICHIGAN
IOWA
ILLINOIS
INDIANA
OHIO
NEW YORK
PENNSYLVANIA
MASSA-CHUSETTES
RHODE ISLAND
CONNECTICUT
NEW JERSEY
DELAWARE
MARYLAND
HAMPTON ROADS
NORFOLK SHIP-YARD
ALBEMARLE SOUND
WEST VIRGINIA
VIRGINIA
MISSOURI
KENTUCKY
TENNESSEE
NORTH CAROLINA
SOUTH CAROLINA
ARKANSAS
MISSISSIPPI
ALABAMA
GEORGIA
LOUISIANA
FLORIDA
RRITORY
ATLANTIC OCEAN
PORT SUMTER
GULF OF MEXICO
THE BAHAMAS
UNION STATES
CONFEDERATE STATES
TERRITORIES
BORDER STATES (PART OF THE UNION)

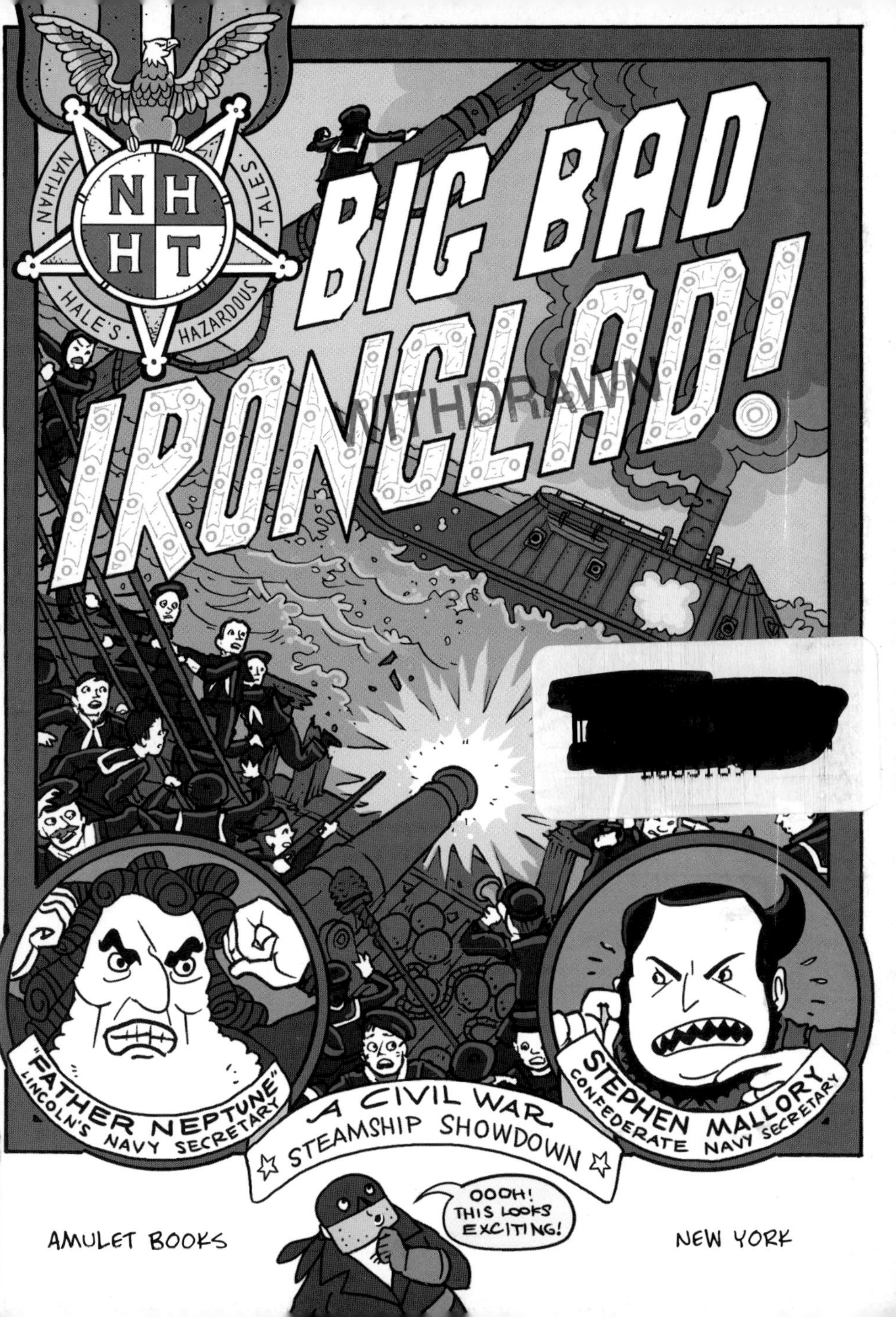
NATHAN HALE'S HAZARDOUS TALES
NH HT
BIG BAD IRONCLAD!
"FATHER NEPTUNE" LINCOLN'S NAVY SECRETARY
STEPHEN MALLORY CONFEDERATE NAVY SECRETARY
A CIVIL WAR STEAMSHIP SHOWDOWN
OOOH! THIS LOOKS EXCITING!

AMULET BOOKS NEW YORK

CATALOGING-IN-PUBLICATION DATA HAS BEEN APPLIED FOR
AND MAY BE OBTAINED FROM THE LIBRARY OF CONGRESS.
ISBN: 978-1-4197-0395-9

TEXT AND ILLUSTRATIONS COPYRIGHT © 2012 NATHAN HALE
BOOK DESIGN BY NATHAN HALE AND CHAD W. BECKERMAN

PRINTED AND BOUND IN CHINA
18

ABRAMS The Art of Books
195 Broadway, New York, NY 10007
abramsbooks.com

TO BENNY

NHHT

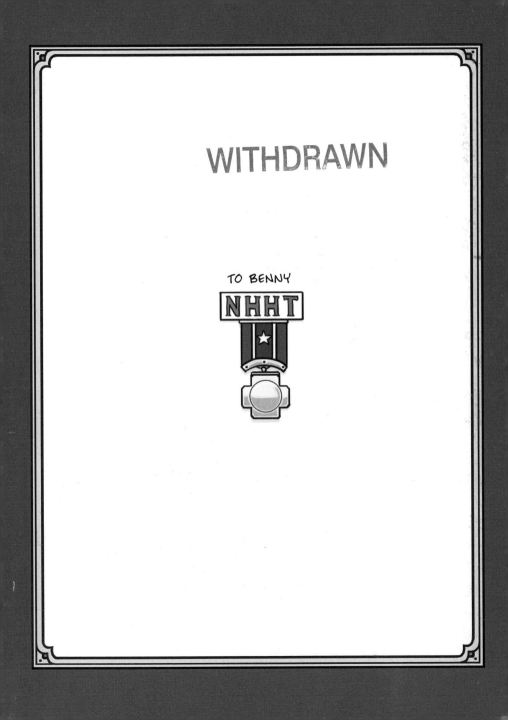

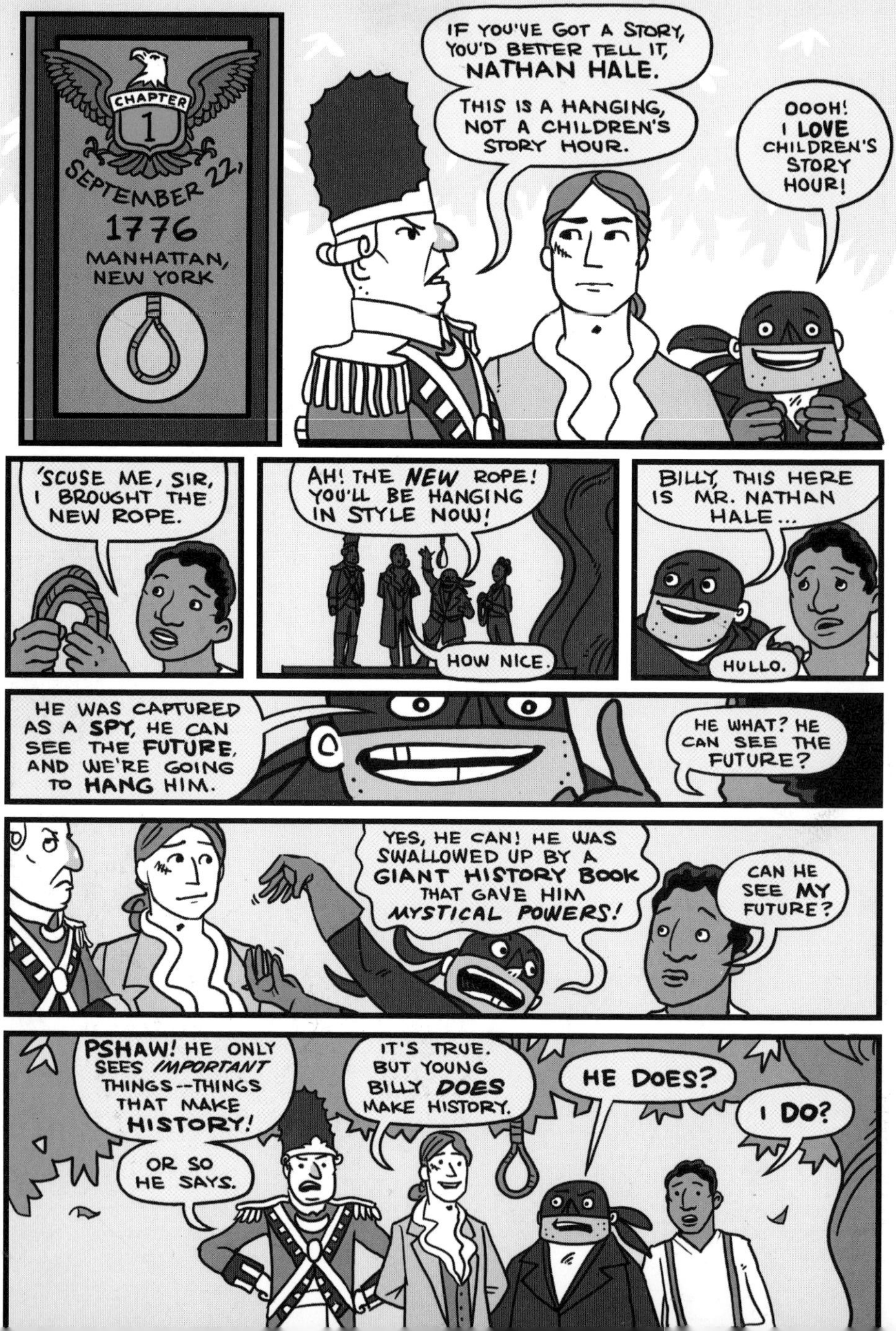
CHAPTER 1
SEPTEMBER 22, 1776
MANHATTAN, NEW YORK
IF YOU'VE GOT A STORY, YOU'D BETTER TELL IT, NATHAN HALE.
THIS IS A HANGING, NOT A CHILDREN'S STORY HOUR.
OOOH! I LOVE CHILDREN'S STORY HOUR!
'SCUSE ME, SIR, I BROUGHT THE NEW ROPE.
AH! THE NEW ROPE! YOU'LL BE HANGING IN STYLE NOW!
HOW NICE.
BILLY, THIS HERE IS MR. NATHAN HALE...
HULLO.
HE WAS CAPTURED AS A SPY, HE CAN SEE THE FUTURE, AND WE'RE GOING TO HANG HIM.
HE WHAT? HE CAN SEE THE FUTURE?
YES, HE CAN! HE WAS SWALLOWED UP BY A GIANT HISTORY BOOK THAT GAVE HIM MYSTICAL POWERS!
CAN HE SEE MY FUTURE?
PSHAW! HE ONLY SEES IMPORTANT THINGS--THINGS THAT MAKE HISTORY!
OR SO HE SAYS.
IT'S TRUE. BUT YOUNG BILLY DOES MAKE HISTORY.
HE DOES?
I DO?

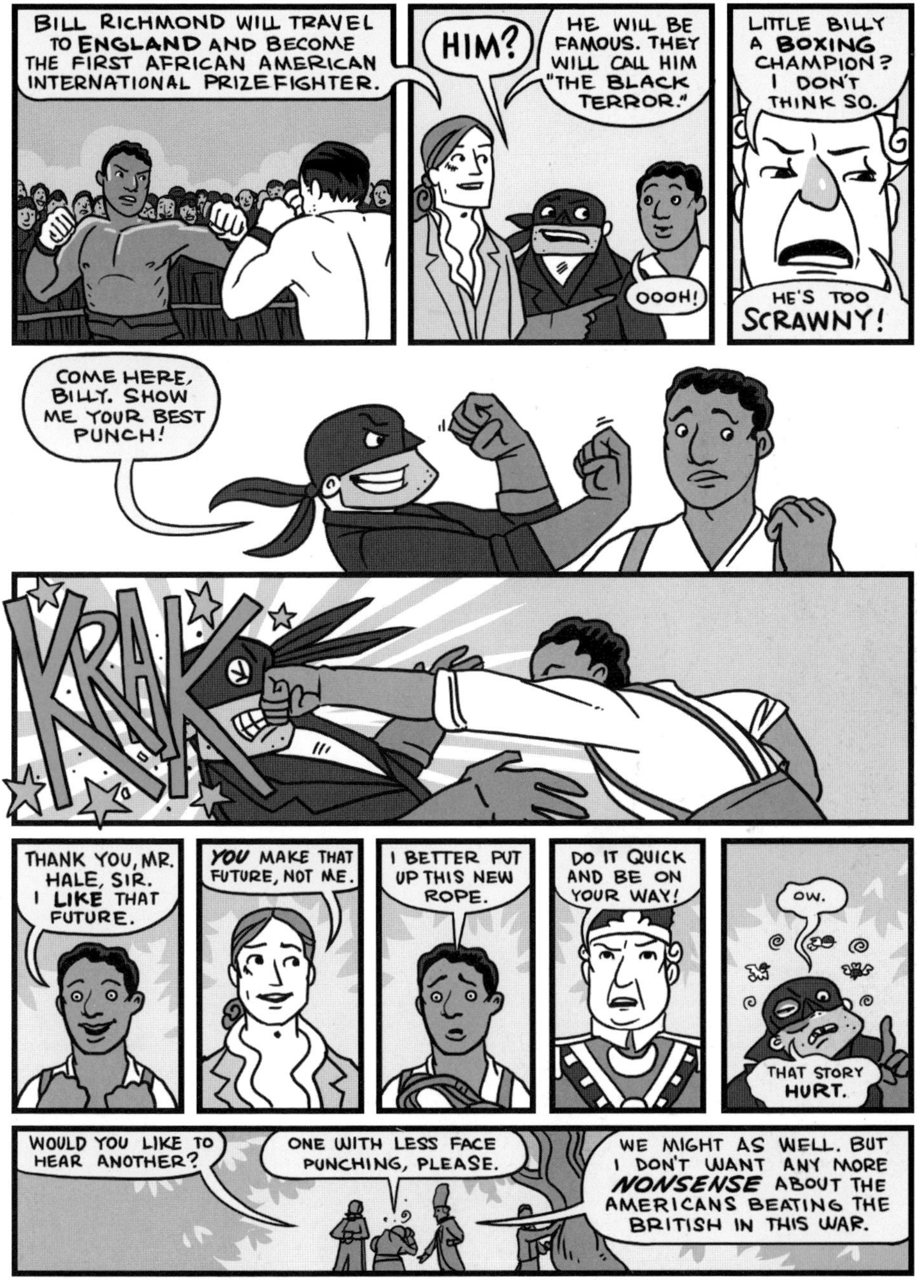
BILL RICHMOND WILL TRAVEL TO ENGLAND AND BECOME THE FIRST AFRICAN AMERICAN INTERNATIONAL PRIZEFIGHTER.
HIM?
HE WILL BE FAMOUS. THEY WILL CALL HIM "THE BLACK TERROR."
OOOH!
LITTLE BILLY A BOXING CHAMPION? I DON'T THINK SO.
HE'S TOO SCRAWNY!
COME HERE, BILLY. SHOW ME YOUR BEST PUNCH!
KRAK
THANK YOU, MR. HALE, SIR. I LIKE THAT FUTURE.
YOU MAKE THAT FUTURE, NOT ME.
I BETTER PUT UP THIS NEW ROPE.
DO IT QUICK AND BE ON YOUR WAY!
OW.
THAT STORY HURT.
WOULD YOU LIKE TO HEAR ANOTHER?
ONE WITH LESS FACE PUNCHING, PLEASE.
WE MIGHT AS WELL. BUT I DON'T WANT ANY MORE NONSENSE ABOUT THE AMERICANS BEATING THE BRITISH IN THIS WAR.

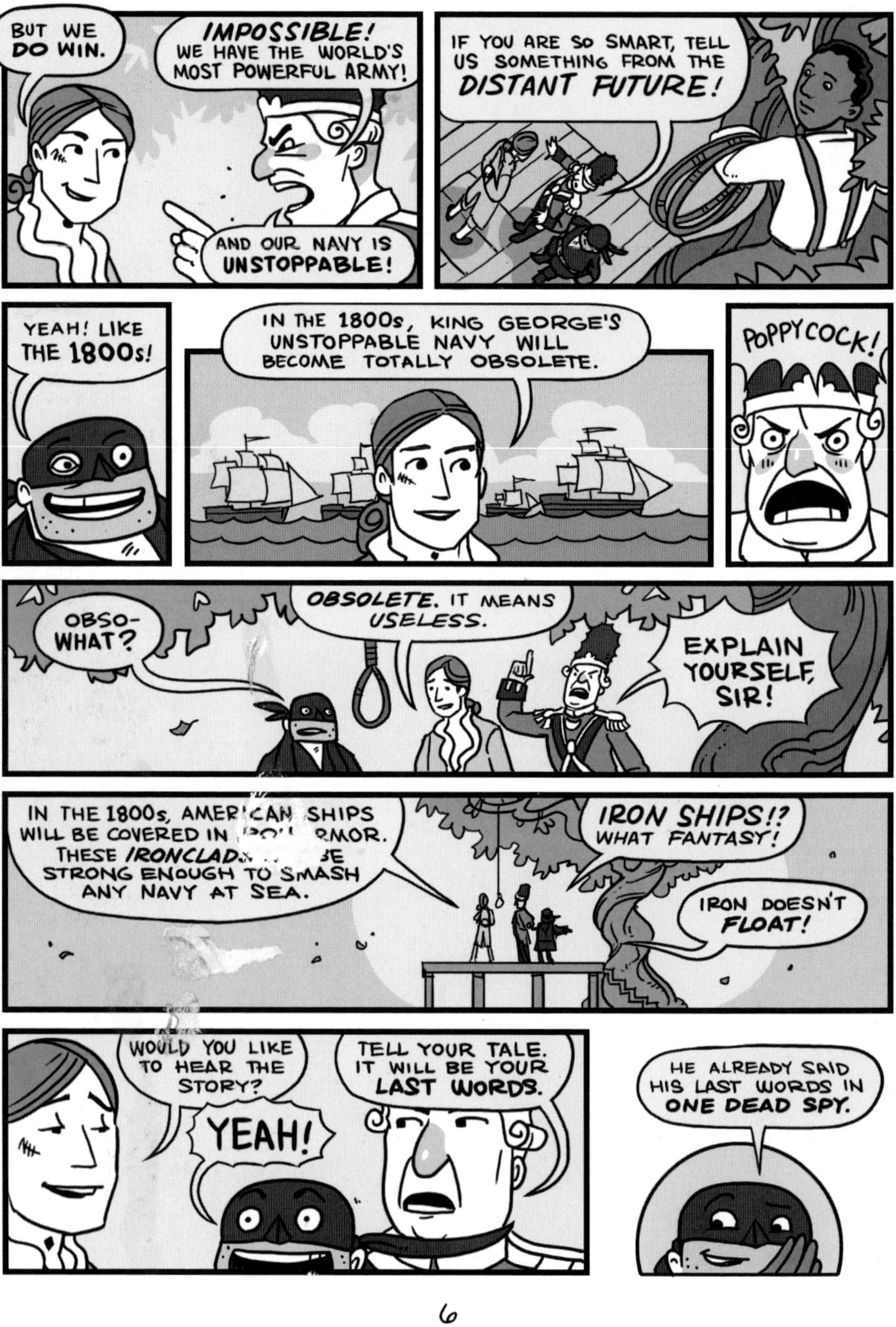

BUT WE DO WIN.
IMPOSSIBLE! WE HAVE THE WORLD'S MOST POWERFUL ARMY!
AND OUR NAVY IS UNSTOPPABLE!
IF YOU ARE SO SMART, TELL US SOMETHING FROM THE DISTANT FUTURE!
YEAH! LIKE THE 1800s!
IN THE 1800s, KING GEORGE'S UNSTOPPABLE NAVY WILL BECOME TOTALLY OBSOLETE.
POPPYCOCK!
OBSO-WHAT?
OBSOLETE. IT MEANS USELESS.
EXPLAIN YOURSELF, SIR!
IN THE 1800s, AMER CAN SHIPS
WILL BE COVERED IN RMOR.
THESE IRONCLADS BE
STRONG ENOUGH TO SMASH ANY NAVY AT SEA.
IRON SHIPS!? WHAT FANTASY!
IRON DOESN'T FLOAT!
WOULD YOU LIKE TO HEAR THE STORY?
YEAH!
TELL YOUR TALE. IT WILL BE YOUR LAST WORDS.
HE ALREADY SAID HIS LAST WORDS IN ONE DEAD SPY.

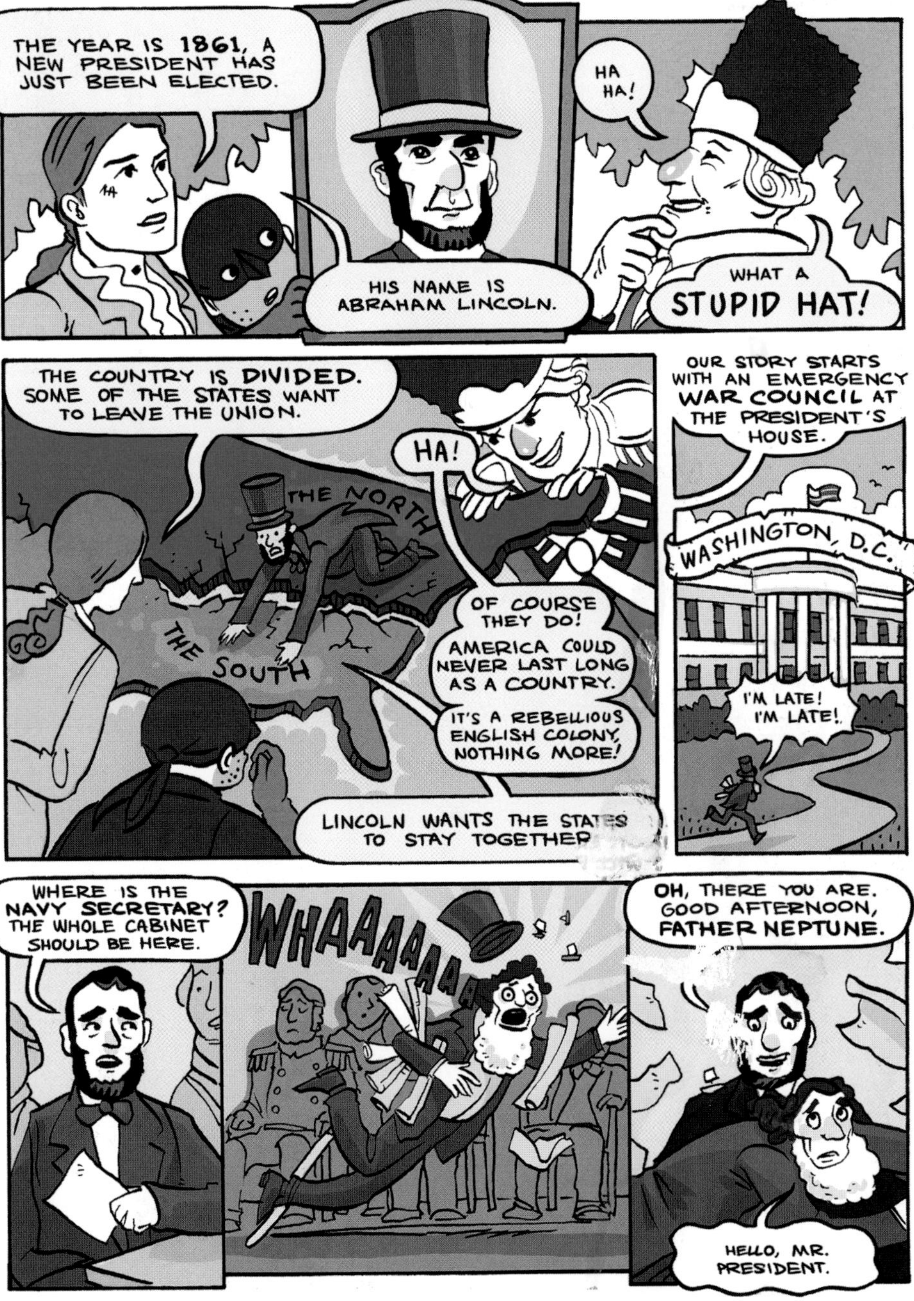
THE YEAR IS 1861, A NEW PRESIDENT HAS JUST BEEN ELECTED.
HIS NAME IS ABRAHAM LINCOLN.
HA HA!
WHAT A STUPID HAT!
THE COUNTRY IS DIVIDED. SOME OF THE STATES WANT TO LEAVE THE UNION.
HA!
THE NORTH
THE SOUTH
OF COURSE THEY DO!
AMERICA COULD NEVER LAST LONG AS A COUNTRY.
IT'S A REBELLIOUS ENGLISH COLONY, NOTHING MORE!
LINCOLN WANTS THE STATES TO STAY TOGETHER
OUR STORY STARTS WITH AN EMERGENCY WAR COUNCIL AT THE PRESIDENT'S HOUSE.
WASHINGTON, D.C.
I'M LATE! I'M LATE!
WHERE IS THE NAVY SECRETARY? THE WHOLE CABINET SHOULD BE HERE.
WHAAAAAAAA
OH, THERE YOU ARE. GOOD AFTERNOON, FATHER NEPTUNE.
HELLO, MR. PRESIDENT.

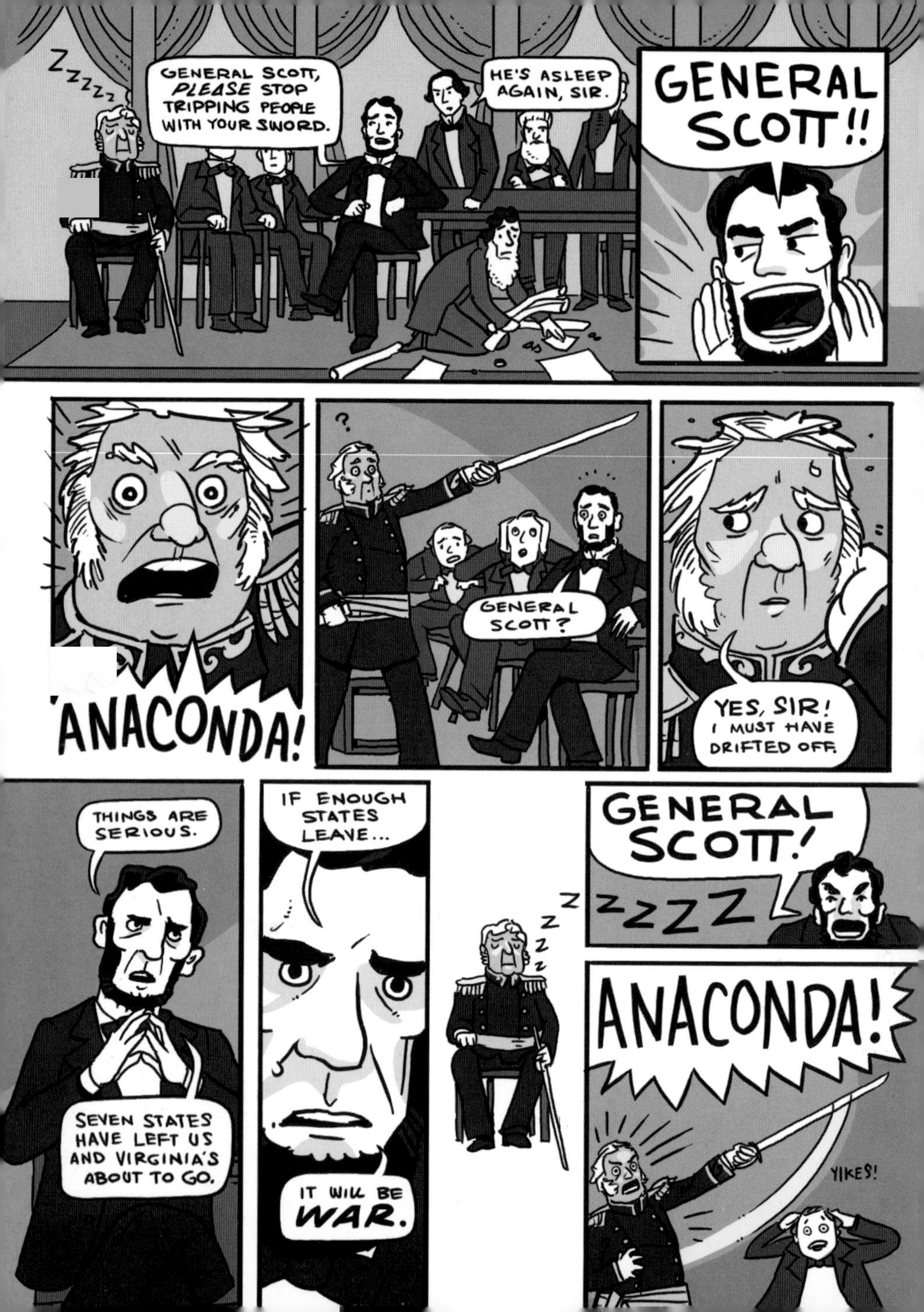
ZZZZZ
GENERAL SCOTT, PLEASE STOP TRIPPING PEOPLE WITH YOUR SWORD.
HE'S ASLEEP AGAIN, SIR.
GENERAL SCOTT!!
ANACONDA!
?
GENERAL SCOTT?
YES, SIR! I MUST HAVE DRIFTED OFF.
THINGS ARE SERIOUS.
SEVEN STATES HAVE LEFT US AND VIRGINIA'S ABOUT TO GO.
IF ENOUGH STATES LEAVE...
IT WILL BE WAR.
ZZZZZZZ
GENERAL SCOTT!
ANACONDA!
YIKES!

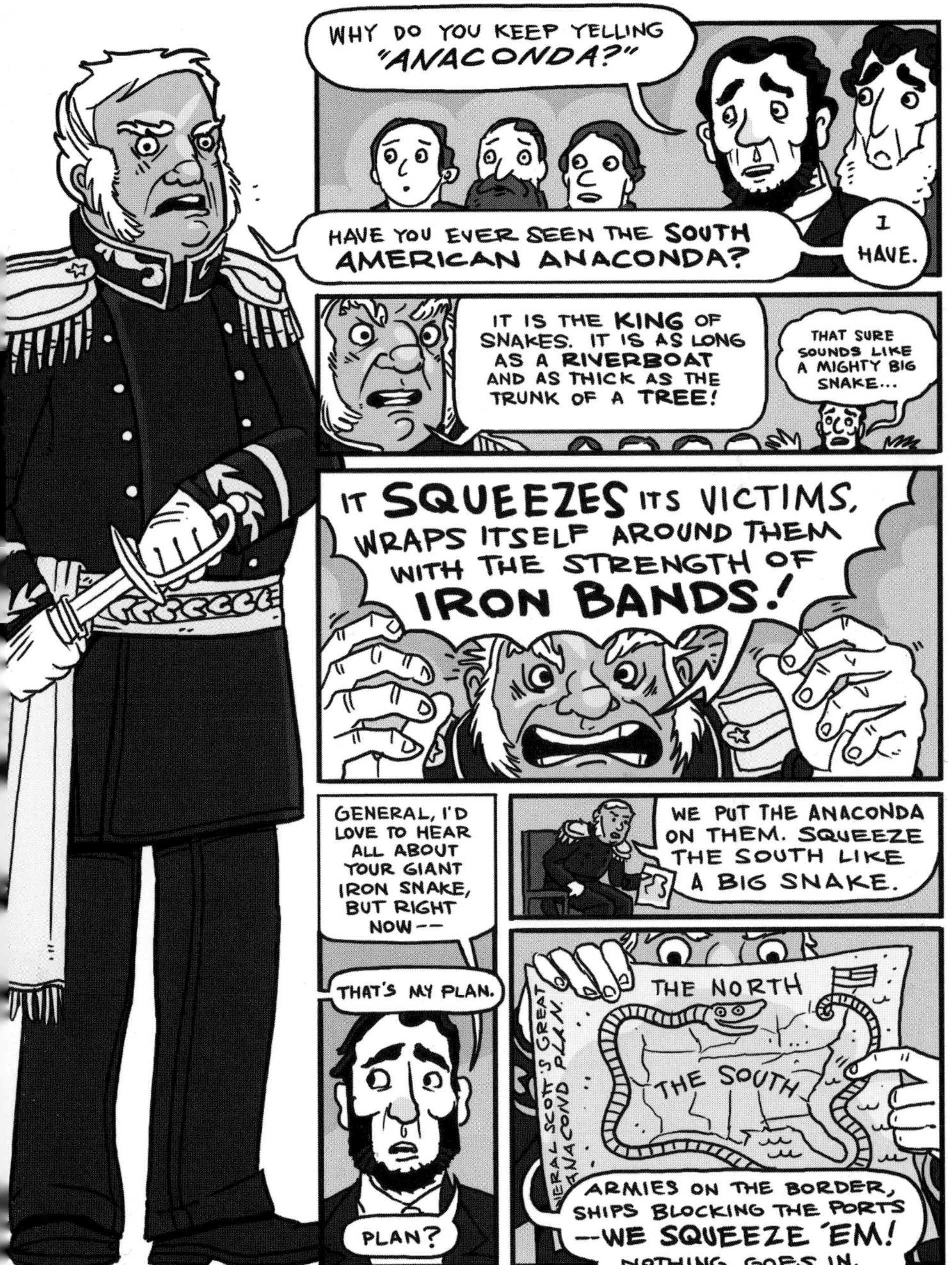

WHY DO YOU KEEP YELLING "ANACONDA?"
HAVE YOU EVER SEEN THE SOUTH AMERICAN ANACONDA?
I HAVE.
IT IS THE KING OF SNAKES. IT IS AS LONG AS A RIVERBOAT AND AS THICK AS THE TRUNK OF A TREE!
THAT SURE SOUNDS LIKE A MIGHTY BIG SNAKE...
IT SQUEEZES ITS VICTIMS, WRAPS ITSELF AROUND THEM WITH THE STRENGTH OF IRON BANDS!
GENERAL, I'D LOVE TO HEAR ALL ABOUT YOUR GIANT IRON SNAKE, BUT RIGHT NOW--
WE PUT THE ANACONDA ON THEM. SQUEEZE THE SOUTH LIKE A BIG SNAKE.
THAT'S MY PLAN.
PLAN?
ERAL SCOTT'S GREAT ANACOND PLAN
THE NORTH
THE SOUTH
ARMIES ON THE BORDER, SHIPS BLOCKING THE PORTS --WE SQUEEZE 'EM!
NOTHING GOES IN, NOTHING COMES OUT.

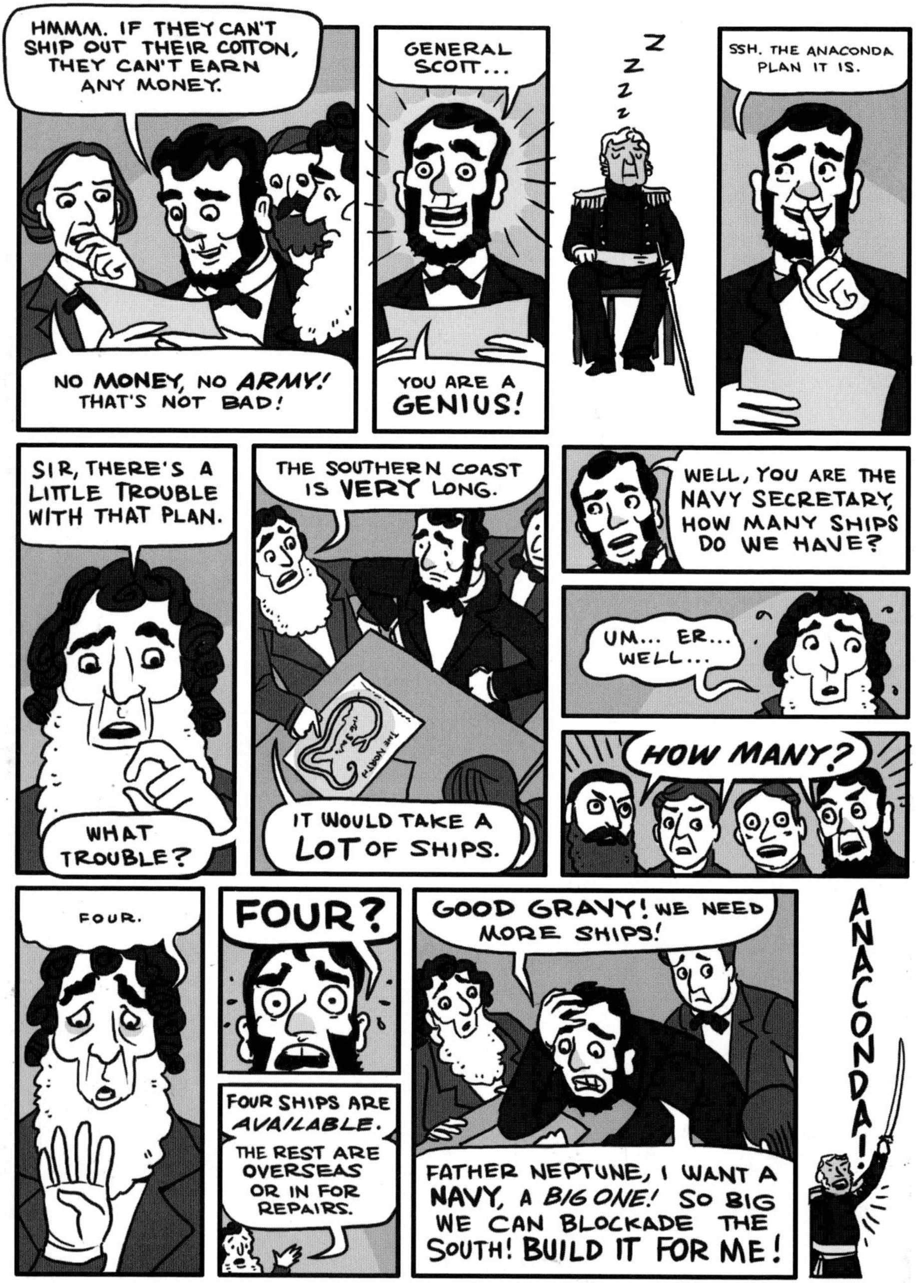
HMMM. IF THEY CAN'T SHIP OUT THEIR COTTON, THEY CAN'T EARN ANY MONEY.
NO MONEY, NO ARMY! THAT'S NOT BAD!
GENERAL SCOTT...
YOU ARE A GENIUS!
Z Z Z Z
SSH. THE ANACONDA PLAN IT IS.
SIR, THERE'S A LITTLE TROUBLE WITH THAT PLAN.
WHAT TROUBLE?
THE SOUTHERN COAST IS VERY LONG.
IT WOULD TAKE A LOT OF SHIPS.
WELL, YOU ARE THE NAVY SECRETARY, HOW MANY SHIPS DO WE HAVE?
UM... ER... WELL...
HOW MANY?
FOUR.
FOUR?
FOUR SHIPS ARE AVAILABLE.
THE REST ARE OVERSEAS OR IN FOR REPAIRS.
GOOD GRAVY! WE NEED MORE SHIPS!
FATHER NEPTUNE, I WANT A NAVY, A BIG ONE! SO BIG WE CAN BLOCKADE THE SOUTH! BUILD IT FOR ME!
ANACONDA!

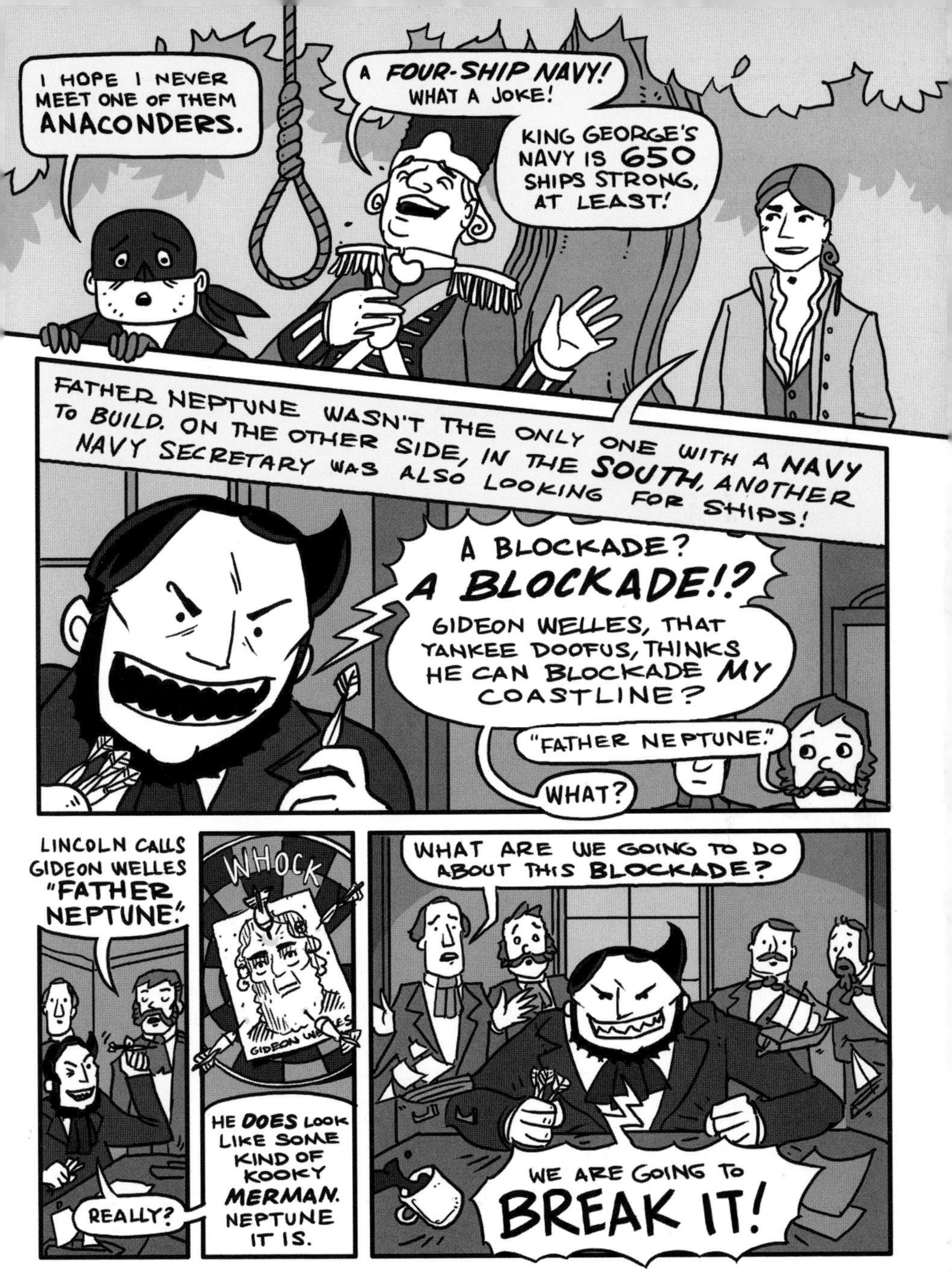
I HOPE I NEVER MEET ONE OF THEM ANACONDERS.
A FOUR-SHIP NAVY! WHAT A JOKE!
KING GEORGE'S NAVY IS 650 SHIPS STRONG, AT LEAST!
FATHER NEPTUNE WASN'T THE ONLY ONE WITH A NAVY TO BUILD. ON THE OTHER SIDE, IN THE SOUTH, ANOTHER NAVY SECRETARY WAS ALSO LOOKING FOR SHIPS!
A BLOCKADE? A BLOCKADE!? GIDEON WELLES, THAT YANKEE DOOFUS, THINKS HE CAN BLOCKADE MY COASTLINE?
"FATHER NEPTUNE."
WHAT?
LINCOLN CALLS GIDEON WELLES "FATHER NEPTUNE."
REALLY?
WHOCK
GIDEON WELLES
HE DOES LOOK LIKE SOME KIND OF KOOKY MERMAN. NEPTUNE IT IS.
WHAT ARE WE GOING TO DO ABOUT THIS BLOCKADE?
WE ARE GOING TO BREAK IT!

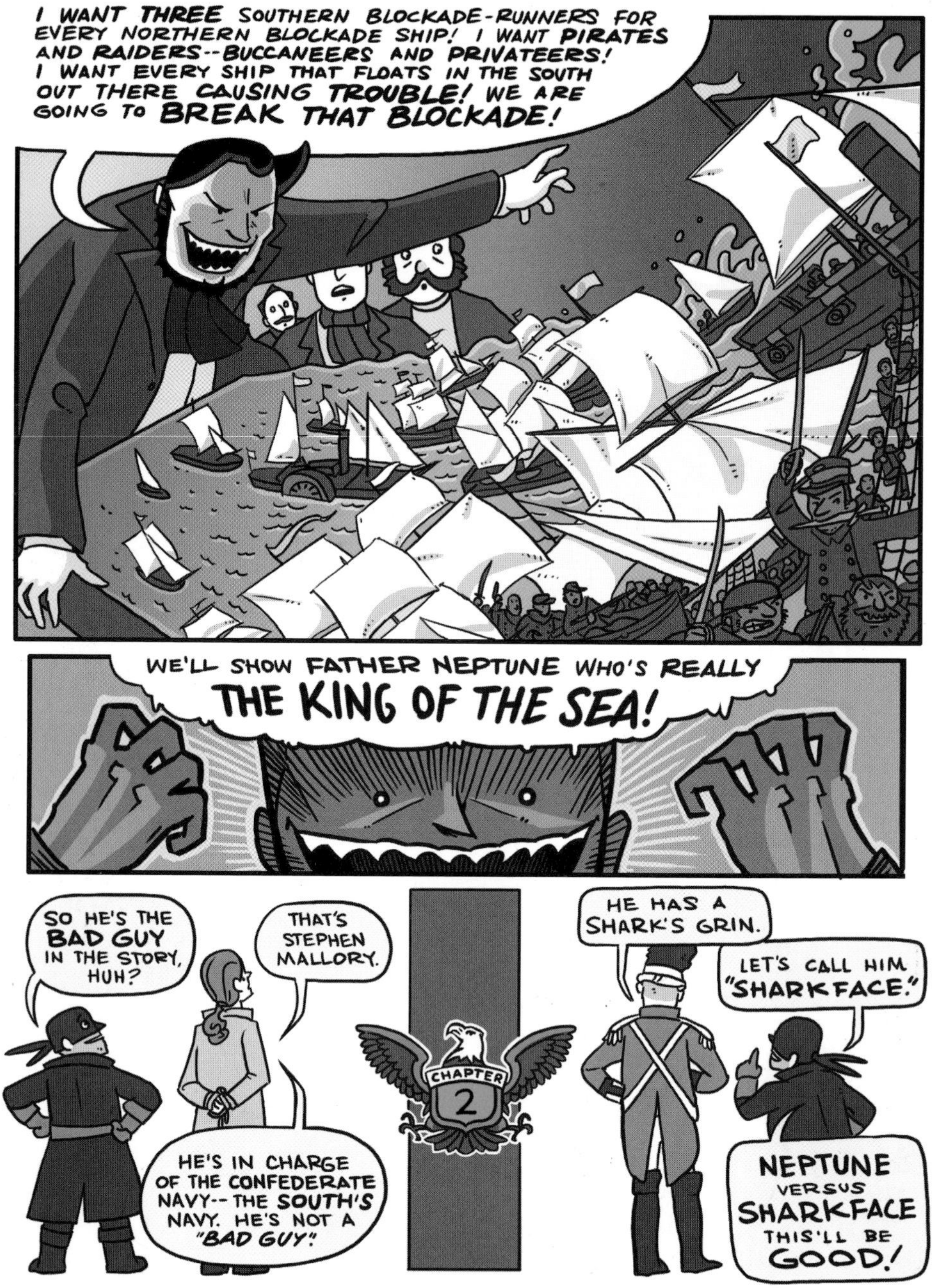
I WANT THREE SOUTHERN BLOCKADE-RUNNERS FOR EVERY NORTHERN BLOCKADE SHIP! I WANT PIRATES AND RAIDERS--BUCCANEERS AND PRIVATEERS! I WANT EVERY SHIP THAT FLOATS IN THE SOUTH OUT THERE CAUSING TROUBLE! WE ARE GOING TO BREAK THAT BLOCKADE!
WE'LL SHOW FATHER NEPTUNE WHO'S REALLY THE KING OF THE SEA!
SO HE'S THE BAD GUY IN THE STORY, HUH?
THAT'S STEPHEN MALLORY.
HE'S IN CHARGE OF THE CONFEDERATE NAVY-- THE SOUTH'S NAVY. HE'S NOT A "BAD GUY".
CHAPTER 2
HE HAS A SHARK'S GRIN.
LET'S CALL HIM "SHARKFACE."
NEPTUNE VERSUS SHARKFACE THIS'LL BE GOOD!

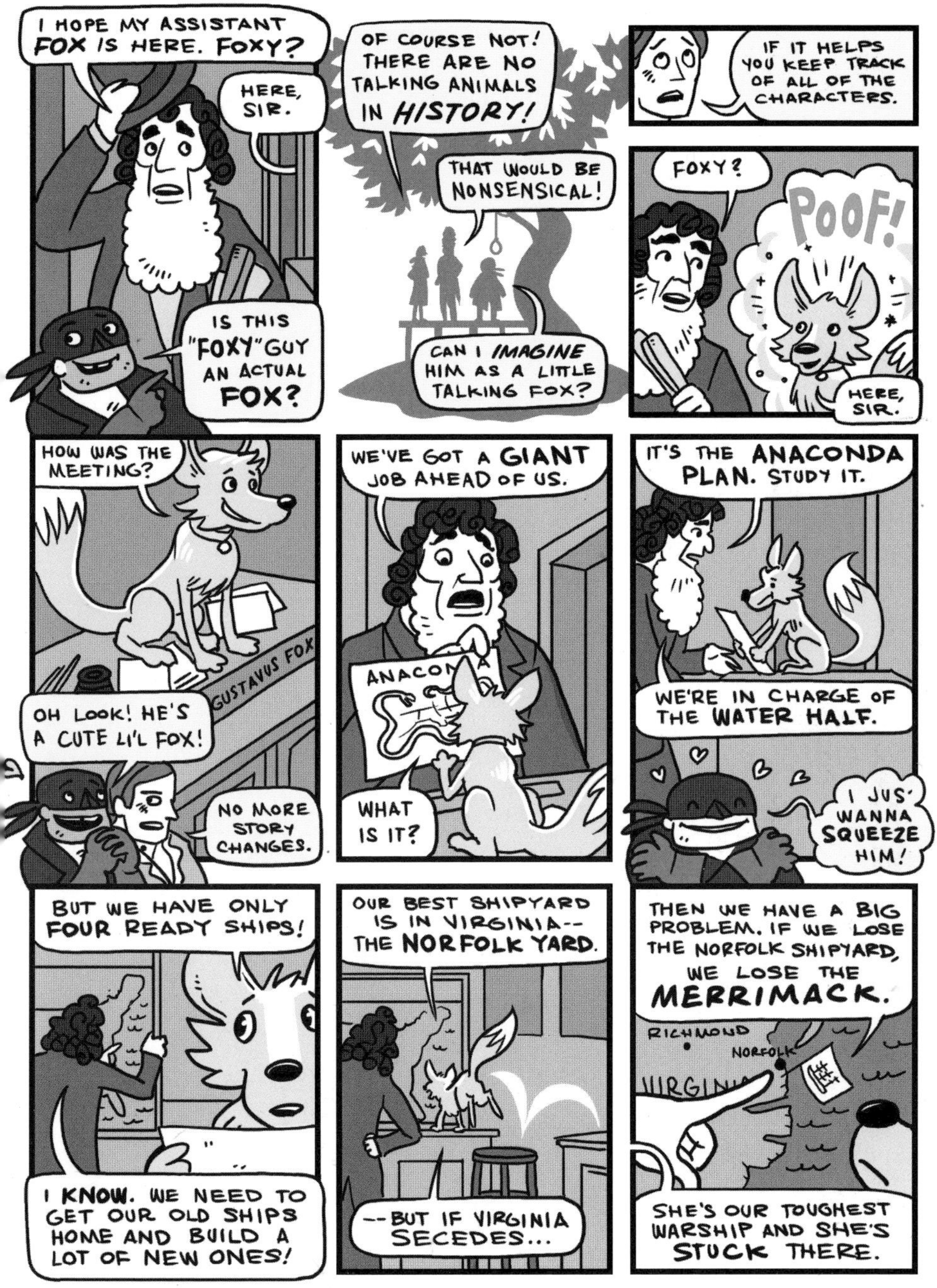

I HOPE MY ASSISTANT FOX IS HERE. FOXY?
HERE, SIR.
IS THIS "FOXY" GUY AN ACTUAL FOX?
OF COURSE NOT! THERE ARE NO TALKING ANIMALS IN HISTORY!
THAT WOULD BE NONSENSICAL!
CAN I IMAGINE HIM AS A LITTLE TALKING FOX?
IF IT HELPS YOU KEEP TRACK OF ALL OF THE CHARACTERS.
FOXY?
POOF!
HERE, SIR.
HOW WAS THE MEETING?
GUSTAVUS FOX
OH LOOK! HE'S A CUTE LI'L FOX!
NO MORE STORY CHANGES.
WE'VE GOT A GIANT JOB AHEAD OF US.
ANACONDA
WHAT IS IT?
IT'S THE ANACONDA PLAN. STUDY IT.
WE'RE IN CHARGE OF THE WATER HALF.
I JUS' WANNA SQUEEZE HIM!
BUT WE HAVE ONLY FOUR READY SHIPS!
I KNOW. WE NEED TO GET OUR OLD SHIPS HOME AND BUILD A LOT OF NEW ONES!
OUR BEST SHIPYARD IS IN VIRGINIA-- THE NORFOLK YARD.
--BUT IF VIRGINIA SECEDES...
THEN WE HAVE A BIG PROBLEM. IF WE LOSE THE NORFOLK SHIPYARD, WE LOSE THE MERRIMACK.
RICHMOND
NORFOLK
VIRGINIA
SHE'S OUR TOUGHEST WARSHIP AND SHE'S STUCK THERE.

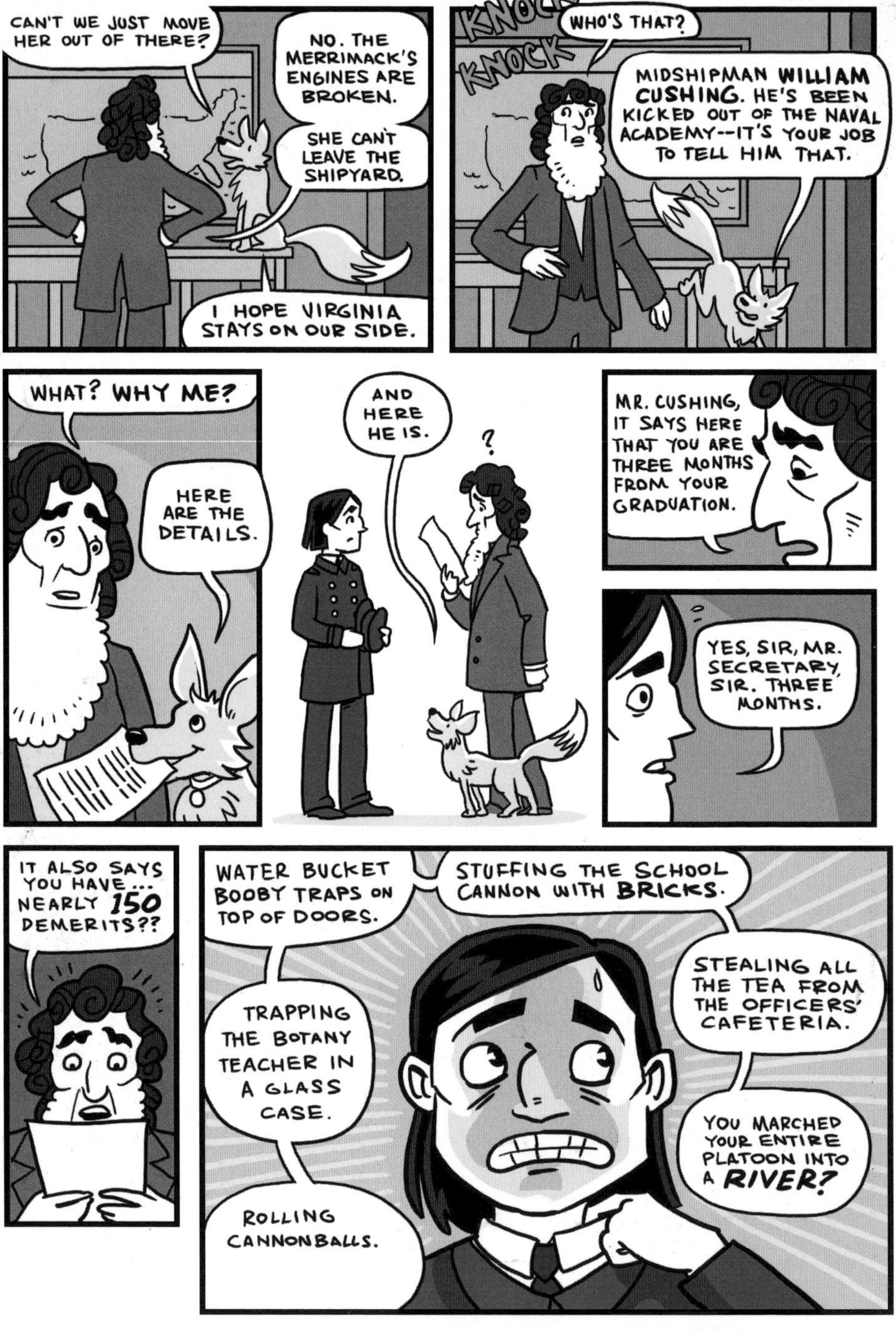
CAN'T WE JUST MOVE HER OUT OF THERE?
NO. THE MERRIMACK'S ENGINES ARE BROKEN.
SHE CAN'T LEAVE THE SHIPYARD.
I HOPE VIRGINIA STAYS ON OUR SIDE.
KNOCK
KNOCK
WHO'S THAT?
MIDSHIPMAN WILLIAM CUSHING. HE'S BEEN KICKED OUT OF THE NAVAL ACADEMY--IT'S YOUR JOB TO TELL HIM THAT.
WHAT? WHY ME?
HERE ARE THE DETAILS.
AND HERE HE IS.
?
MR. CUSHING, IT SAYS HERE THAT YOU ARE THREE MONTHS FROM YOUR GRADUATION.
YES, SIR, MR. SECRETARY, SIR. THREE MONTHS.
IT ALSO SAYS YOU HAVE... NEARLY 150 DEMERITS??
WATER BUCKET BOOBY TRAPS ON TOP OF DOORS.
STUFFING THE SCHOOL CANNON WITH BRICKS.
TRAPPING THE BOTANY TEACHER IN A GLASS CASE.
STEALING ALL THE TEA FROM THE OFFICERS' CAFETERIA.
ROLLING CANNONBALLS.
YOU MARCHED YOUR ENTIRE PLATOON INTO A RIVER?

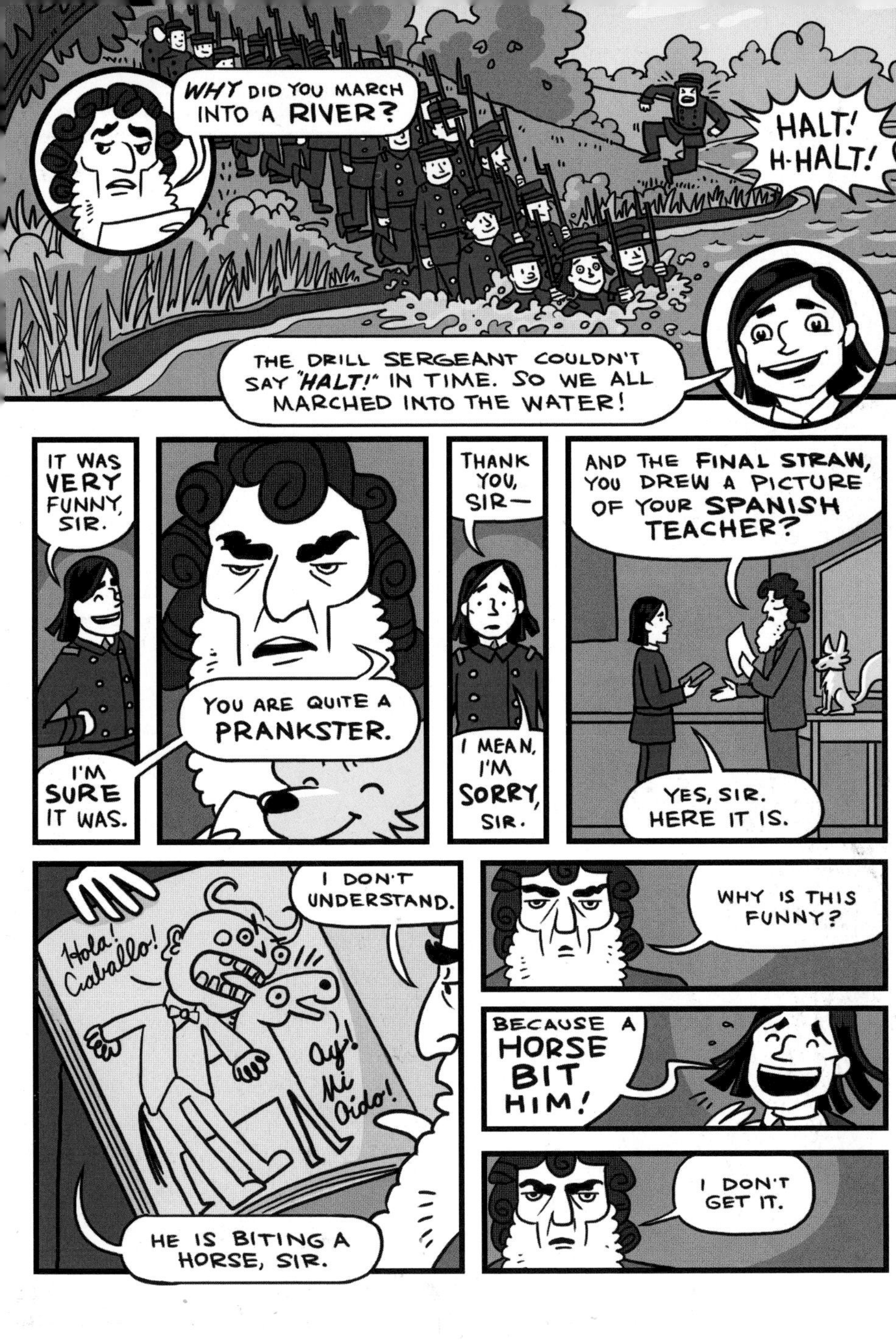
WHY DID YOU MARCH INTO A RIVER?
HALT! H-HALT!
THE DRILL SERGEANT COULDN'T SAY "HALT!" IN TIME. SO WE ALL MARCHED INTO THE WATER!
IT WAS VERY FUNNY, SIR.
I'M SURE IT WAS.
YOU ARE QUITE A PRANKSTER.
THANK YOU, SIR—
I MEAN, I'M SORRY, SIR.
AND THE FINAL STRAW, YOU DREW A PICTURE OF YOUR SPANISH TEACHER?
YES, SIR. HERE IT IS.
Hola! Caballo!
Ay! Mi Oído!
I DON'T UNDERSTAND.
HE IS BITING A HORSE, SIR.
WHY IS THIS FUNNY?
BECAUSE A HORSE BIT HIM!
I DON'T GET IT.

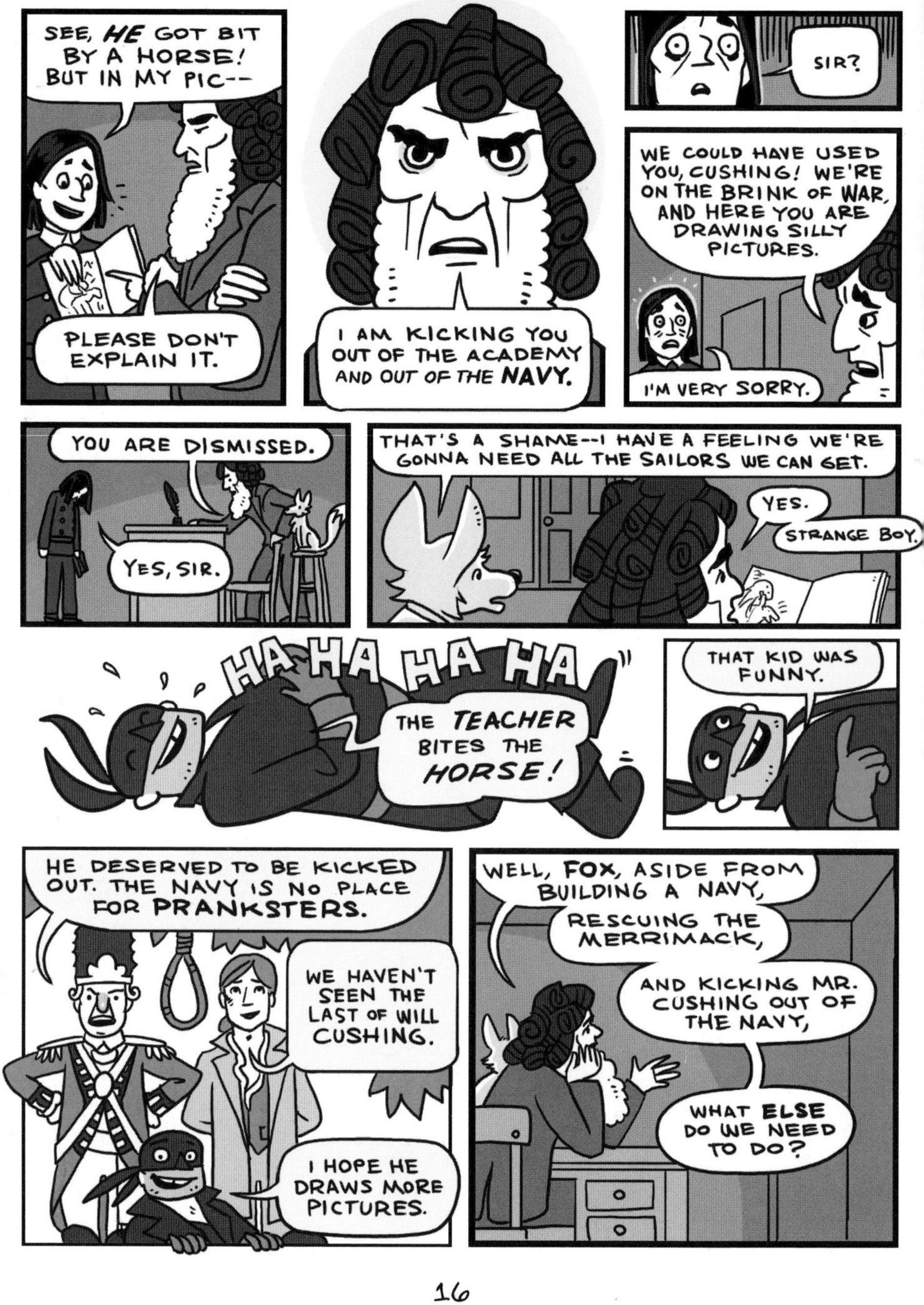
SEE, HE GOT BIT BY A HORSE! BUT IN MY PIC--
PLEASE DON'T EXPLAIN IT.
I AM KICKING YOU OUT OF THE ACADEMY AND OUT OF THE NAVY.
SIR?
WE COULD HAVE USED YOU, CUSHING! WE'RE ON THE BRINK OF WAR, AND HERE YOU ARE DRAWING SILLY PICTURES.
I'M VERY SORRY.
YOU ARE DISMISSED.
YES, SIR.
THAT'S A SHAME--I HAVE A FEELING WE'RE GONNA NEED ALL THE SAILORS WE CAN GET.
YES.
STRANGE BOY.
HA HA HA HA
THE TEACHER BITES THE HORSE!
THAT KID WAS FUNNY.
HE DESERVED TO BE KICKED OUT. THE NAVY IS NO PLACE FOR PRANKSTERS.
WE HAVEN'T SEEN THE LAST OF WILL CUSHING.
I HOPE HE DRAWS MORE PICTURES.
WELL, FOX, ASIDE FROM BUILDING A NAVY,
RESCUING THE MERRIMACK,
AND KICKING MR. CUSHING OUT OF THE NAVY,
WHAT ELSE DO WE NEED TO DO?

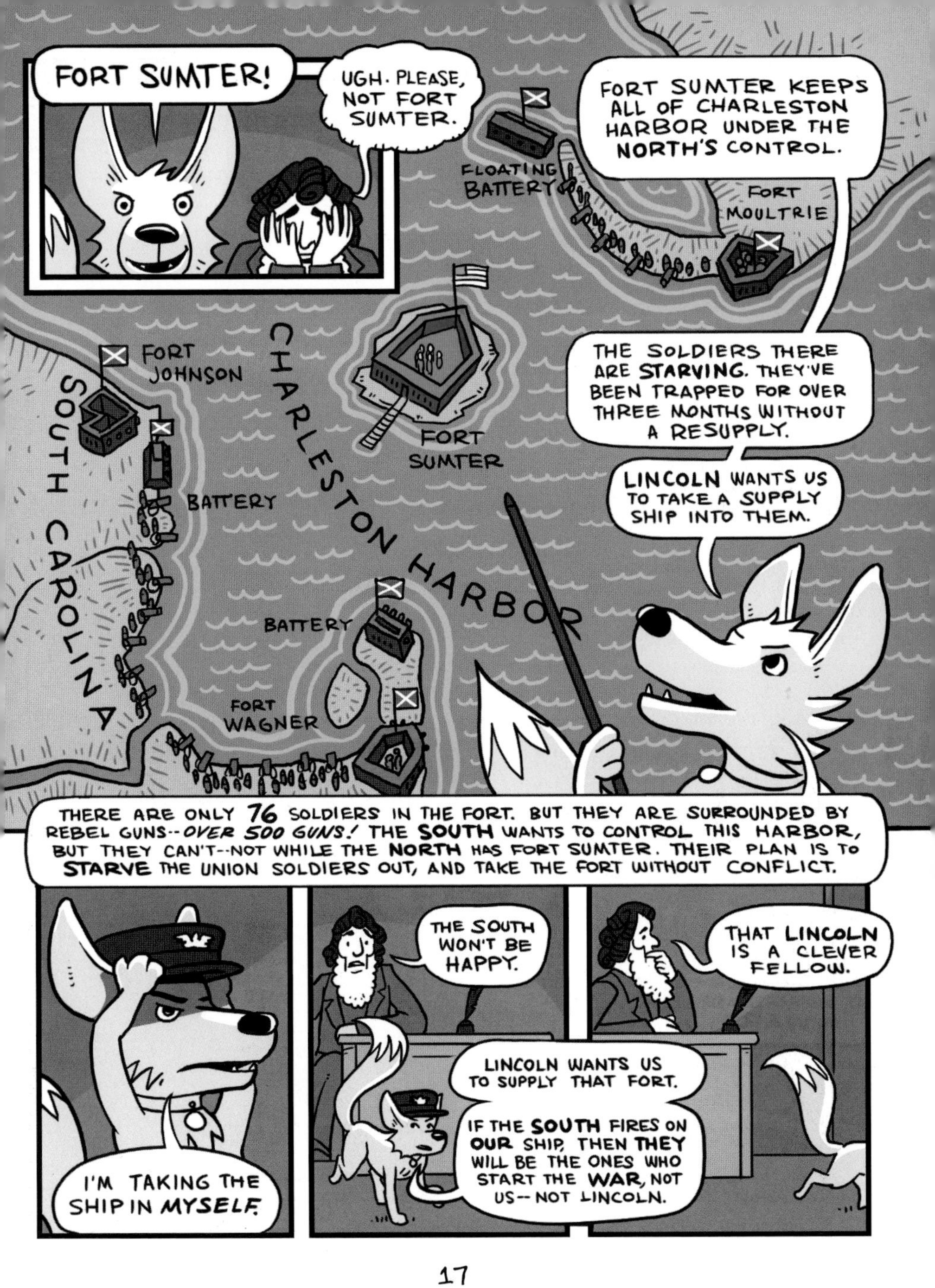
FORT SUMTER!
UGH. PLEASE, NOT FORT SUMTER.
FORT SUMTER KEEPS ALL OF CHARLESTON HARBOR UNDER THE NORTH'S CONTROL.
FLOATING BATTERY
FORT MOULTRIE
FORT JOHNSON
SOUTH CAROLINA
CHARLESTON HARBOR
FORT SUMTER
BATTERY
BATTERY
FORT WAGNER
THE SOLDIERS THERE ARE STARVING. THEY'VE BEEN TRAPPED FOR OVER THREE MONTHS WITHOUT A RESUPPLY.
LINCOLN WANTS US TO TAKE A SUPPLY SHIP INTO THEM.
THERE ARE ONLY 76 SOLDIERS IN THE FORT. BUT THEY ARE SURROUNDED BY REBEL GUNS--OVER 500 GUNS! THE SOUTH WANTS TO CONTROL THIS HARBOR, BUT THEY CAN'T--NOT WHILE THE NORTH HAS FORT SUMTER. THEIR PLAN IS TO STARVE THE UNION SOLDIERS OUT, AND TAKE THE FORT WITHOUT CONFLICT.
I'M TAKING THE SHIP IN MYSELF.
THE SOUTH WON'T BE HAPPY.
LINCOLN WANTS US TO SUPPLY THAT FORT.
IF THE SOUTH FIRES ON OUR SHIP, THEN THEY WILL BE THE ONES WHO START THE WAR, NOT US-- NOT LINCOLN.
THAT LINCOLN IS A CLEVER FELLOW.

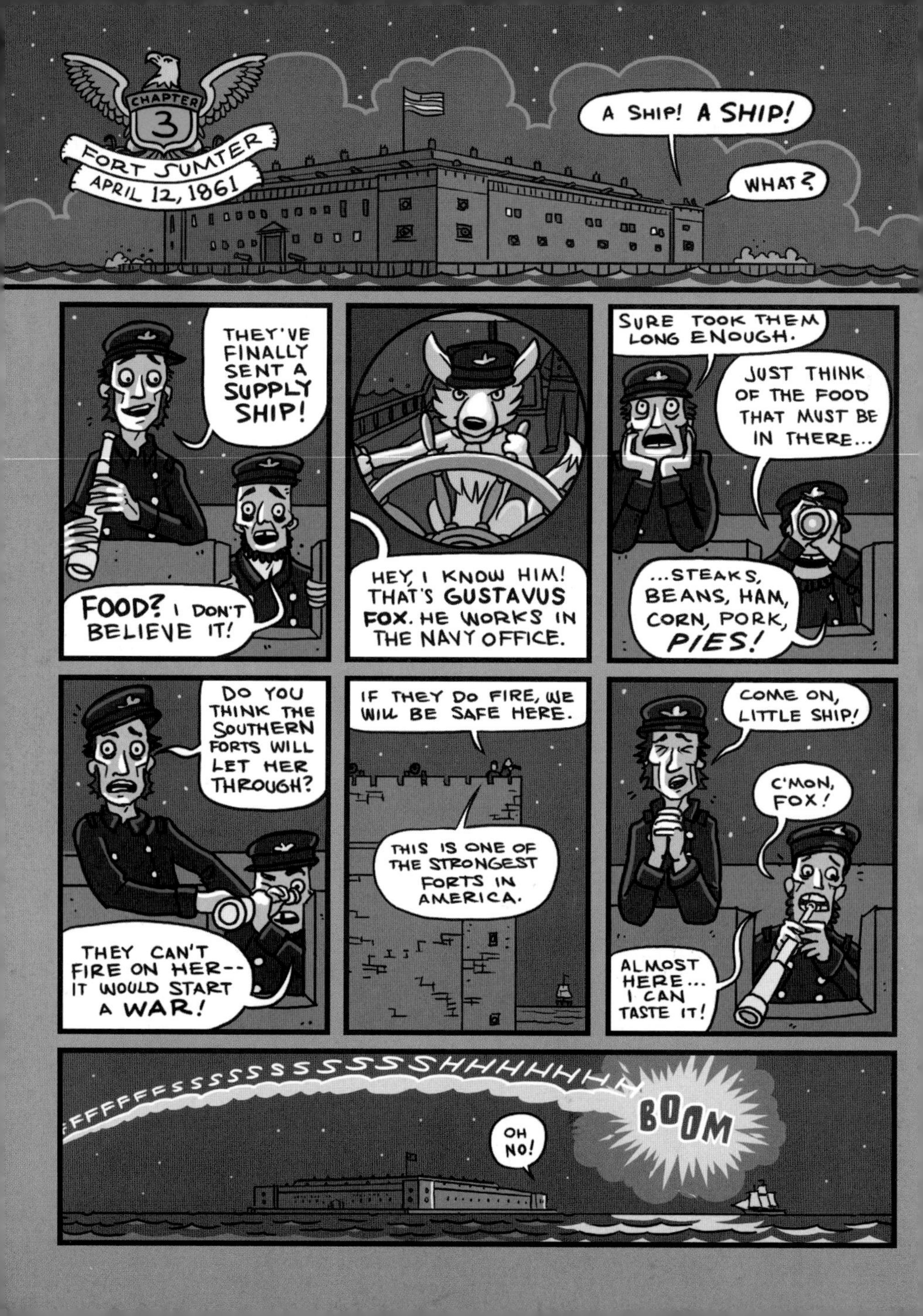
CHAPTER 3
FORT SUMTER
APRIL 12, 1861
A SHIP! A SHIP!
WHAT?
THEY'VE FINALLY SENT A SUPPLY SHIP!
FOOD? I DON'T BELIEVE IT!
HEY, I KNOW HIM! THAT'S GUSTAVUS FOX. HE WORKS IN THE NAVY OFFICE.
SURE TOOK THEM LONG ENOUGH.
JUST THINK OF THE FOOD THAT MUST BE IN THERE...
...STEAKS, BEANS, HAM, CORN, PORK, PIES!
DO YOU THINK THE SOUTHERN FORTS WILL LET HER THROUGH?
THEY CAN'T FIRE ON HER-- IT WOULD START A WAR!
IF THEY DO FIRE, WE WILL BE SAFE HERE.
THIS IS ONE OF THE STRONGEST FORTS IN AMERICA.
COME ON, LITTLE SHIP!
C'MON, FOX!
ALMOST HERE... I CAN TASTE IT!
FFFFFFFSSSSSSSSSSSSSHHHHHHH
BOOM
OH NO!

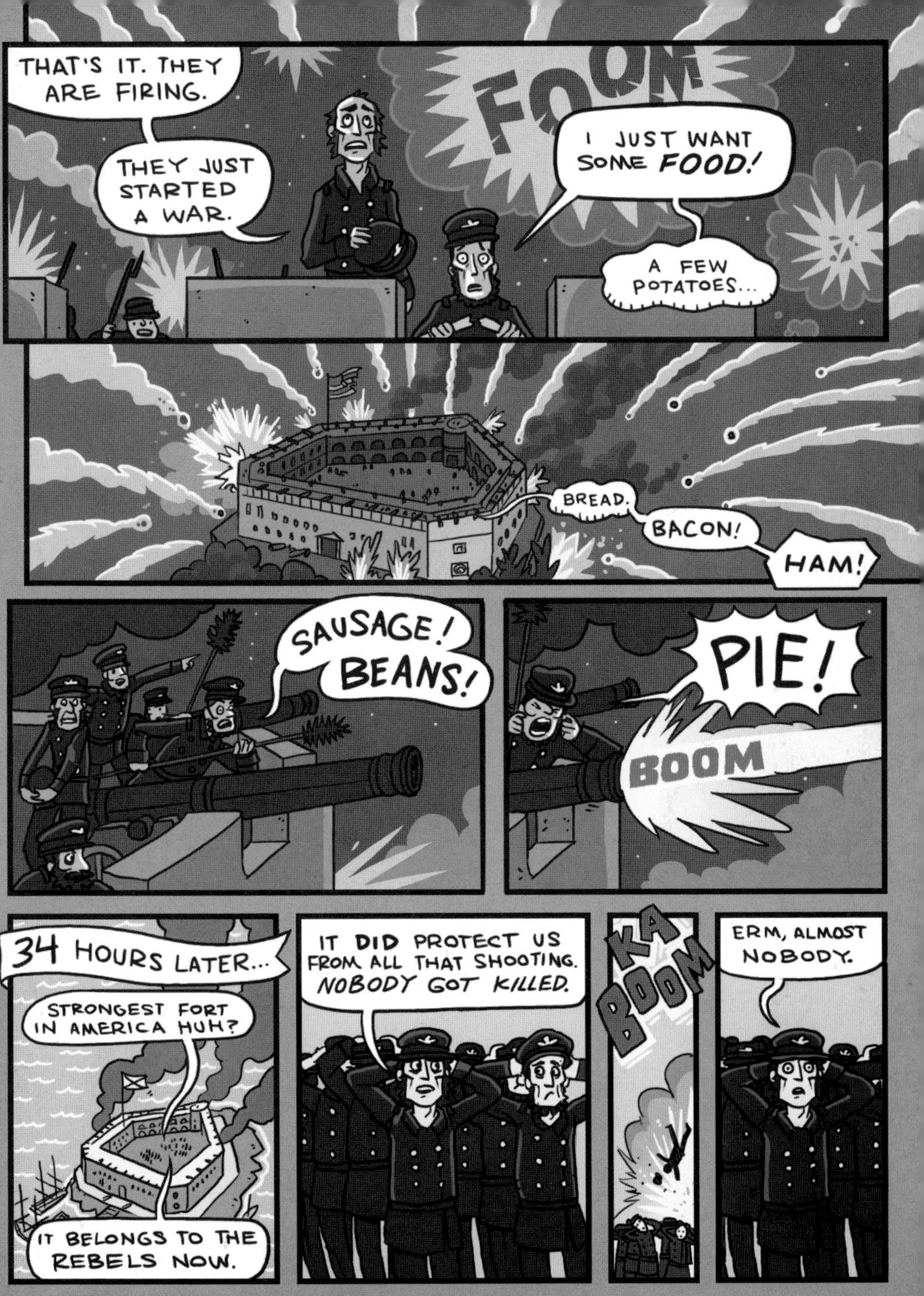
THAT'S IT. THEY ARE FIRING.
THEY JUST STARTED A WAR.
FOOM
I JUST WANT SOME FOOD!
A FEW POTATOES...
BREAD.
BACON!
HAM!
SAUSAGE! BEANS!
PIE!
BOOM
34 HOURS LATER...
STRONGEST FORT IN AMERICA HUH?
IT BELONGS TO THE REBELS NOW.
IT DID PROTECT US FROM ALL THAT SHOOTING. NOBODY GOT KILLED.
KA BOOM
ERM, ALMOST NOBODY.

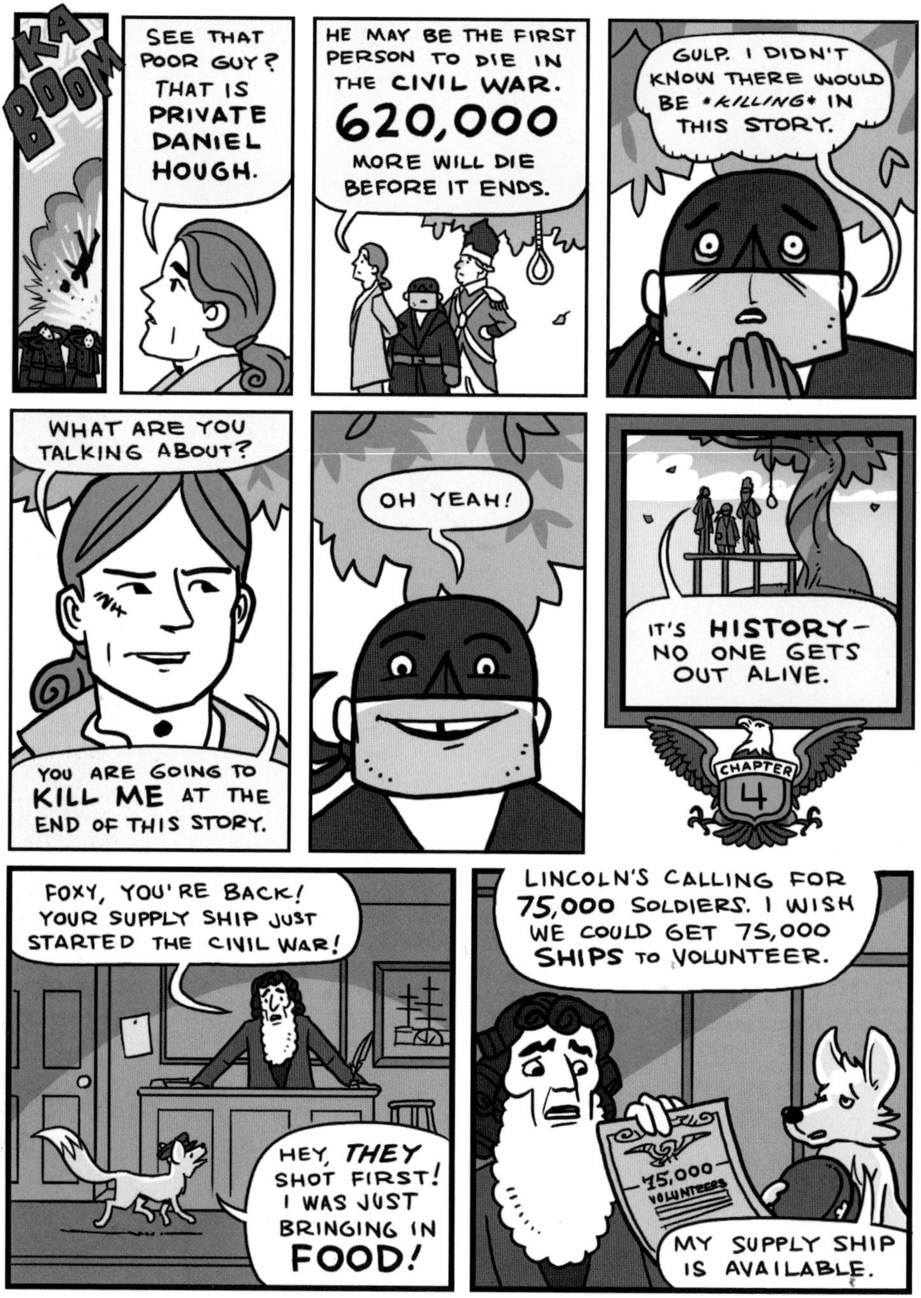
KA BOOM
SEE THAT POOR GUY? THAT IS PRIVATE DANIEL HOUGH.
HE MAY BE THE FIRST PERSON TO DIE IN THE CIVIL WAR. 620,000 MORE WILL DIE BEFORE IT ENDS.
GULP. I DIDN'T KNOW THERE WOULD BE *KILLING* IN THIS STORY.
WHAT ARE YOU TALKING ABOUT?
YOU ARE GOING TO KILL ME AT THE END OF THIS STORY.
OH YEAH!
IT'S HISTORY— NO ONE GETS OUT ALIVE.
CHAPTER 4
FOXY, YOU'RE BACK! YOUR SUPPLY SHIP JUST STARTED THE CIVIL WAR!
HEY, THEY SHOT FIRST! I WAS JUST BRINGING IN FOOD!
LINCOLN'S CALLING FOR 75,000 SOLDIERS. I WISH WE COULD GET 75,000 SHIPS TO VOLUNTEER.
75,000 VOLUNTEERS
MY SUPPLY SHIP IS AVAILABLE.

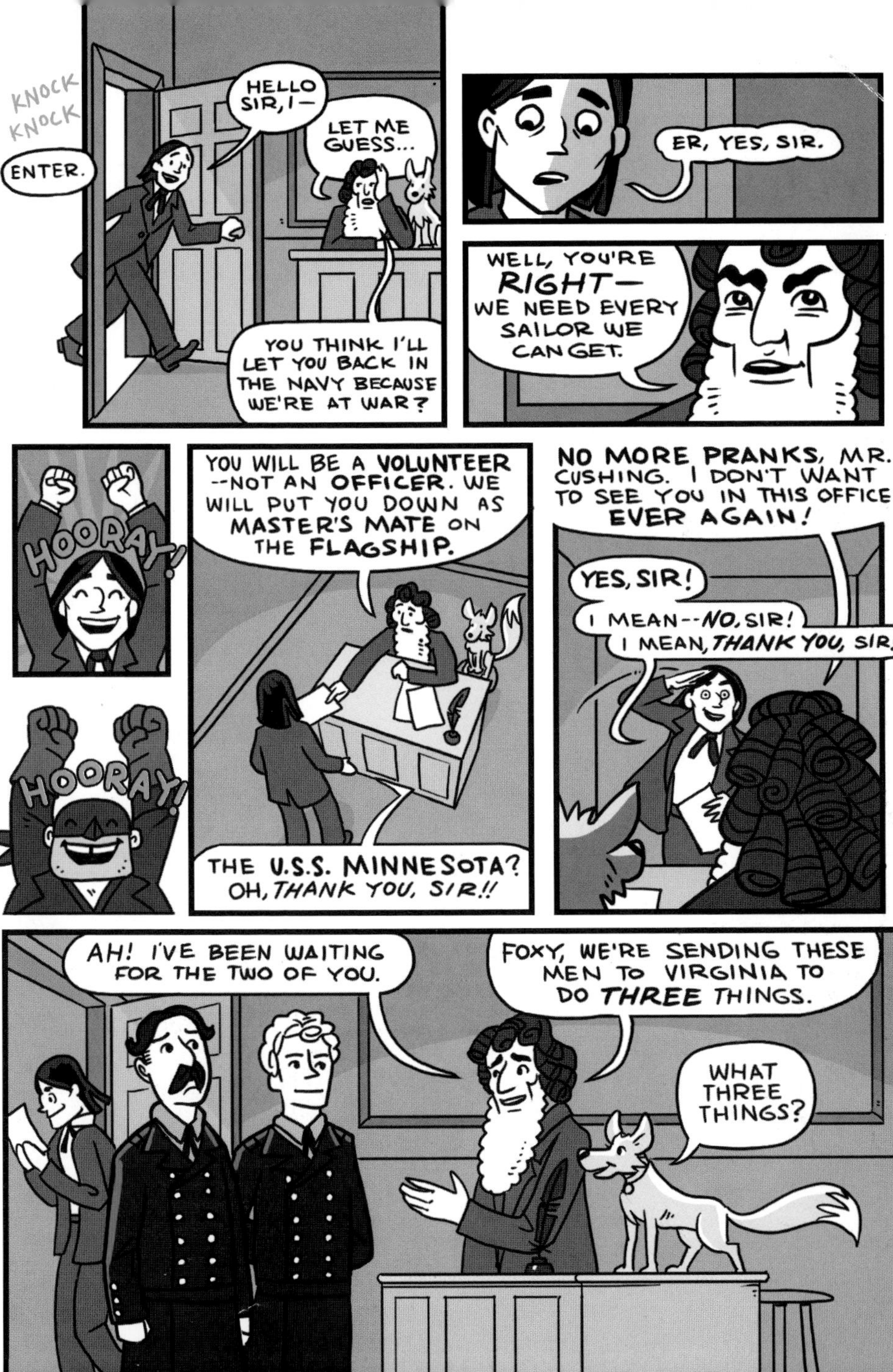
KNOCK KNOCK
ENTER.
HELLO SIR, I—
LET ME GUESS...
YOU THINK I'LL LET YOU BACK IN THE NAVY BECAUSE WE'RE AT WAR?
ER, YES, SIR.
WELL, YOU'RE RIGHT— WE NEED EVERY SAILOR WE CAN GET.
HOORAY!
HOORAY!
YOU WILL BE A VOLUNTEER --NOT AN OFFICER. WE WILL PUT YOU DOWN AS MASTER'S MATE ON THE FLAGSHIP.
THE U.S.S. MINNESOTA? OH, THANK YOU, SIR!!
NO MORE PRANKS, MR. CUSHING. I DON'T WANT TO SEE YOU IN THIS OFFICE EVER AGAIN!
YES, SIR!
I MEAN--NO, SIR!
I MEAN, THANK YOU, SIR!
AH! I'VE BEEN WAITING FOR THE TWO OF YOU.
FOXY, WE'RE SENDING THESE MEN TO VIRGINIA TO DO THREE THINGS.
WHAT THREE THINGS?

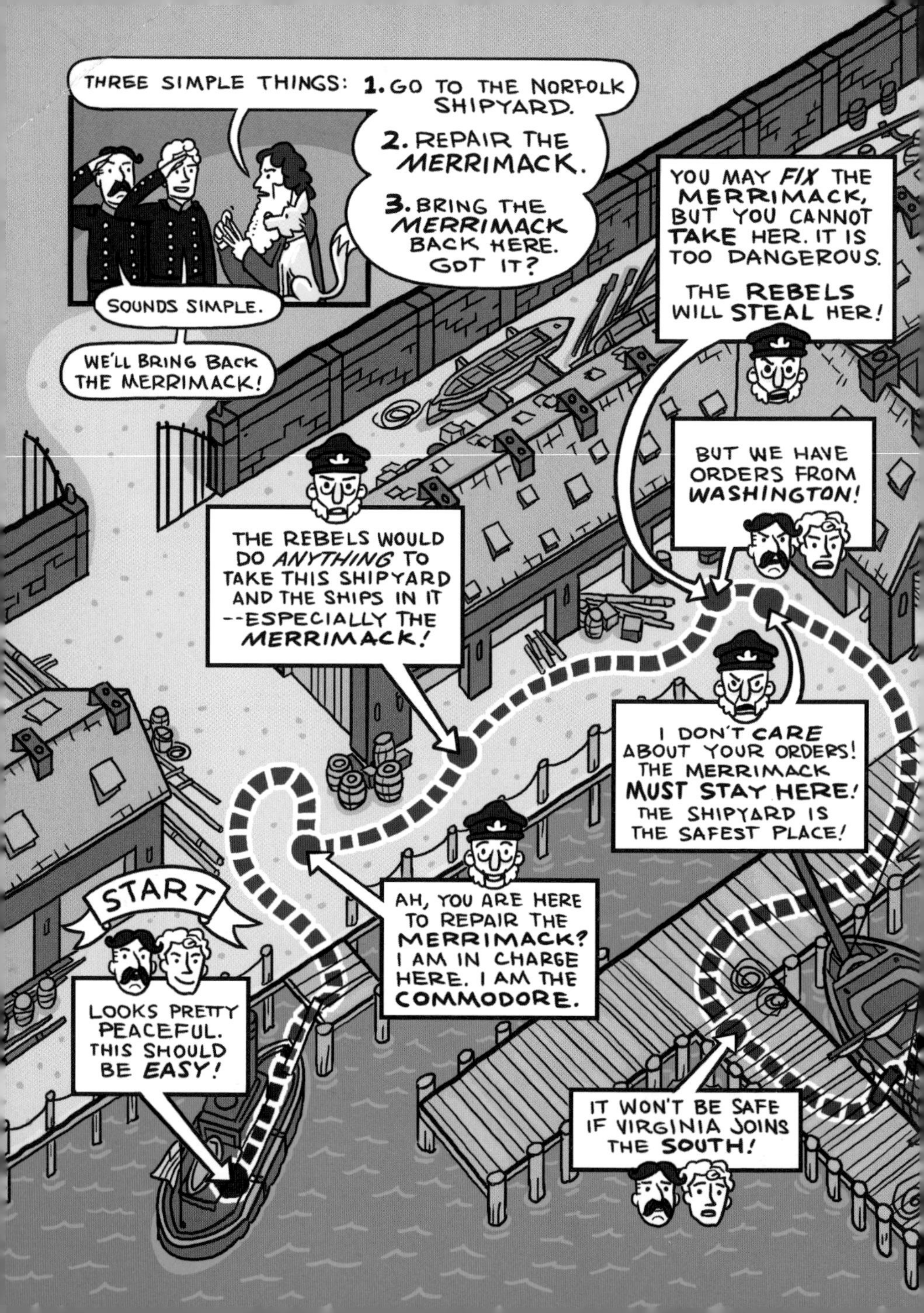
THREE SIMPLE THINGS: 1. GO TO THE NORFOLK SHIPYARD.
2. REPAIR THE MERRIMACK.
3. BRING THE MERRIMACK BACK HERE. GOT IT?
SOUNDS SIMPLE.
WE'LL BRING BACK THE MERRIMACK!
START
LOOKS PRETTY PEACEFUL. THIS SHOULD BE EASY!
AH, YOU ARE HERE TO REPAIR THE MERRIMACK? I AM IN CHARGE HERE. I AM THE COMMODORE.
THE REBELS WOULD DO ANYTHING TO TAKE THIS SHIPYARD AND THE SHIPS IN IT --ESPECIALLY THE MERRIMACK!
BUT WE HAVE ORDERS FROM WASHINGTON!
YOU MAY FIX THE MERRIMACK, BUT YOU CANNOT TAKE HER. IT IS TOO DANGEROUS.
THE REBELS WILL STEAL HER!
I DON'T CARE ABOUT YOUR ORDERS! THE MERRIMACK MUST STAY HERE! THE SHIPYARD IS THE SAFEST PLACE!
IT WON'T BE SAFE IF VIRGINIA JOINS THE SOUTH!

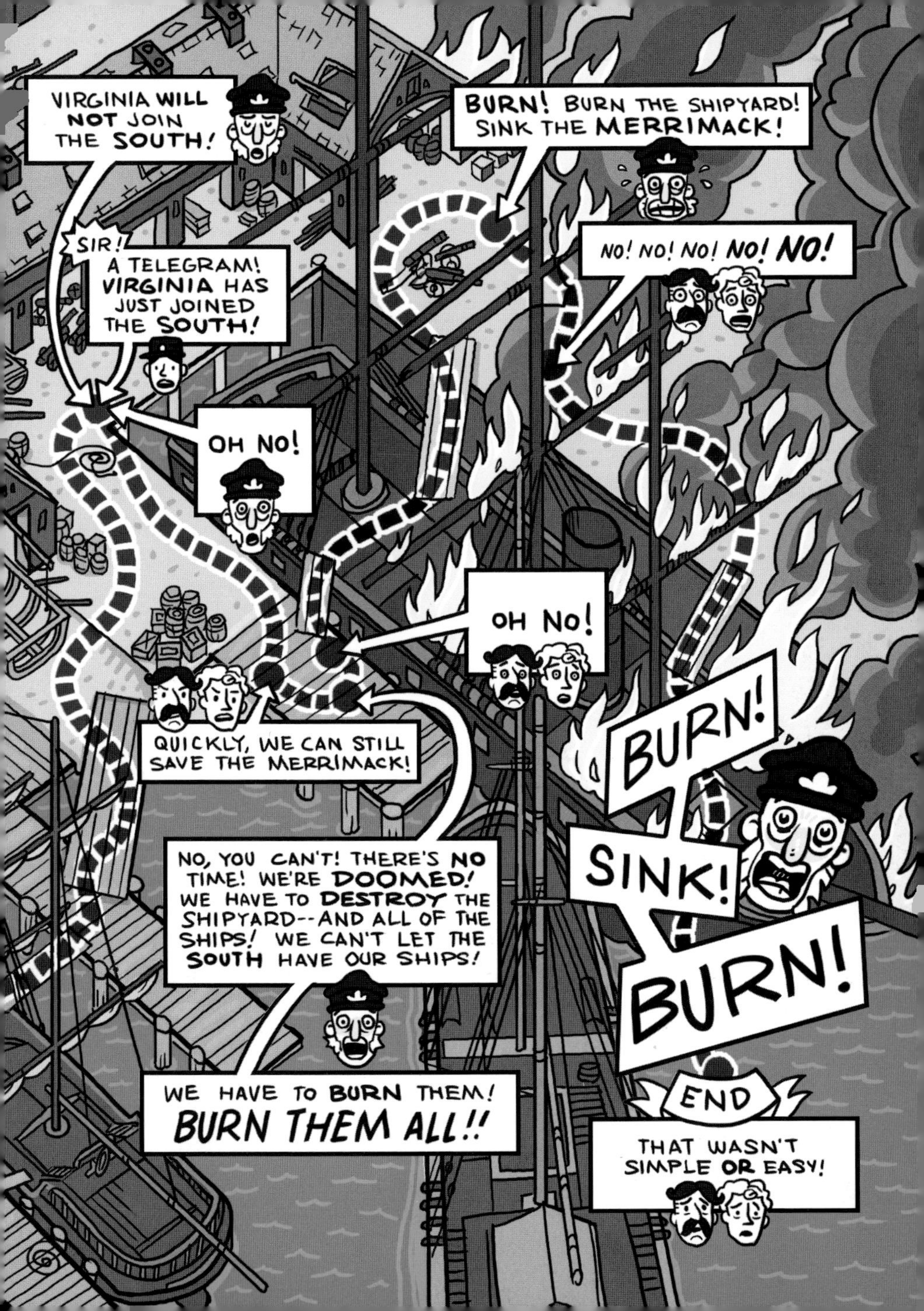
VIRGINIA WILL NOT JOIN THE SOUTH!
SIR!
A TELEGRAM! VIRGINIA HAS JUST JOINED THE SOUTH!
OH NO!
QUICKLY, WE CAN STILL SAVE THE MERRIMACK!
OH NO!
NO, YOU CAN'T! THERE'S NO TIME! WE'RE DOOMED! WE HAVE TO DESTROY THE SHIPYARD--AND ALL OF THE SHIPS! WE CAN'T LET THE SOUTH HAVE OUR SHIPS!
WE HAVE TO BURN THEM! BURN THEM ALL!!
BURN! BURN THE SHIPYARD! SINK THE MERRIMACK!
NO! NO! NO! NO! NO!
BURN!
SINK!
BURN!
END
THAT WASN'T SIMPLE OR EASY!

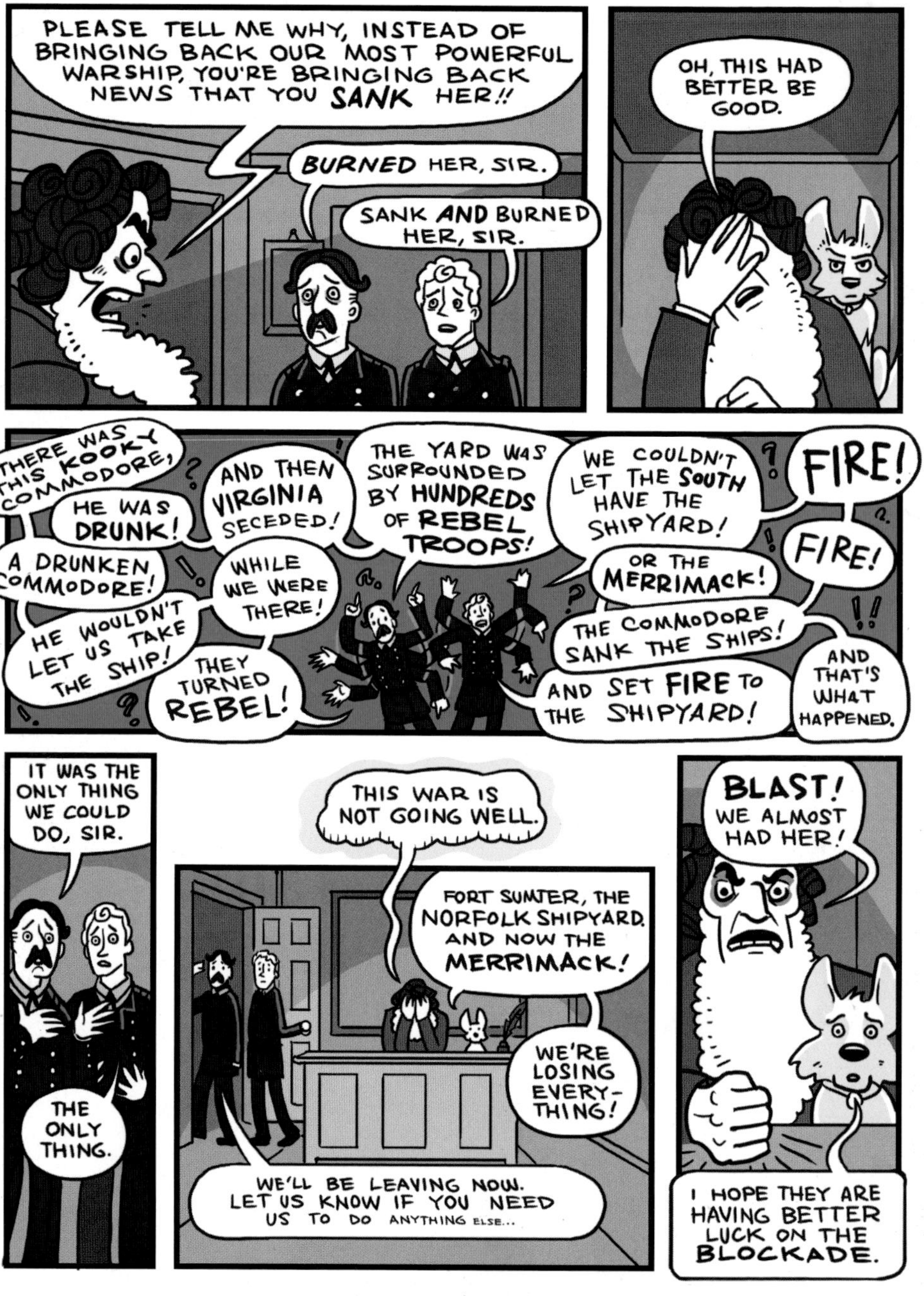
PLEASE TELL ME WHY, INSTEAD OF BRINGING BACK OUR MOST POWERFUL WARSHIP, YOU'RE BRINGING BACK NEWS THAT YOU SANK HER!!
BURNED HER, SIR.
SANK AND BURNED HER, SIR.
OH, THIS HAD BETTER BE GOOD.
THERE WAS THIS KOOKY COMMODORE,
HE WAS DRUNK!
A DRUNKEN COMMODORE!
HE WOULDN'T LET US TAKE THE SHIP!
AND THEN VIRGINIA SECEDED!
WHILE WE WERE THERE!
THEY TURNED REBEL!
THE YARD WAS SURROUNDED BY HUNDREDS OF REBEL TROOPS!
WE COULDN'T LET THE SOUTH HAVE THE SHIPYARD!
OR THE MERRIMACK!
THE COMMODORE SANK THE SHIPS!
AND SET FIRE TO THE SHIPYARD!
FIRE!
FIRE!
AND THAT'S WHAT HAPPENED.
IT WAS THE ONLY THING WE COULD DO, SIR.
THE ONLY THING.
THIS WAR IS NOT GOING WELL.
FORT SUMTER, THE NORFOLK SHIPYARD, AND NOW THE MERRIMACK!
WE'RE LOSING EVERYTHING!
WE'LL BE LEAVING NOW. LET US KNOW IF YOU NEED US TO DO ANYTHING ELSE...
BLAST! WE ALMOST HAD HER!
I HOPE THEY ARE HAVING BETTER LUCK ON THE BLOCKADE.

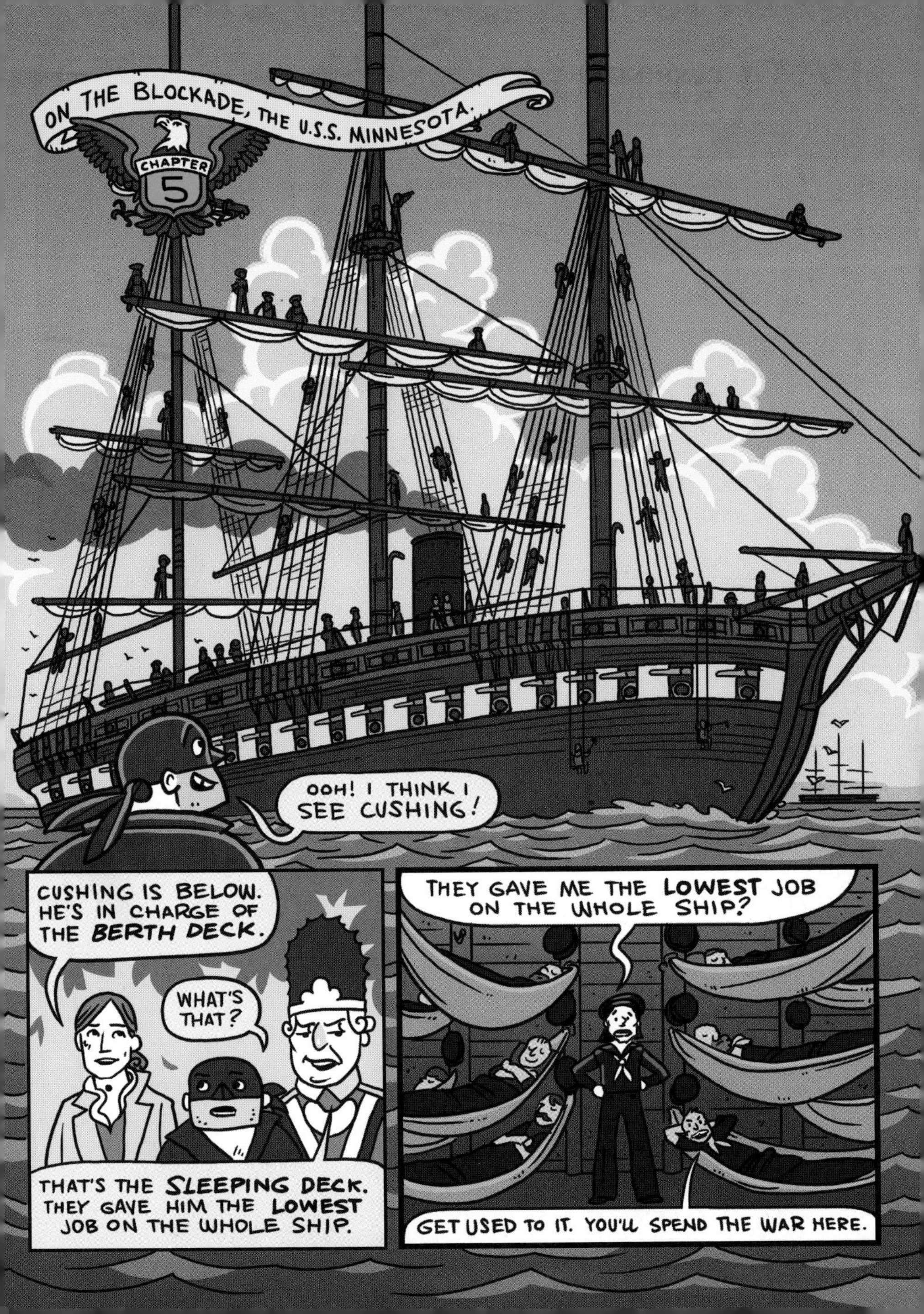
ON THE BLOCKADE, THE U.S.S. MINNESOTA.
CHAPTER 5
OOH! I THINK I SEE CUSHING!
CUSHING IS BELOW. HE'S IN CHARGE OF THE BERTH DECK.
WHAT'S THAT?
THAT'S THE SLEEPING DECK. THEY GAVE HIM THE LOWEST JOB ON THE WHOLE SHIP.
THEY GAVE ME THE LOWEST JOB ON THE WHOLE SHIP?
GET USED TO IT. YOU'LL SPEND THE WAR HERE.

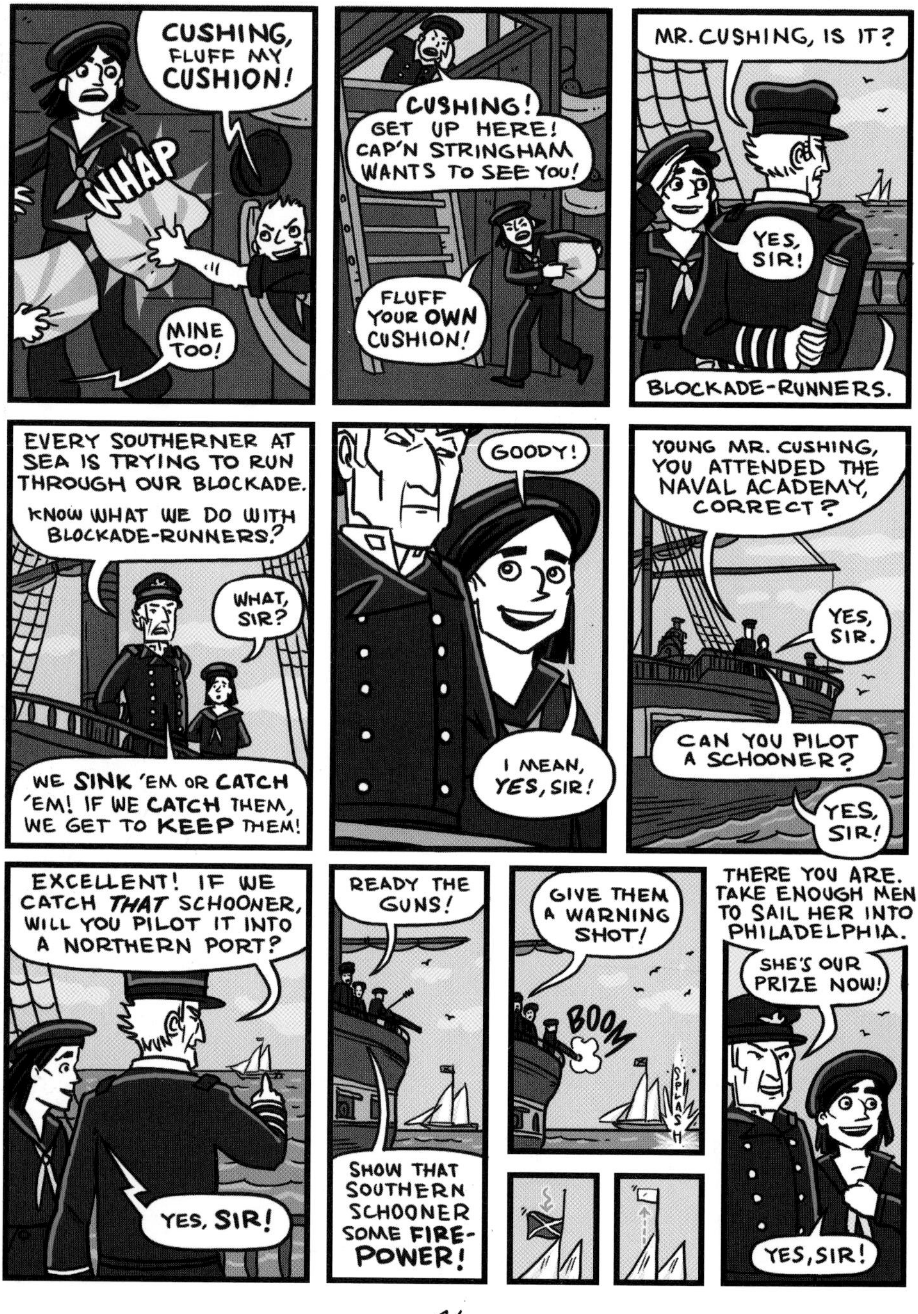
CUSHING, FLUFF MY CUSHION!
WHAP
MINE TOO!
CUSHING! GET UP HERE! CAP'N STRINGHAM WANTS TO SEE YOU!
FLUFF YOUR OWN CUSHION!
MR. CUSHING, IS IT?
YES, SIR!
BLOCKADE-RUNNERS.
EVERY SOUTHERNER AT SEA IS TRYING TO RUN THROUGH OUR BLOCKADE.
KNOW WHAT WE DO WITH BLOCKADE-RUNNERS?
WHAT, SIR?
WE SINK 'EM OR CATCH 'EM! IF WE CATCH THEM, WE GET TO KEEP THEM!
GOODY!
I MEAN, YES, SIR!
YOUNG MR. CUSHING, YOU ATTENDED THE NAVAL ACADEMY, CORRECT?
YES, SIR.
CAN YOU PILOT A SCHOONER?
YES, SIR!
EXCELLENT! IF WE CATCH THAT SCHOONER, WILL YOU PILOT IT INTO A NORTHERN PORT?
YES, SIR!
READY THE GUNS!
SHOW THAT SOUTHERN SCHOONER SOME FIRE-POWER!
GIVE THEM A WARNING SHOT!
BOOM
SPLASH
THERE YOU ARE. TAKE ENOUGH MEN TO SAIL HER INTO PHILADELPHIA.
SHE'S OUR PRIZE NOW!
YES, SIR!

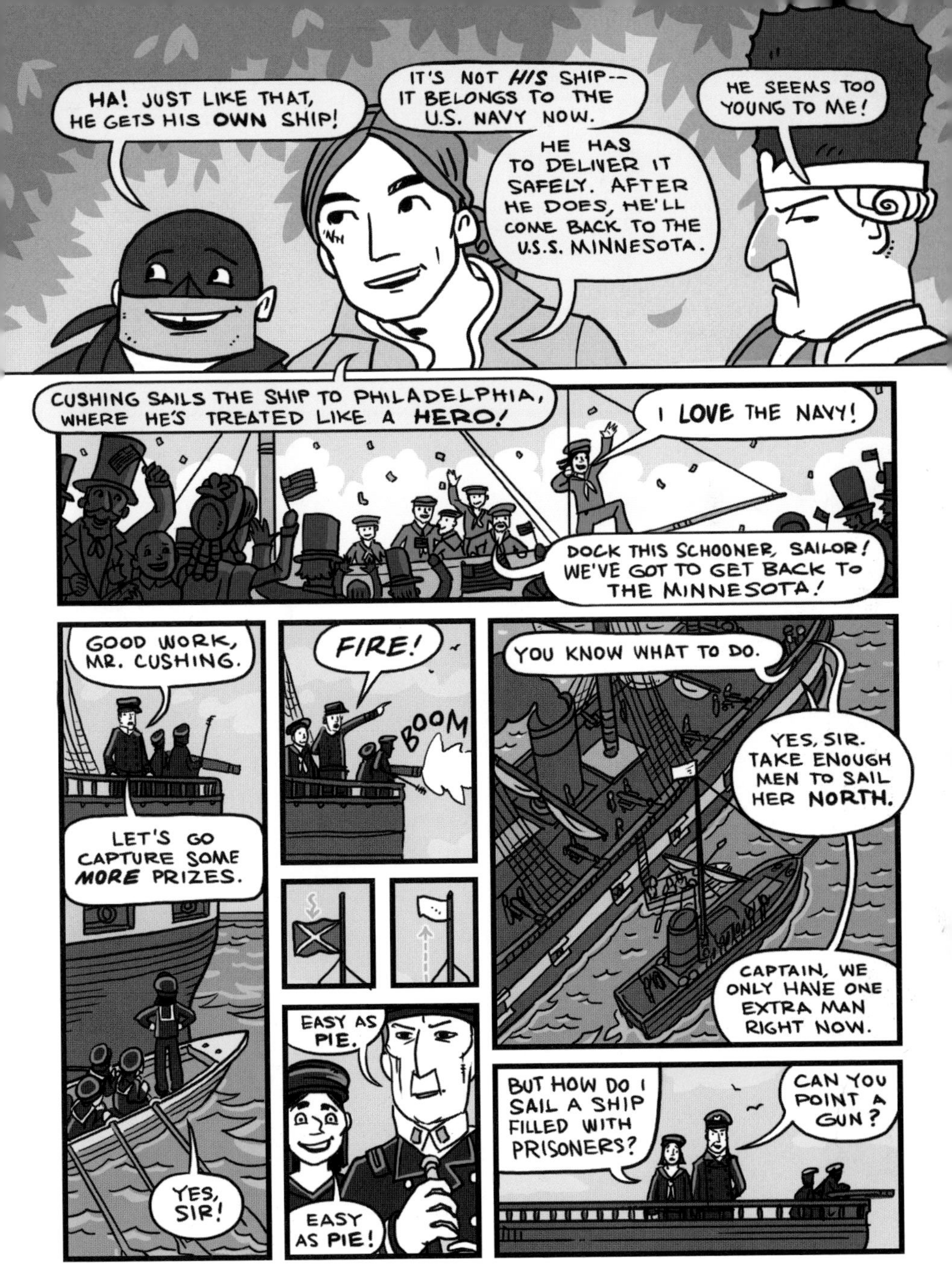

HA! JUST LIKE THAT, HE GETS HIS OWN SHIP!
IT'S NOT HIS SHIP-- IT BELONGS TO THE U.S. NAVY NOW.
HE HAS TO DELIVER IT SAFELY. AFTER HE DOES, HE'LL COME BACK TO THE U.S.S. MINNESOTA.
HE SEEMS TOO YOUNG TO ME!
CUSHING SAILS THE SHIP TO PHILADELPHIA, WHERE HE'S TREATED LIKE A HERO!
I LOVE THE NAVY!
DOCK THIS SCHOONER, SAILOR! WE'VE GOT TO GET BACK TO THE MINNESOTA!
GOOD WORK, MR. CUSHING.
LET'S GO CAPTURE SOME MORE PRIZES.
YES, SIR!
FIRE!
BOOM
EASY AS PIE.
EASY AS PIE!
YOU KNOW WHAT TO DO.
YES, SIR. TAKE ENOUGH MEN TO SAIL HER NORTH.
CAPTAIN, WE ONLY HAVE ONE EXTRA MAN RIGHT NOW.
BUT HOW DO I SAIL A SHIP FILLED WITH PRISONERS?
CAN YOU POINT A GUN?

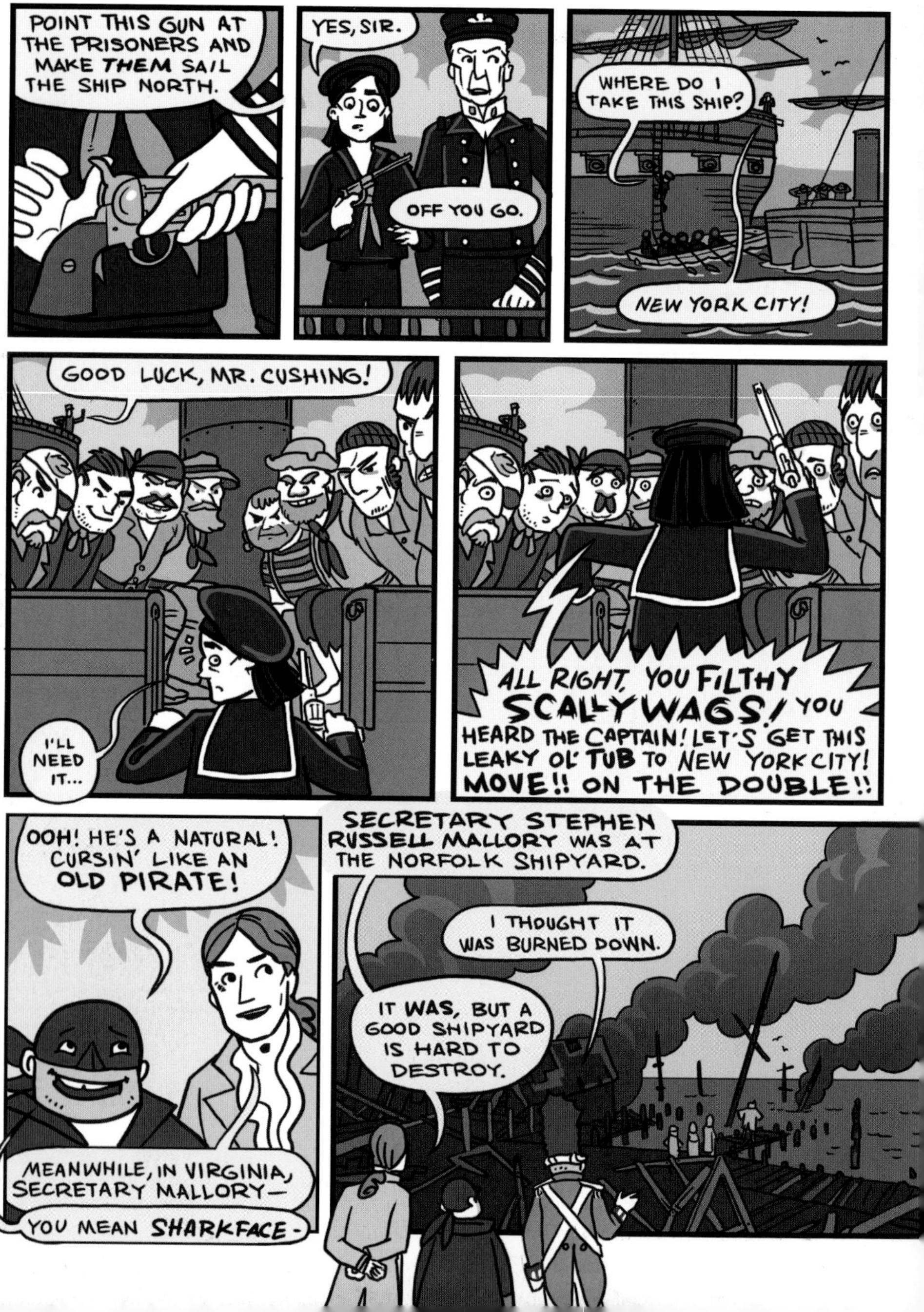

POINT THIS GUN AT THE PRISONERS AND MAKE *THEM* SAIL THE SHIP NORTH.
YES, SIR.
OFF YOU GO.
WHERE DO I TAKE THIS SHIP?
NEW YORK CITY!
GOOD LUCK, MR. CUSHING!
I'LL NEED IT...
ALL RIGHT, YOU FILTHY SCALLYWAGS! YOU HEARD THE CAPTAIN! LET'S GET THIS LEAKY OL' TUB TO NEW YORK CITY! MOVE!! ON THE DOUBLE!!
OOH! HE'S A NATURAL! CURSIN' LIKE AN OLD PIRATE!
MEANWHILE, IN VIRGINIA, SECRETARY MALLORY—
YOU MEAN SHARKFACE-
SECRETARY STEPHEN RUSSELL MALLORY WAS AT THE NORFOLK SHIPYARD.
I THOUGHT IT WAS BURNED DOWN.
IT WAS, BUT A GOOD SHIPYARD IS HARD TO DESTROY.

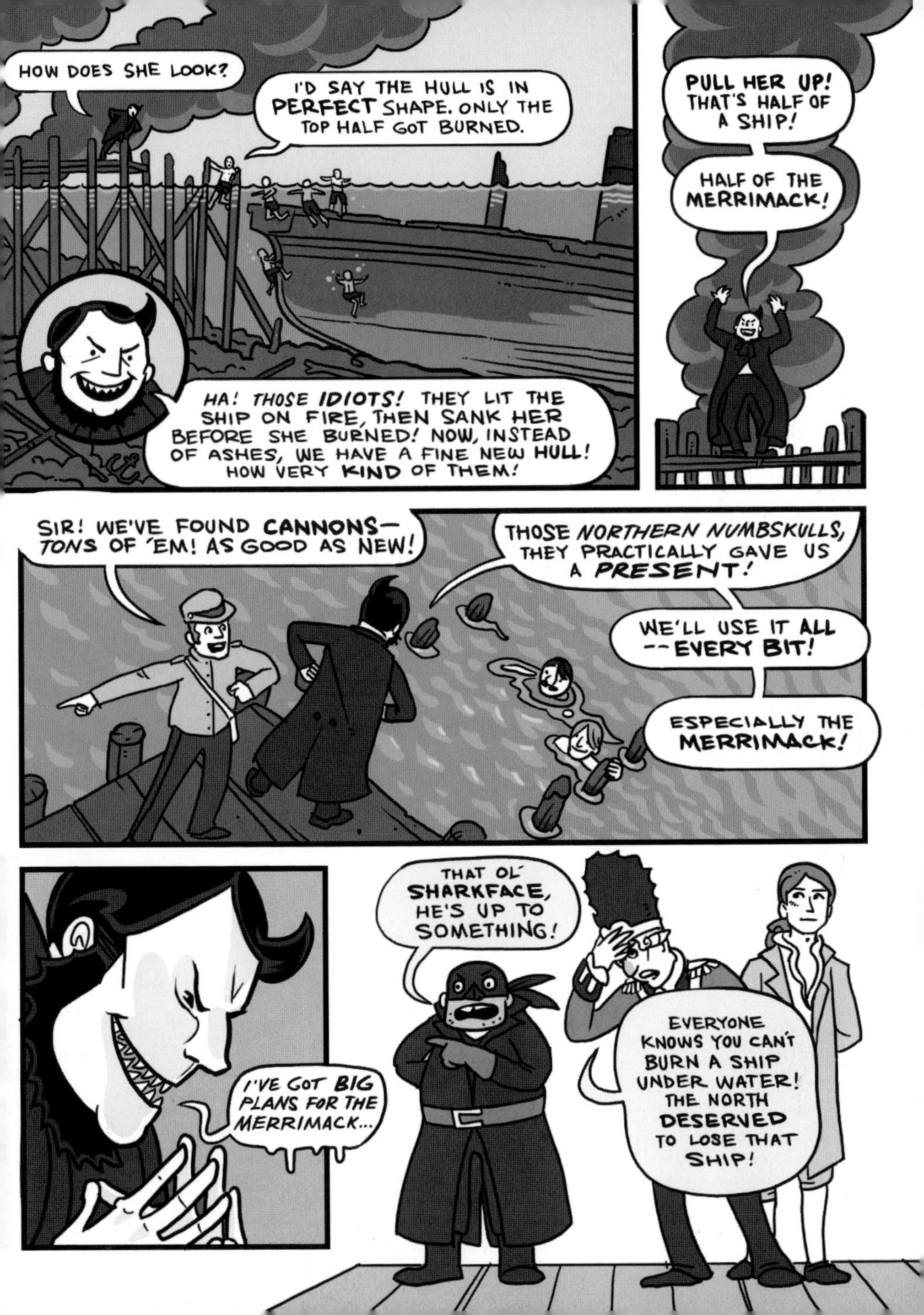
HOW DOES SHE LOOK?
I'D SAY THE HULL IS IN PERFECT SHAPE. ONLY THE TOP HALF GOT BURNED.
HA! THOSE IDIOTS! THEY LIT THE SHIP ON FIRE, THEN SANK HER BEFORE SHE BURNED! NOW, INSTEAD OF ASHES, WE HAVE A FINE NEW HULL! HOW VERY KIND OF THEM!
PULL HER UP! THAT'S HALF OF A SHIP!
HALF OF THE MERRIMACK!
SIR! WE'VE FOUND CANNONS—TONS OF 'EM! AS GOOD AS NEW!
THOSE NORTHERN NUMBSKULLS, THEY PRACTICALLY GAVE US A PRESENT!
WE'LL USE IT ALL --EVERY BIT!
ESPECIALLY THE MERRIMACK!
I'VE GOT BIG PLANS FOR THE MERRIMACK...
THAT OL' SHARKFACE, HE'S UP TO SOMETHING!
EVERYONE KNOWS YOU CAN'T BURN A SHIP UNDER WATER! THE NORTH DESERVED TO LOSE THAT SHIP!

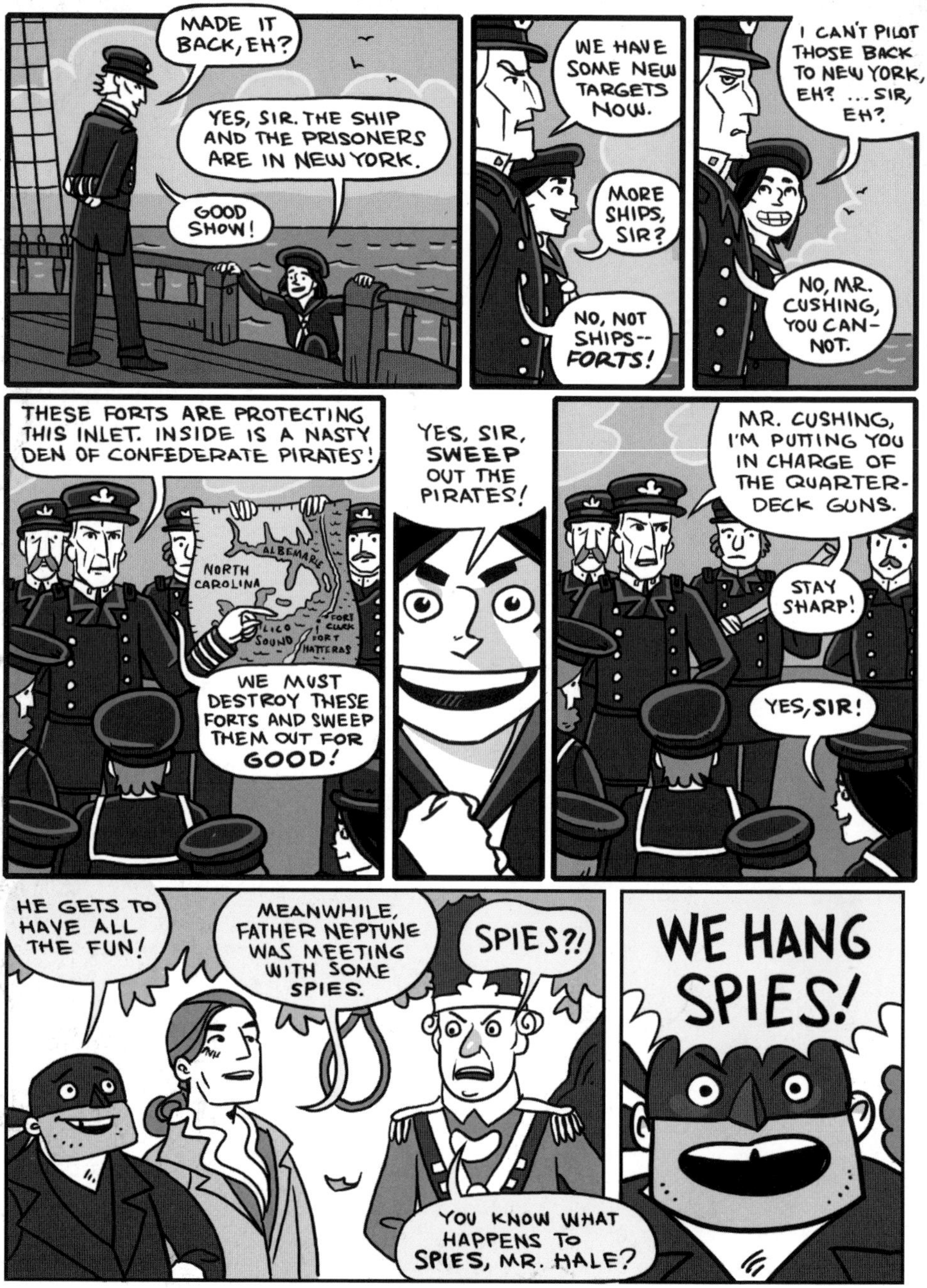

MADE IT BACK, EH?
YES, SIR. THE SHIP AND THE PRISONERS ARE IN NEW YORK.
GOOD SHOW!
WE HAVE SOME NEW TARGETS NOW.
MORE SHIPS, SIR?
NO, NOT SHIPS-- FORTS!
I CAN'T PILOT THOSE BACK TO NEW YORK, EH? ... SIR, EH?
NO, MR. CUSHING, YOU CAN-NOT.
THESE FORTS ARE PROTECTING THIS INLET. INSIDE IS A NASTY DEN OF CONFEDERATE PIRATES!
ALBEMARLE
NORTH CAROLINA
FORT CLARK
FORT HATTERAS
SOUND
WE MUST DESTROY THESE FORTS AND SWEEP THEM OUT FOR GOOD!
YES, SIR, SWEEP OUT THE PIRATES!
MR. CUSHING, I'M PUTTING YOU IN CHARGE OF THE QUARTER-DECK GUNS.
STAY SHARP!
YES, SIR!
HE GETS TO HAVE ALL THE FUN!
MEANWHILE, FATHER NEPTUNE WAS MEETING WITH SOME SPIES.
SPIES?!
YOU KNOW WHAT HAPPENS TO SPIES, MR. HALE?
WE HANG SPIES!

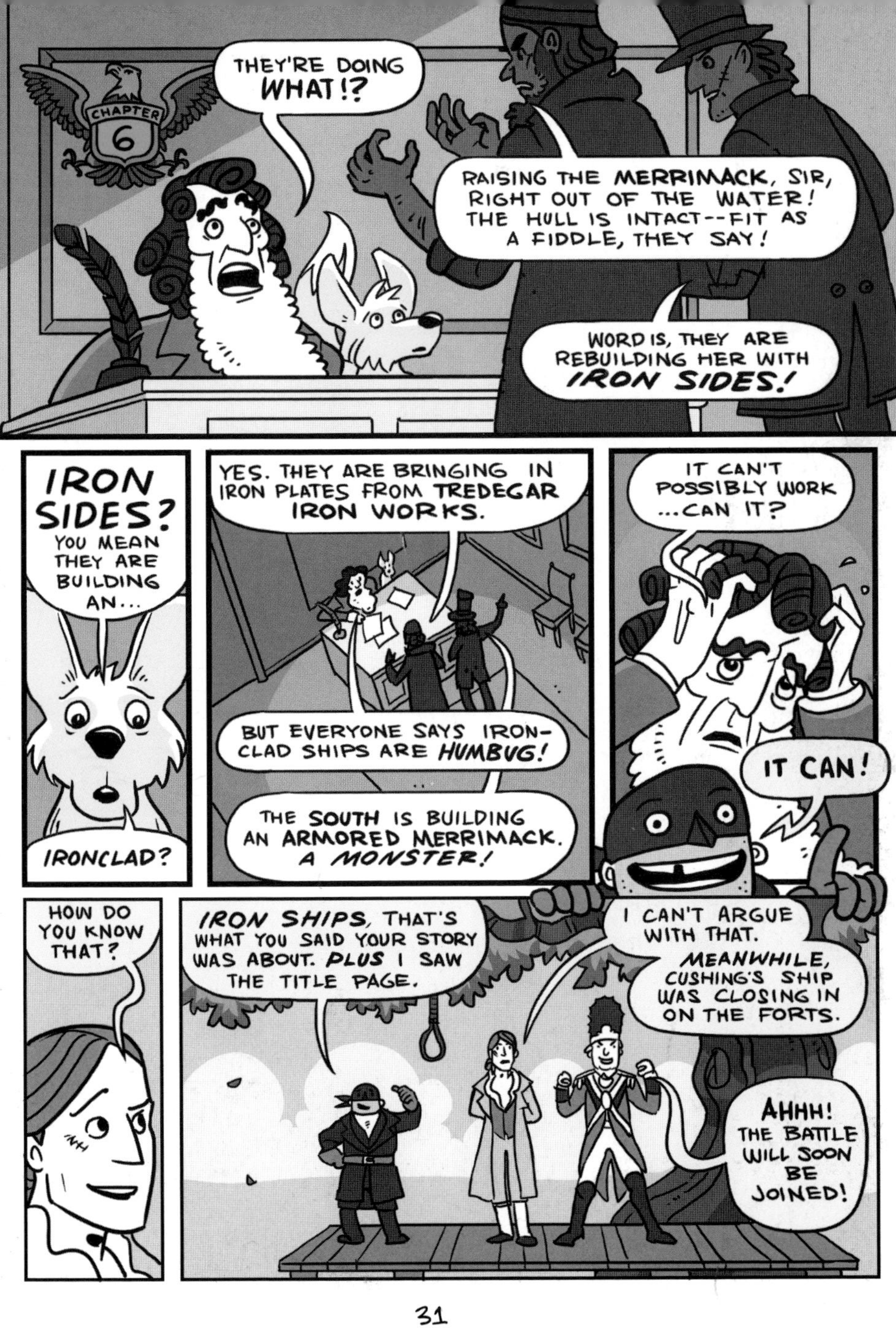
CHAPTER 6
THEY'RE DOING WHAT!?
RAISING THE MERRIMACK, SIR, RIGHT OUT OF THE WATER! THE HULL IS INTACT--FIT AS A FIDDLE, THEY SAY!
WORD IS, THEY ARE REBUILDING HER WITH IRON SIDES!
IRON SIDES? YOU MEAN THEY ARE BUILDING AN...
IRONCLAD?
YES. THEY ARE BRINGING IN IRON PLATES FROM TREDEGAR IRON WORKS.
BUT EVERYONE SAYS IRON-CLAD SHIPS ARE HUMBUG!
THE SOUTH IS BUILDING AN ARMORED MERRIMACK. A MONSTER!
IT CAN'T POSSIBLY WORK ...CAN IT?
IT CAN!
HOW DO YOU KNOW THAT?
IRON SHIPS, THAT'S WHAT YOU SAID YOUR STORY WAS ABOUT. PLUS I SAW THE TITLE PAGE.
I CAN'T ARGUE WITH THAT.
MEANWHILE, CUSHING'S SHIP WAS CLOSING IN ON THE FORTS.
AHHH! THE BATTLE WILL SOON BE JOINED!

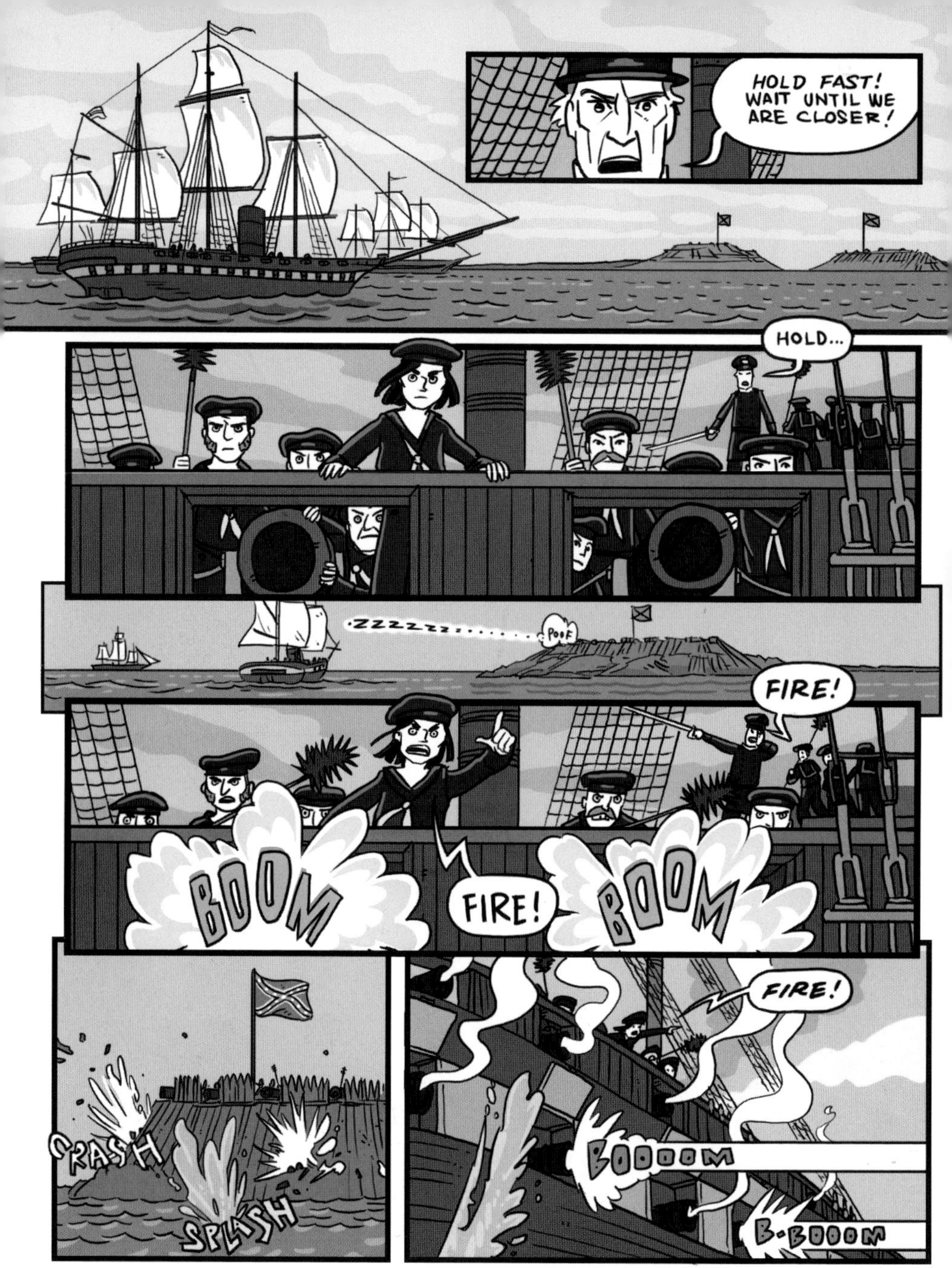
HOLD FAST! WAIT UNTIL WE ARE CLOSER!
HOLD...
ZZZZZZZ
POOF
FIRE!
BOOM
FIRE!
BOOM
CRASH
SPLASH
FIRE!
BOOOOM
B-BOOOM

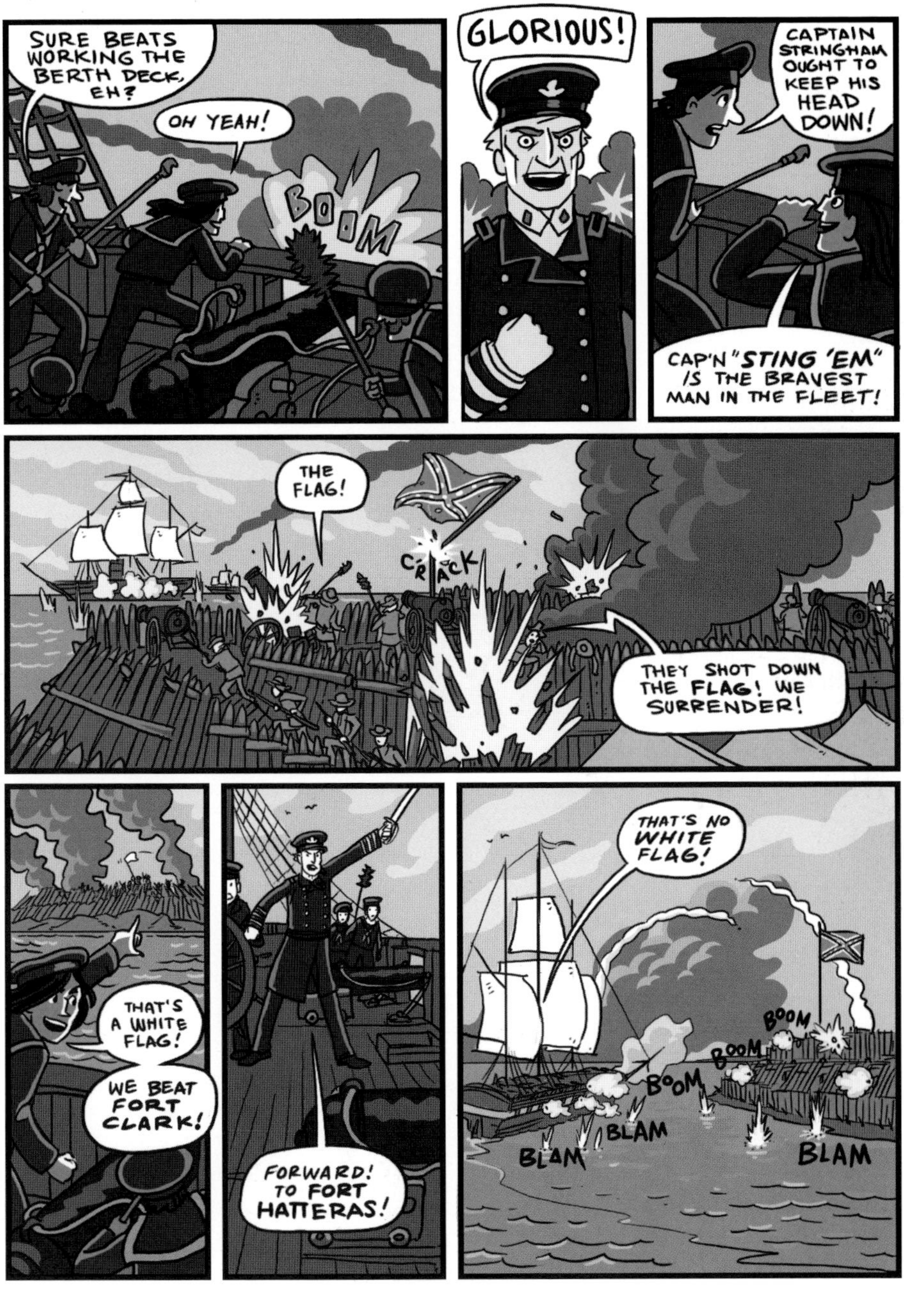
SURE BEATS WORKING THE BERTH DECK, EH?
OH YEAH!
BOOM
GLORIOUS!
CAPTAIN STRINGHAM OUGHT TO KEEP HIS HEAD DOWN!
CAP'N "STING 'EM" IS THE BRAVEST MAN IN THE FLEET!
THE FLAG!
CRACK
THEY SHOT DOWN THE FLAG! WE SURRENDER!
THAT'S A WHITE FLAG!
WE BEAT FORT CLARK!
FORWARD! TO FORT HATTERAS!
THAT'S NO WHITE FLAG!
BOOM
BOOM
BOOM
BLAM
BLAM
BLAM

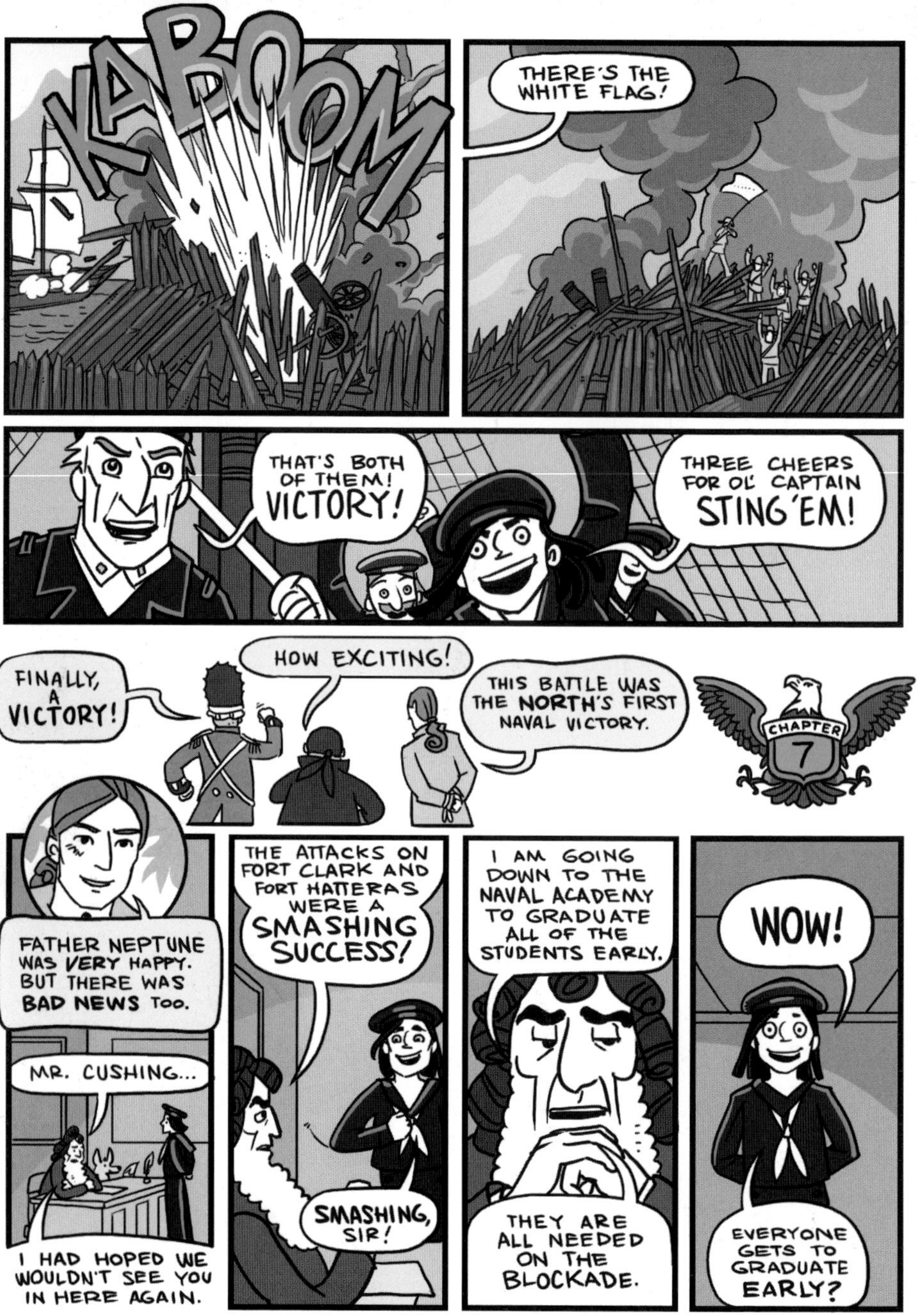
KABOOM
THERE'S THE WHITE FLAG!
THAT'S BOTH OF THEM! VICTORY!
THREE CHEERS FOR OL' CAPTAIN STING'EM!
FINALLY, A VICTORY!
HOW EXCITING!
THIS BATTLE WAS THE NORTH'S FIRST NAVAL VICTORY.
CHAPTER 7
FATHER NEPTUNE WAS VERY HAPPY. BUT THERE WAS BAD NEWS TOO.
MR. CUSHING...
I HAD HOPED WE WOULDN'T SEE YOU IN HERE AGAIN.
THE ATTACKS ON FORT CLARK AND FORT HATTERAS WERE A SMASHING SUCCESS!
SMASHING, SIR!
I AM GOING DOWN TO THE NAVAL ACADEMY TO GRADUATE ALL OF THE STUDENTS EARLY.
THEY ARE ALL NEEDED ON THE BLOCKADE.
WOW!
EVERYONE GETS TO GRADUATE EARLY?

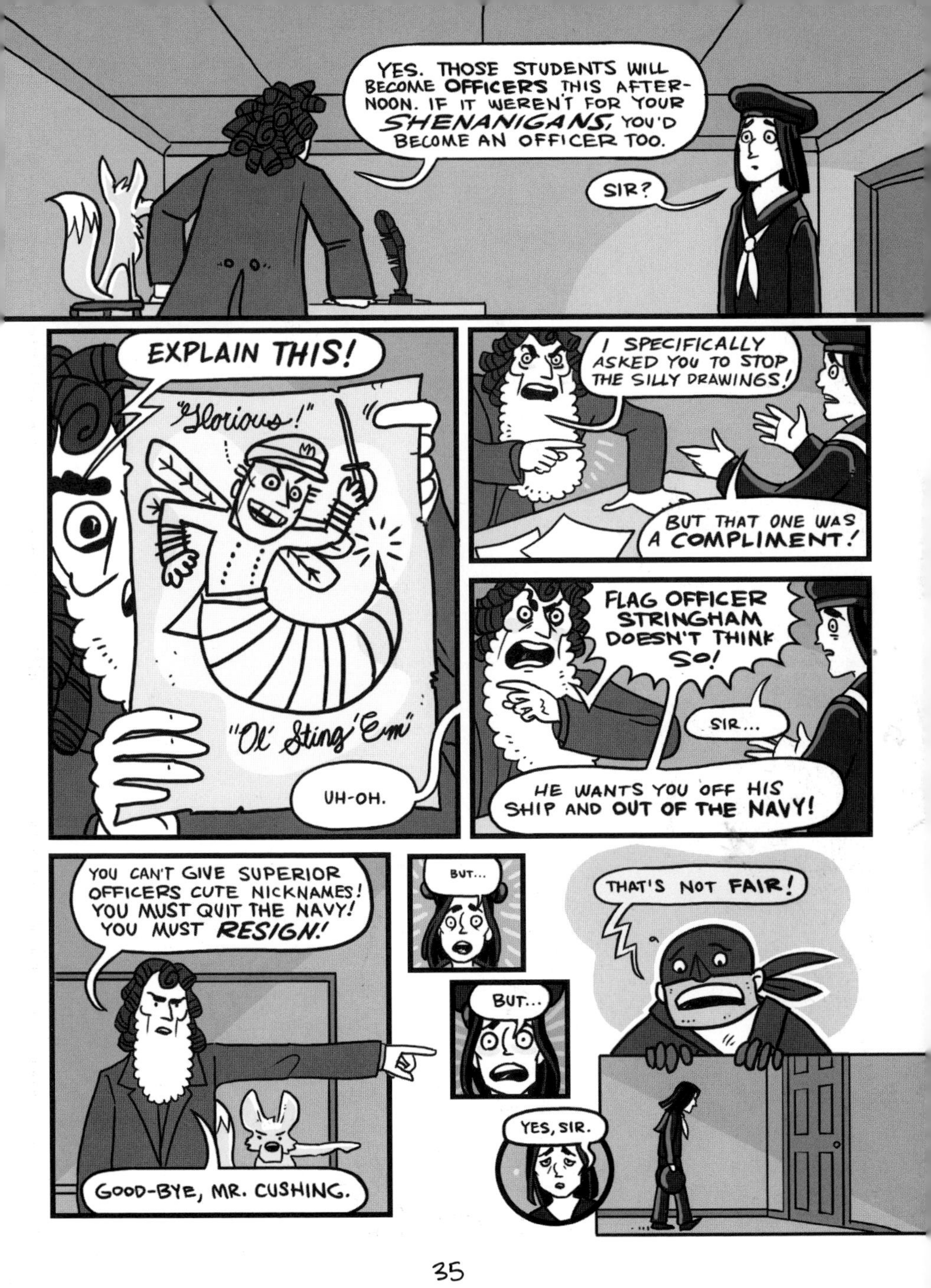
YES. THOSE STUDENTS WILL BECOME OFFICERS THIS AFTER-NOON. IF IT WEREN'T FOR YOUR SHENANIGANS, YOU'D BECOME AN OFFICER TOO.
SIR?
EXPLAIN THIS!
"Glorious!"
"Ol' Sting 'Em"
UH-OH.
I SPECIFICALLY ASKED YOU TO STOP THE SILLY DRAWINGS!
BUT THAT ONE WAS A COMPLIMENT!
FLAG OFFICER STRINGHAM DOESN'T THINK SO!
SIR...
HE WANTS YOU OFF HIS SHIP AND OUT OF THE NAVY!
YOU CAN'T GIVE SUPERIOR OFFICERS CUTE NICKNAMES! YOU MUST QUIT THE NAVY! YOU MUST RESIGN!
GOOD-BYE, MR. CUSHING.
BUT...
BUT...
YES, SIR.
THAT'S NOT FAIR!

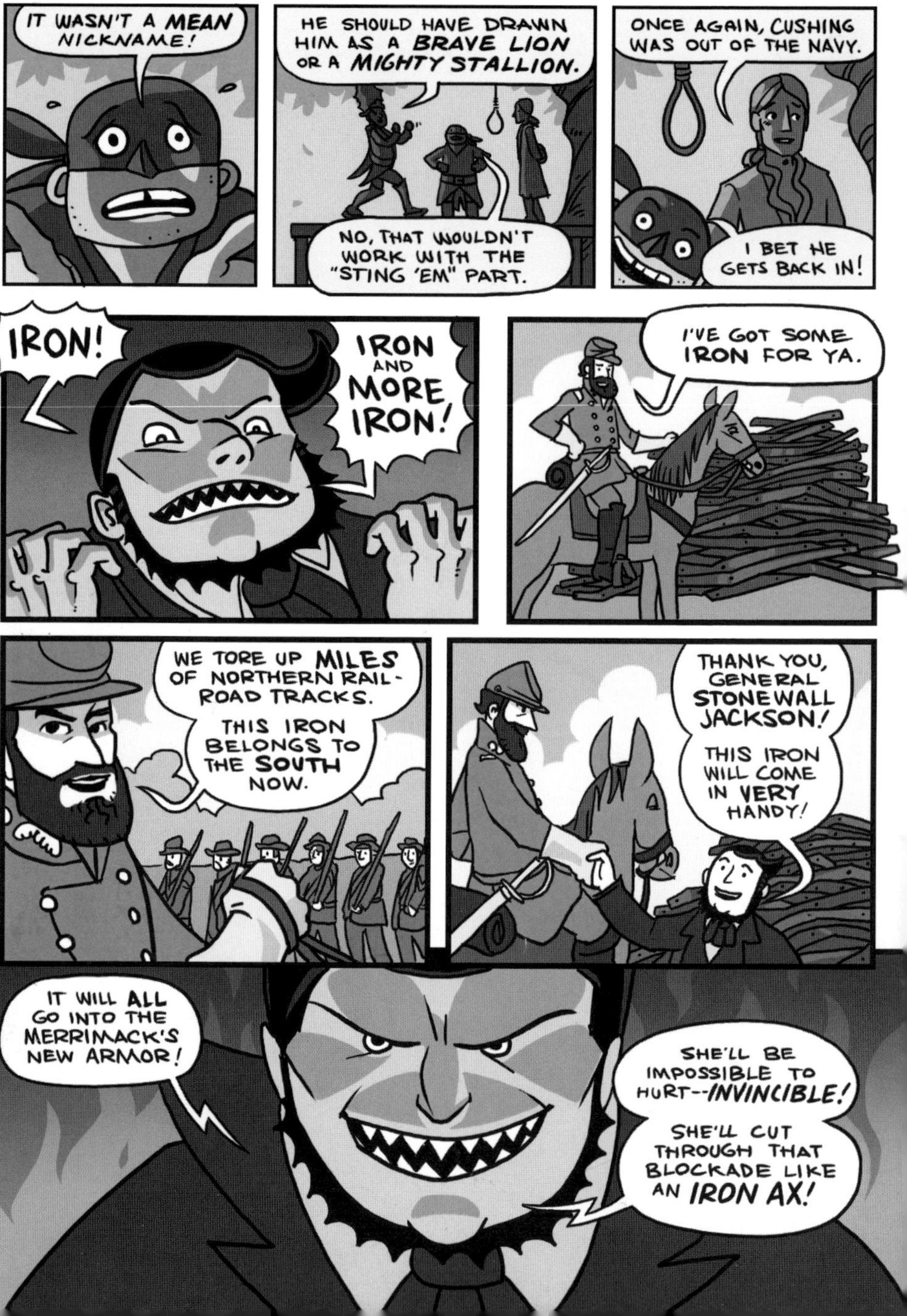

IT WASN'T A MEAN NICKNAME!
HE SHOULD HAVE DRAWN HIM AS A BRAVE LION OR A MIGHTY STALLION.
NO, THAT WOULDN'T WORK WITH THE "STING 'EM" PART.
ONCE AGAIN, CUSHING WAS OUT OF THE NAVY.
I BET HE GETS BACK IN!
IRON!
IRON AND MORE IRON!
I'VE GOT SOME IRON FOR YA.
WE TORE UP MILES OF NORTHERN RAIL-ROAD TRACKS.
THIS IRON BELONGS TO THE SOUTH NOW.
THANK YOU, GENERAL STONEWALL JACKSON!
THIS IRON WILL COME IN VERY HANDY!
IT WILL ALL GO INTO THE MERRIMACK'S NEW ARMOR!
SHE'LL BE IMPOSSIBLE TO HURT--INVINCIBLE!
SHE'LL CUT THROUGH THAT BLOCKADE LIKE AN IRON AX!

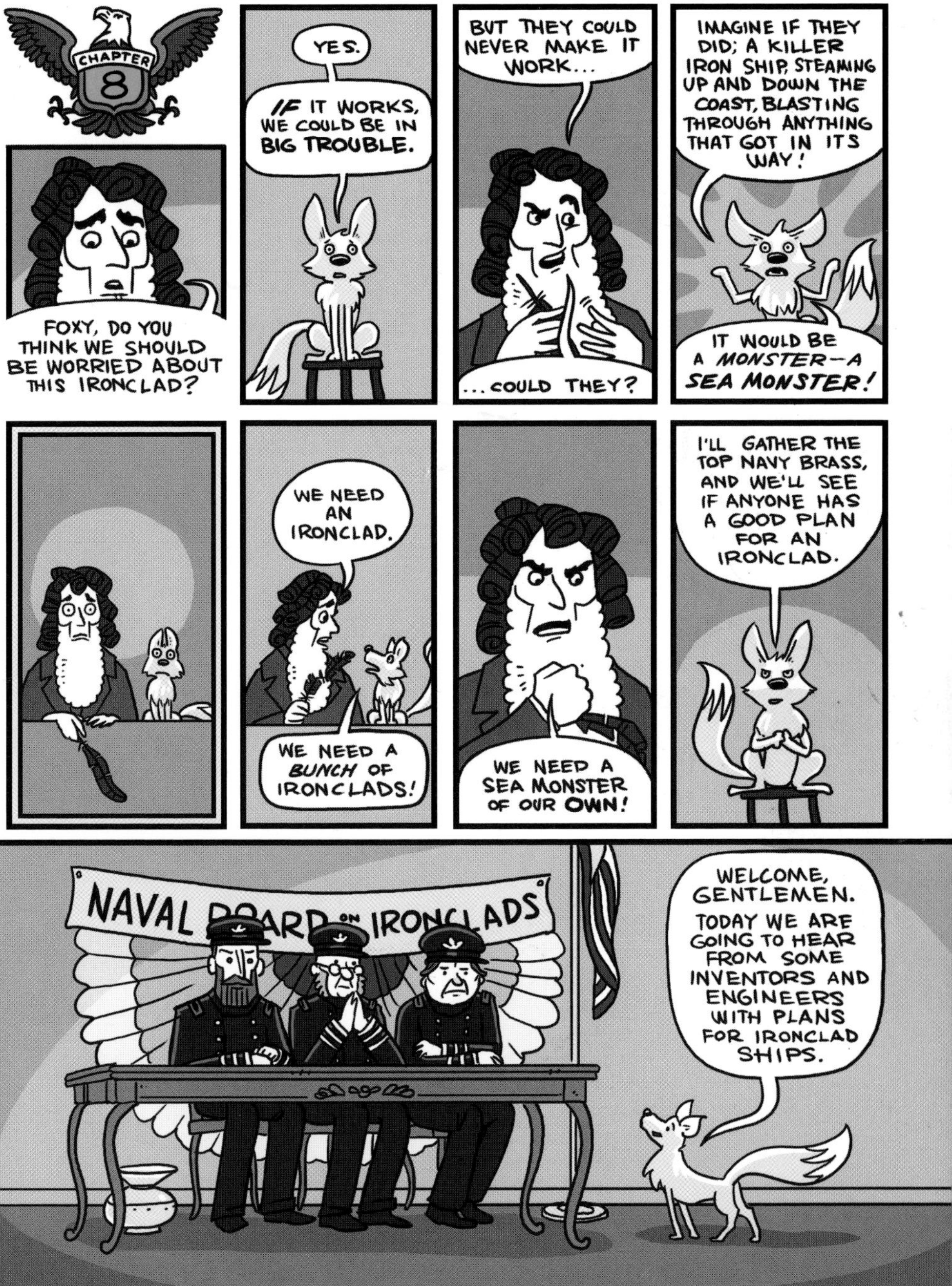
CHAPTER 8
FOXY, DO YOU THINK WE SHOULD BE WORRIED ABOUT THIS IRONCLAD?
YES.
IF IT WORKS, WE COULD BE IN **BIG TROUBLE.**
BUT THEY COULD NEVER MAKE IT WORK...
...COULD THEY?
IMAGINE IF THEY DID; A KILLER IRON SHIP, STEAMING UP AND DOWN THE *COAST*, BLASTING THROUGH ANYTHING THAT GOT IN ITS WAY!
IT WOULD BE A *MONSTER*—A ***SEA MONSTER!***
WE NEED AN IRONCLAD.
WE NEED A *BUNCH* OF IRONCLADS!
WE NEED A SEA MONSTER OF OUR **OWN!**
I'LL GATHER THE TOP NAVY BRASS, AND WE'LL SEE IF ANYONE HAS A GOOD PLAN FOR AN IRONCLAD.
NAVAL BOARD ON IRONCLADS
WELCOME, GENTLEMEN.
TODAY WE ARE GOING TO HEAR FROM SOME INVENTORS AND ENGINEERS WITH PLANS FOR IRONCLAD SHIPS.

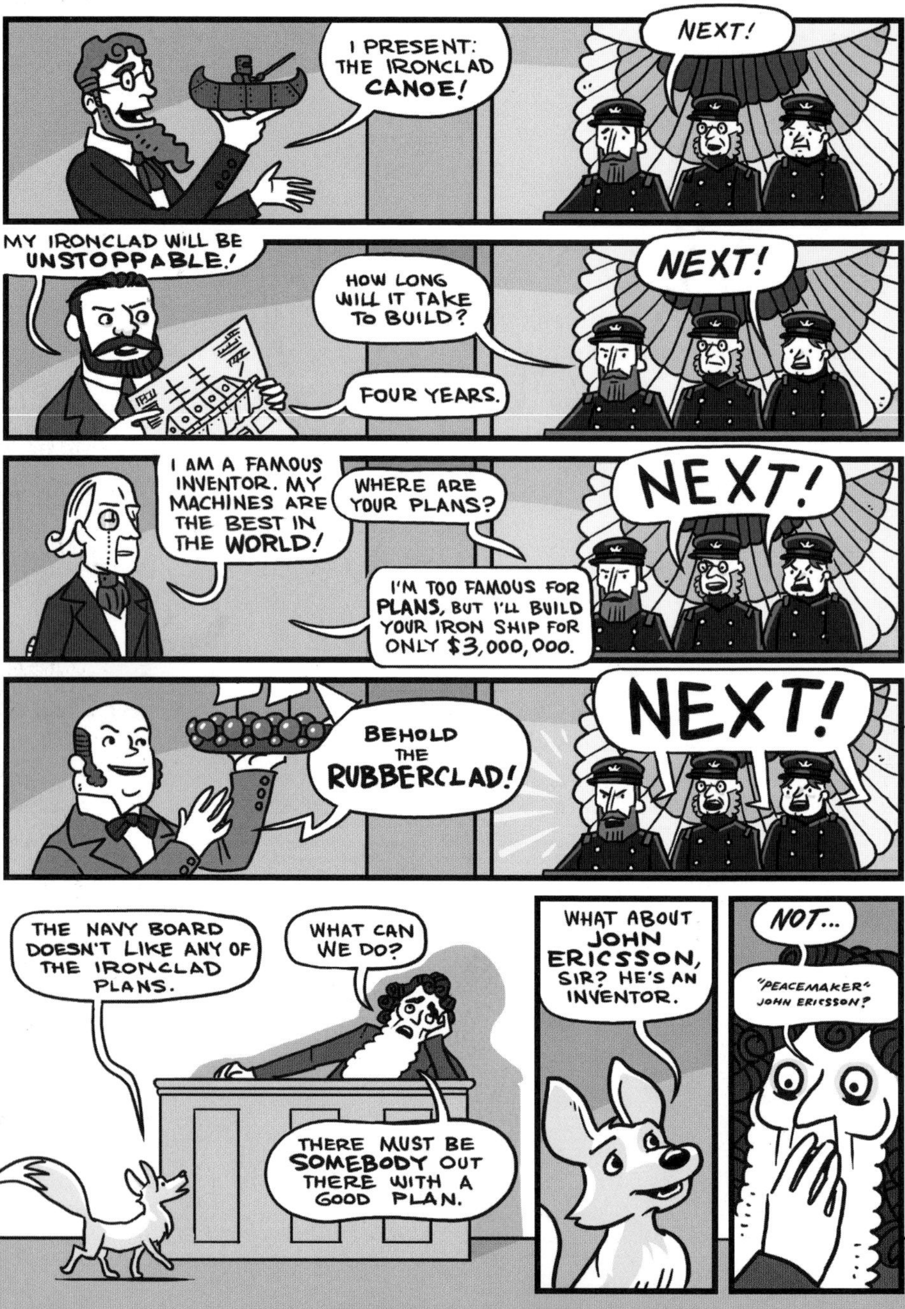
I PRESENT: THE IRONCLAD CANOE!
NEXT!
MY IRONCLAD WILL BE UNSTOPPABLE!
HOW LONG WILL IT TAKE TO BUILD?
FOUR YEARS.
NEXT!
I AM A FAMOUS INVENTOR. MY MACHINES ARE THE BEST IN THE WORLD!
WHERE ARE YOUR PLANS?
I'M TOO FAMOUS FOR PLANS, BUT I'LL BUILD YOUR IRON SHIP FOR ONLY $3,000,000.
NEXT!
BEHOLD THE RUBBERCLAD!
NEXT!
THE NAVY BOARD DOESN'T LIKE ANY OF THE IRONCLAD PLANS.
WHAT CAN WE DO?
THERE MUST BE SOMEBODY OUT THERE WITH A GOOD PLAN.
WHAT ABOUT JOHN ERICSSON, SIR? HE'S AN INVENTOR.
NOT...
"PEACEMAKER" JOHN ERICSSON?

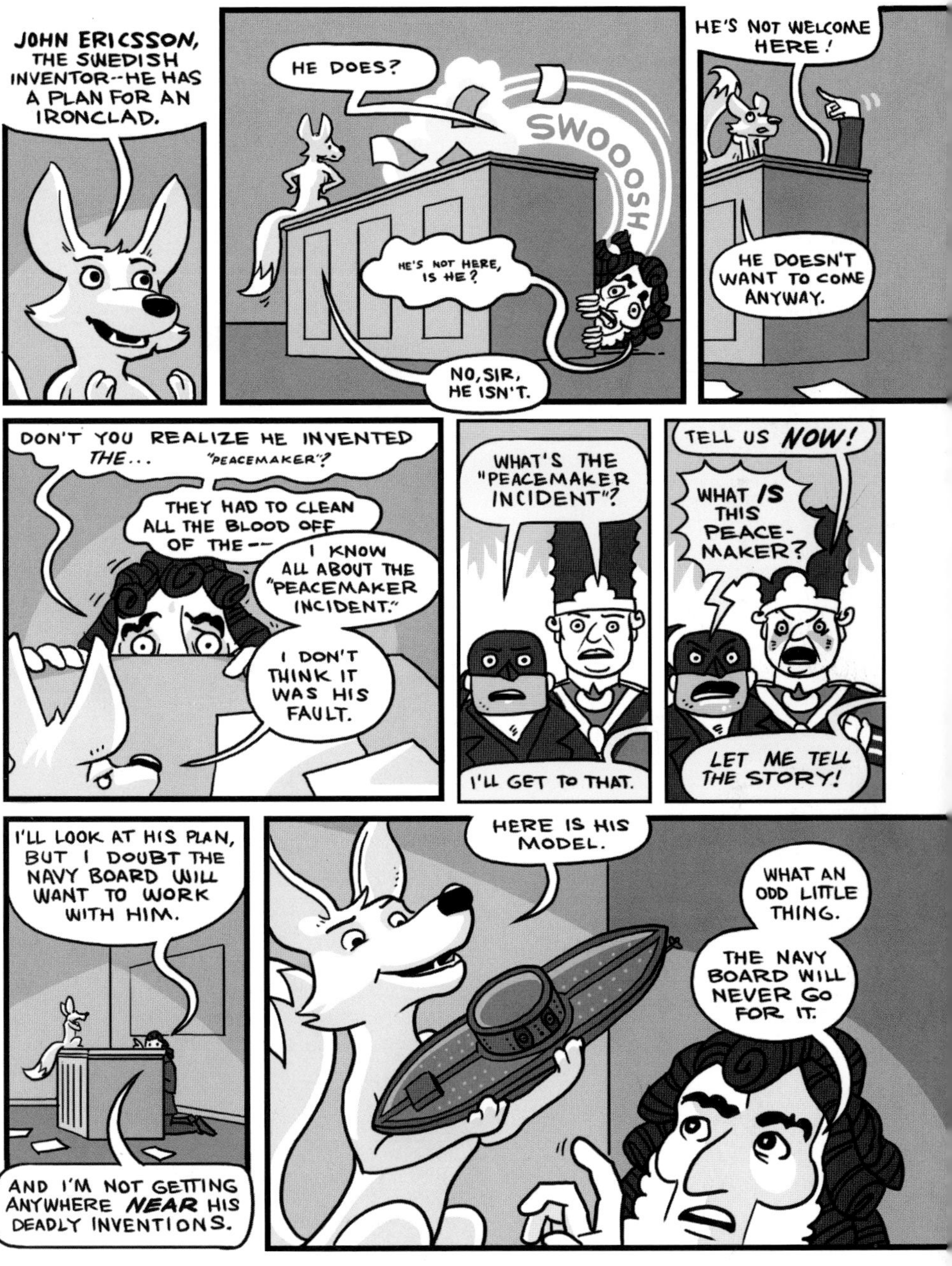
JOHN ERICSSON, THE SWEDISH INVENTOR--HE HAS A PLAN FOR AN IRONCLAD.
HE DOES?
SWOOOOSH
HE'S NOT HERE, IS HE?
NO, SIR, HE ISN'T.
HE'S NOT WELCOME HERE!
HE DOESN'T WANT TO COME ANYWAY.
DON'T YOU REALIZE HE INVENTED THE... "PEACEMAKER"?
THEY HAD TO CLEAN ALL THE BLOOD OFF OF THE--
I KNOW ALL ABOUT THE "PEACEMAKER INCIDENT."
I DON'T THINK IT WAS HIS FAULT.
WHAT'S THE "PEACEMAKER INCIDENT"?
I'LL GET TO THAT.
TELL US NOW!
WHAT IS THIS PEACEMAKER?
LET ME TELL THE STORY!
I'LL LOOK AT HIS PLAN, BUT I DOUBT THE NAVY BOARD WILL WANT TO WORK WITH HIM.
AND I'M NOT GETTING ANYWHERE NEAR HIS DEADLY INVENTIONS.
HERE IS HIS MODEL.
WHAT AN ODD LITTLE THING.
THE NAVY BOARD WILL NEVER GO FOR IT.

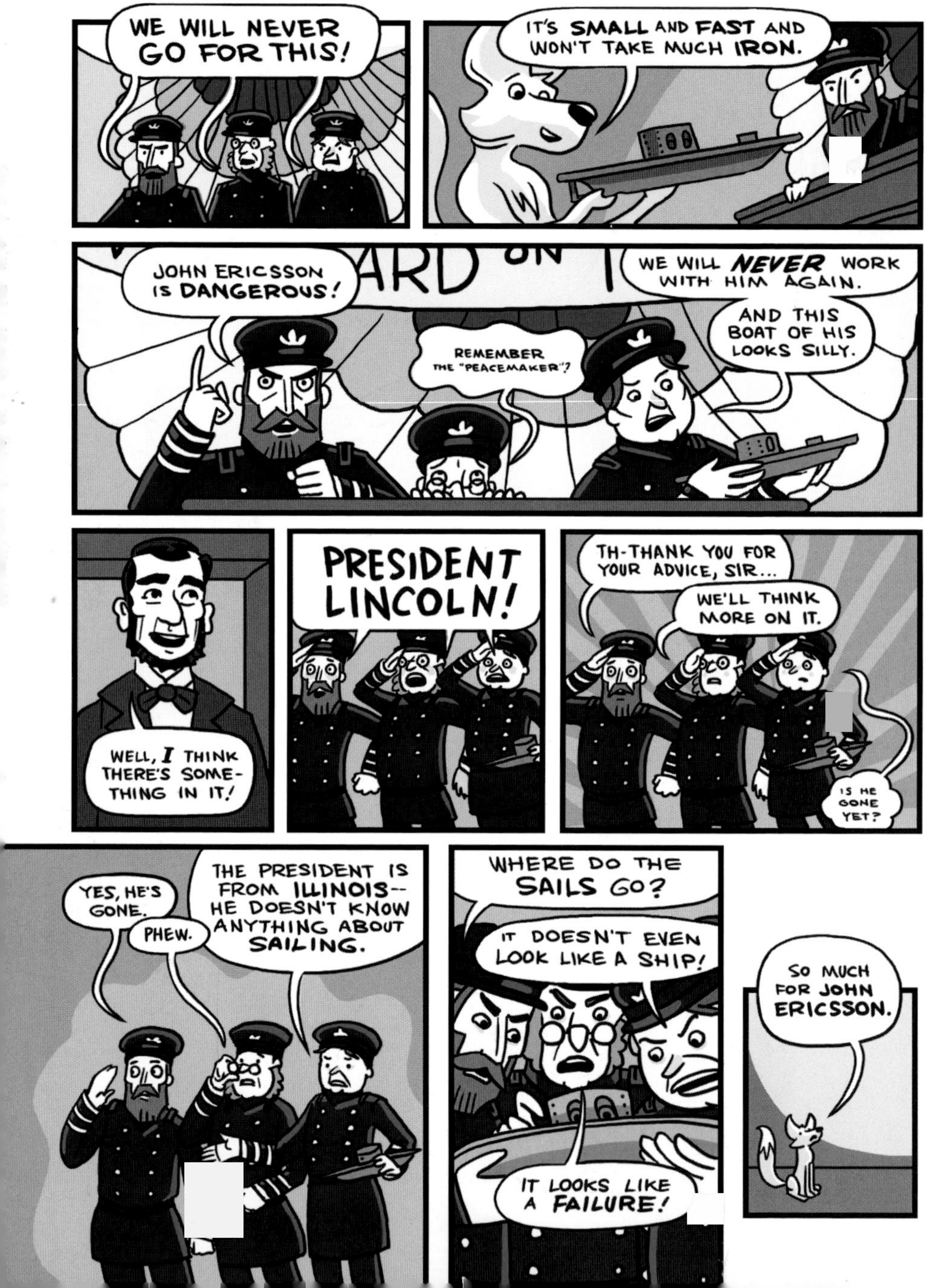
WE WILL NEVER GO FOR THIS!
IT'S SMALL AND FAST AND WON'T TAKE MUCH IRON.
JOHN ERICSSON IS DANGEROUS!
REMEMBER THE "PEACEMAKER"?
WE WILL NEVER WORK WITH HIM AGAIN.
AND THIS BOAT OF HIS LOOKS SILLY.
WELL, I THINK THERE'S SOME-THING IN IT!
PRESIDENT LINCOLN!
TH-THANK YOU FOR YOUR ADVICE, SIR...
WE'LL THINK MORE ON IT.
IS HE GONE YET?
YES, HE'S GONE.
PHEW.
THE PRESIDENT IS FROM ILLINOIS-- HE DOESN'T KNOW ANYTHING ABOUT SAILING.
WHERE DO THE SAILS GO?
IT DOESN'T EVEN LOOK LIKE A SHIP!
IT LOOKS LIKE A FAILURE!
SO MUCH FOR JOHN ERICSSON.

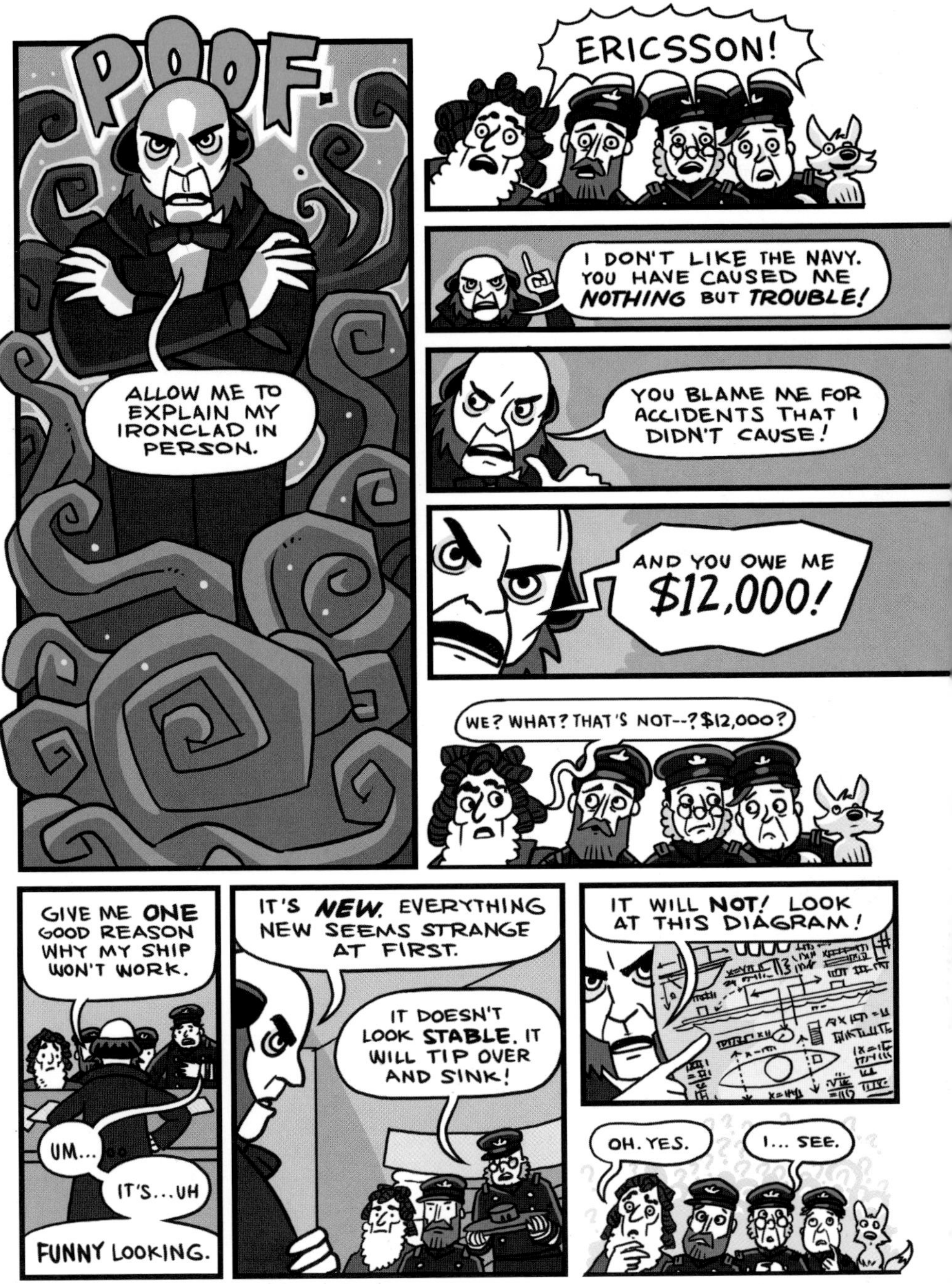
POOF!
ALLOW ME TO EXPLAIN MY IRONCLAD IN PERSON.
ERICSSON!
I DON'T LIKE THE NAVY. YOU HAVE CAUSED ME NOTHING BUT TROUBLE!
YOU BLAME ME FOR ACCIDENTS THAT I DIDN'T CAUSE!
AND YOU OWE ME $12,000!
WE? WHAT? THAT'S NOT--? $12,000?
GIVE ME ONE GOOD REASON WHY MY SHIP WON'T WORK.
UM...
IT'S...UH
FUNNY LOOKING.
IT'S NEW. EVERYTHING NEW SEEMS STRANGE AT FIRST.
IT DOESN'T LOOK STABLE. IT WILL TIP OVER AND SINK!
IT WILL NOT! LOOK AT THIS DIAGRAM!
OH. YES.
I... SEE.

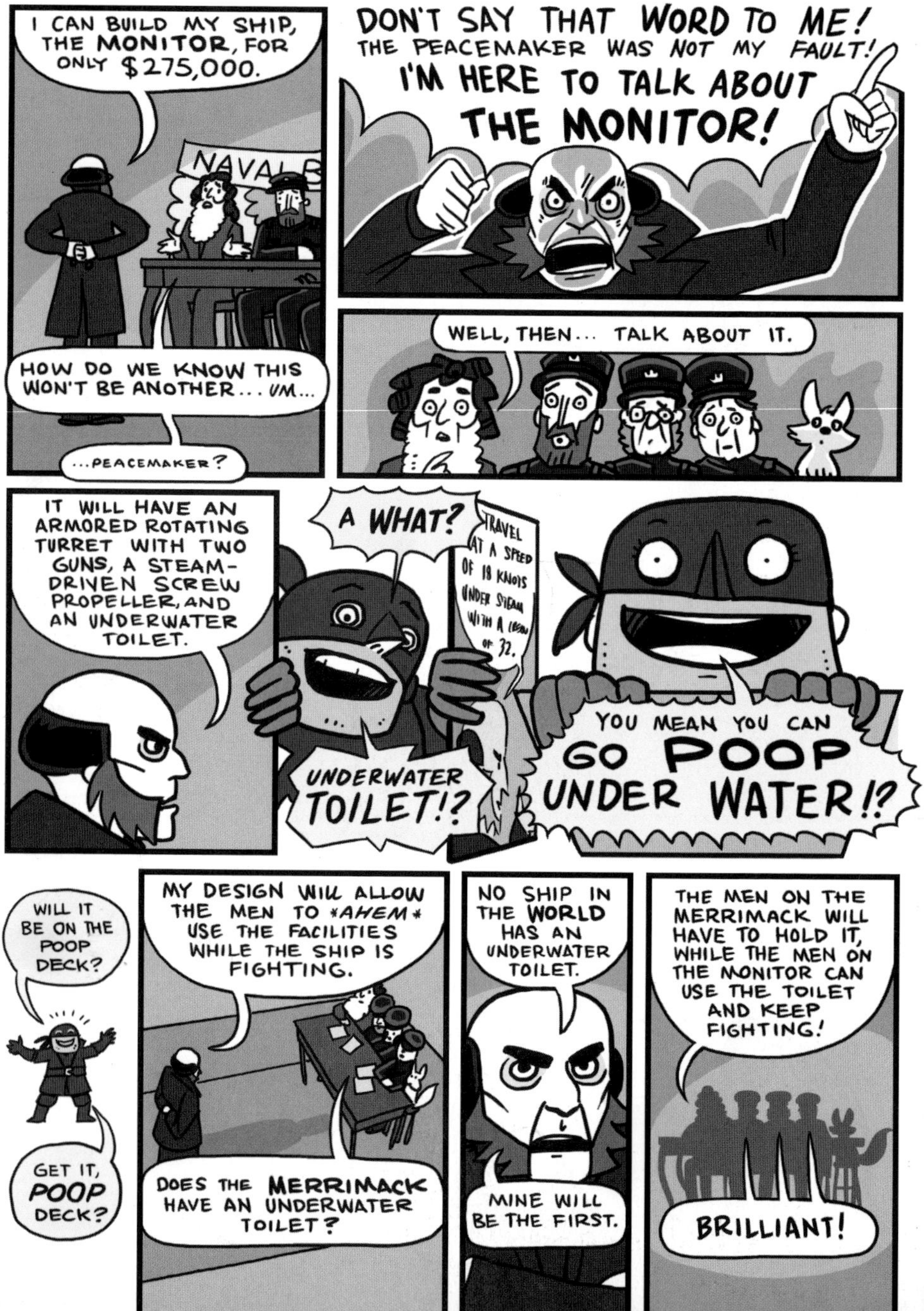
I CAN BUILD MY SHIP, THE MONITOR, FOR ONLY $275,000.
NAVAL
HOW DO WE KNOW THIS WON'T BE ANOTHER... UM...
...PEACEMAKER?
DON'T SAY THAT WORD TO ME! THE PEACEMAKER WAS NOT MY FAULT! I'M HERE TO TALK ABOUT THE MONITOR!
WELL, THEN... TALK ABOUT IT.
IT WILL HAVE AN ARMORED ROTATING TURRET WITH TWO GUNS, A STEAM-DRIVEN SCREW PROPELLER, AND AN UNDERWATER TOILET.
A WHAT?
TRAVEL AT A SPEED OF 18 KNOTS UNDER STEAM WITH A CREW OF 32.
UNDERWATER TOILET!?
YOU MEAN YOU CAN GO POOP UNDER WATER!?
WILL IT BE ON THE POOP DECK?
GET IT, POOP DECK?
MY DESIGN WILL ALLOW THE MEN TO *AHEM* USE THE FACILITIES WHILE THE SHIP IS FIGHTING.
DOES THE MERRIMACK HAVE AN UNDERWATER TOILET?
NO SHIP IN THE WORLD HAS AN UNDERWATER TOILET.
MINE WILL BE THE FIRST.
THE MEN ON THE MERRIMACK WILL HAVE TO HOLD IT, WHILE THE MEN ON THE MONITOR CAN USE THE TOILET AND KEEP FIGHTING!
BRILLIANT!

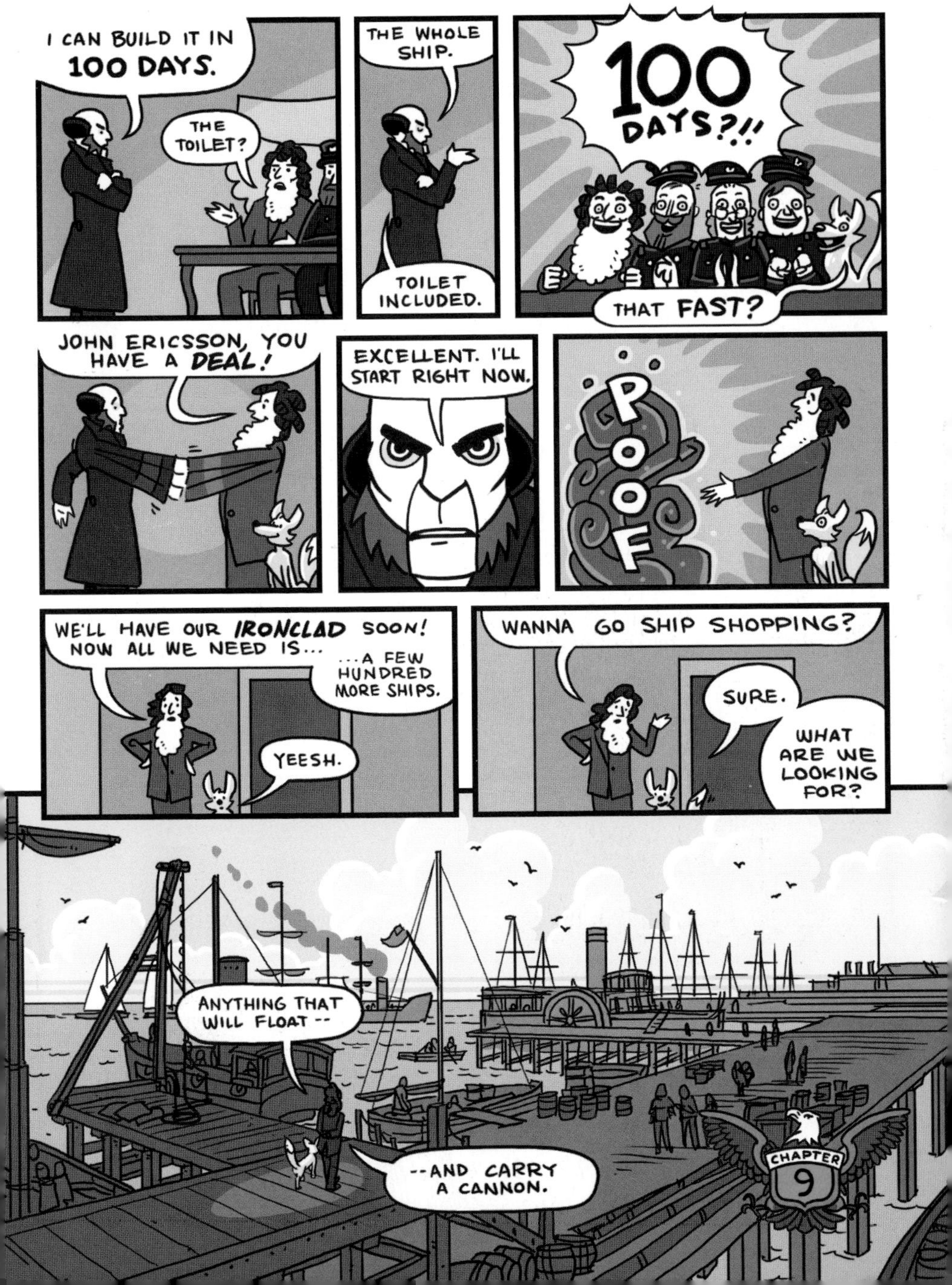
I CAN BUILD IT IN 100 DAYS.
THE TOILET?
THE WHOLE SHIP.
TOILET INCLUDED.
100 DAYS?!!
THAT FAST?
JOHN ERICSSON, YOU HAVE A DEAL!
EXCELLENT. I'LL START RIGHT NOW.
POOF
WE'LL HAVE OUR IRONCLAD SOON! NOW ALL WE NEED IS...
...A FEW HUNDRED MORE SHIPS.
YEESH.
WANNA GO SHIP SHOPPING?
SURE.
WHAT ARE WE LOOKING FOR?
ANYTHING THAT WILL FLOAT --
--AND CARRY A CANNON.
CHAPTER 9

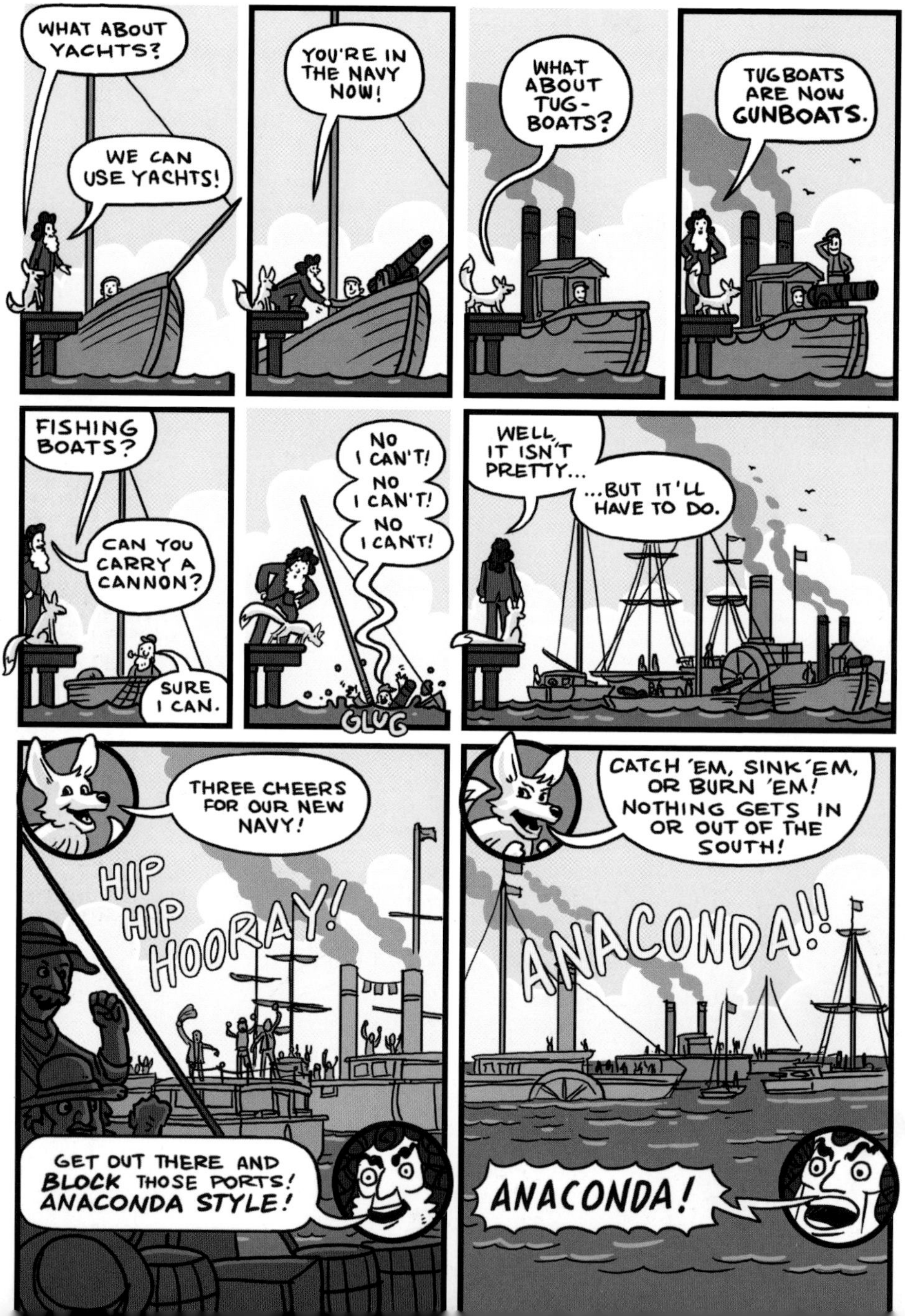

WHAT ABOUT YACHTS?
WE CAN USE YACHTS!
YOU'RE IN THE NAVY NOW!
WHAT ABOUT TUG-BOATS?
TUGBOATS ARE NOW GUNBOATS.
FISHING BOATS?
CAN YOU CARRY A CANNON?
SURE I CAN.
NO I CAN'T!
NO I CAN'T!
NO I CAN'T!
GLUG
WELL, IT ISN'T PRETTY...
...BUT IT'LL HAVE TO DO.
THREE CHEERS FOR OUR NEW NAVY!
HIP HIP HOORAY!
GET OUT THERE AND BLOCK THOSE PORTS! ANACONDA STYLE!
CATCH 'EM, SINK 'EM, OR BURN 'EM! NOTHING GETS IN OR OUT OF THE SOUTH!
ANACONDA!!
ANACONDA!

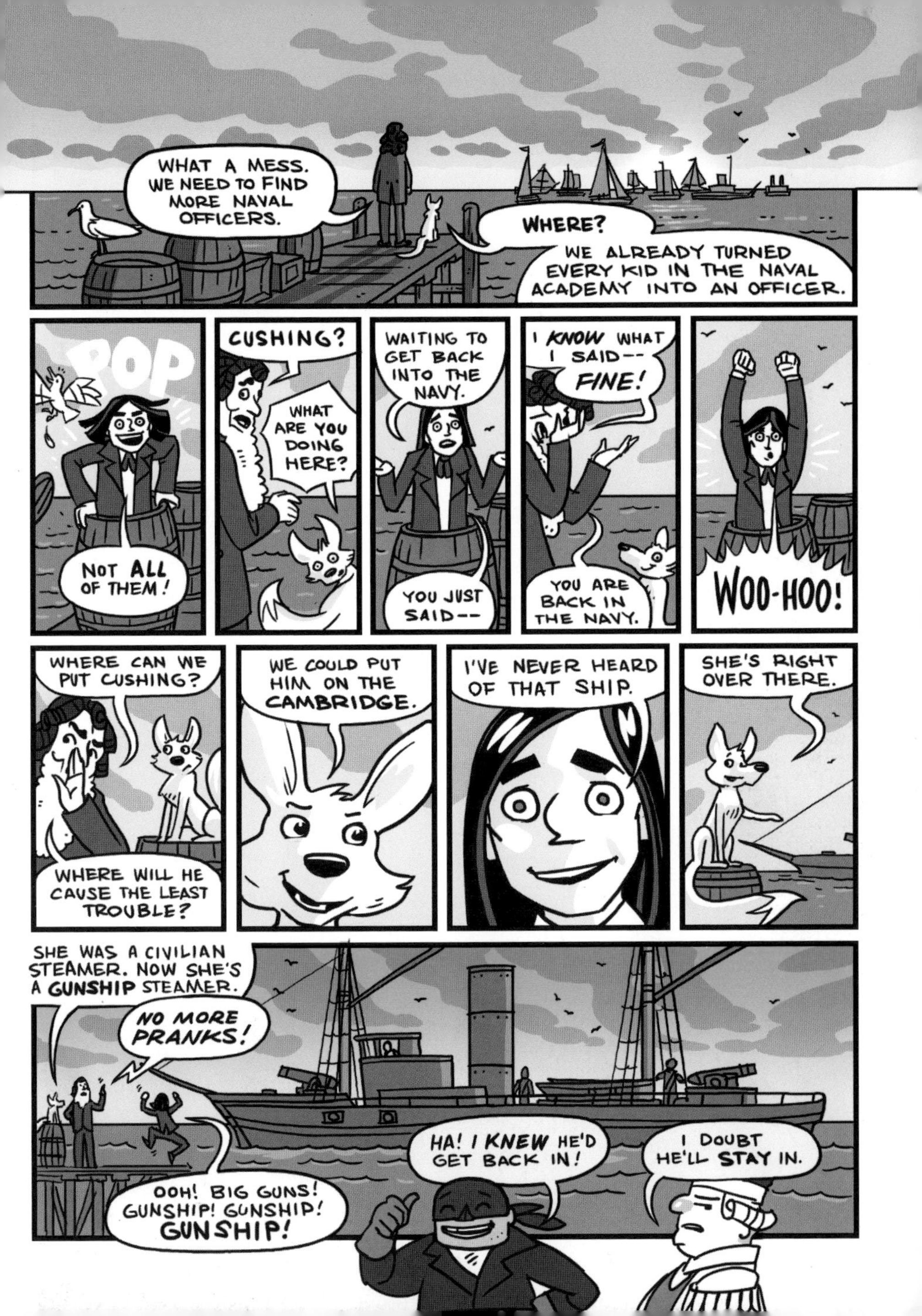
WHAT A MESS. WE NEED TO FIND MORE NAVAL OFFICERS.
WHERE?
WE ALREADY TURNED EVERY KID IN THE NAVAL ACADEMY INTO AN OFFICER.
POP
NOT ALL OF THEM!
CUSHING?
WHAT ARE YOU DOING HERE?
WAITING TO GET BACK INTO THE NAVY.
YOU JUST SAID--
I KNOW WHAT I SAID-- FINE!
YOU ARE BACK IN THE NAVY.
WOO-HOO!
WHERE CAN WE PUT CUSHING?
WHERE WILL HE CAUSE THE LEAST TROUBLE?
WE COULD PUT HIM ON THE CAMBRIDGE.
I'VE NEVER HEARD OF THAT SHIP.
SHE'S RIGHT OVER THERE.
SHE WAS A CIVILIAN STEAMER. NOW SHE'S A GUNSHIP STEAMER.
NO MORE PRANKS!
OOH! BIG GUNS! GUNSHIP! GUNSHIP! GUNSHIP!
HA! I KNEW HE'D GET BACK IN!
I DOUBT HE'LL STAY IN.

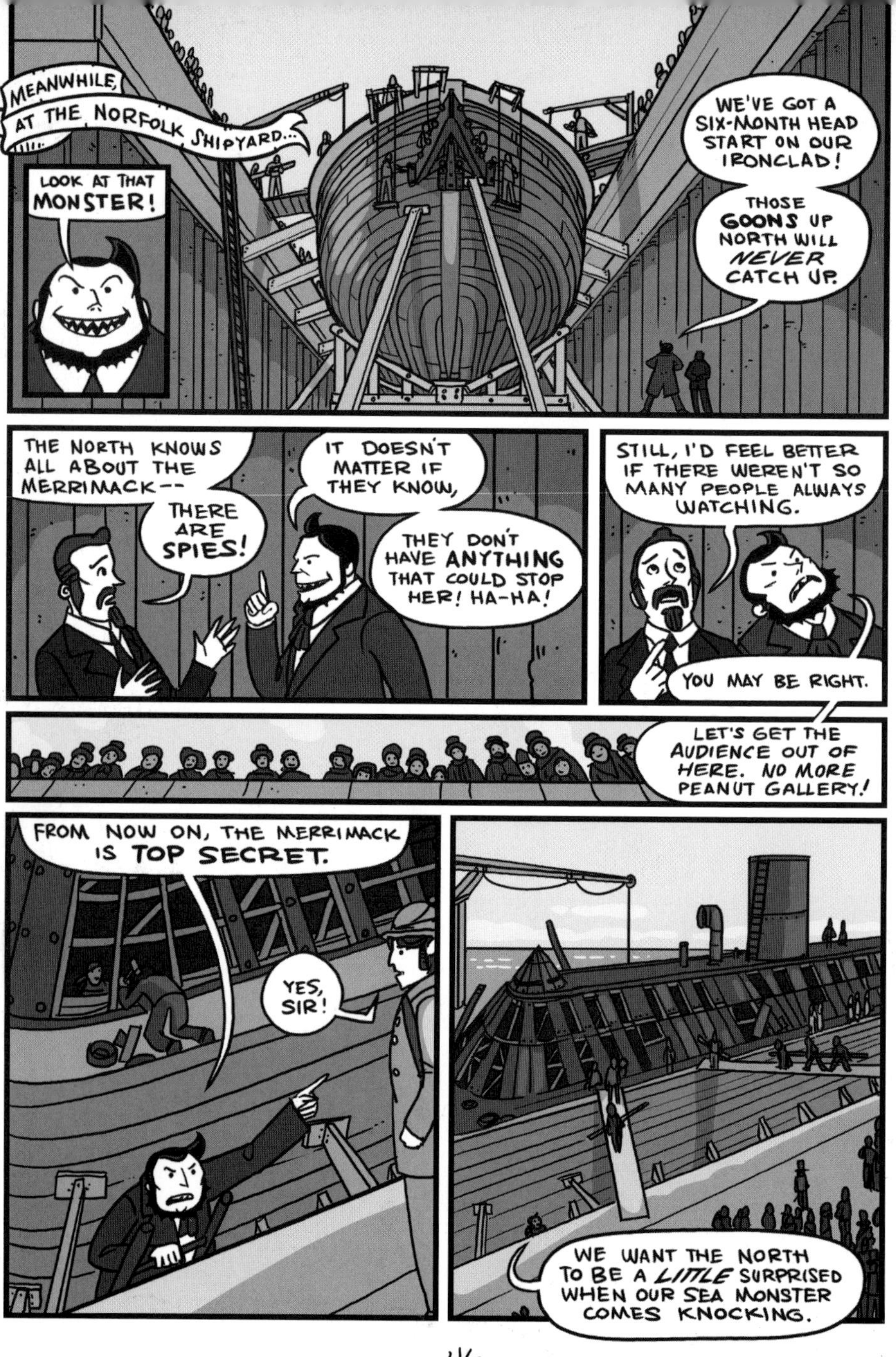
MEANWHILE, AT THE NORFOLK SHIPYARD...
LOOK AT THAT MONSTER!
WE'VE GOT A SIX-MONTH HEAD START ON OUR IRONCLAD!
THOSE GOONS UP NORTH WILL NEVER CATCH UP.
THE NORTH KNOWS ALL ABOUT THE MERRIMACK--
THERE ARE SPIES!
IT DOESN'T MATTER IF THEY KNOW,
THEY DON'T HAVE ANYTHING THAT COULD STOP HER! HA-HA!
STILL, I'D FEEL BETTER IF THERE WEREN'T SO MANY PEOPLE ALWAYS WATCHING.
YOU MAY BE RIGHT.
LET'S GET THE AUDIENCE OUT OF HERE. NO MORE PEANUT GALLERY!
FROM NOW ON, THE MERRIMACK IS TOP SECRET.
YES, SIR!
WE WANT THE NORTH TO BE A LITTLE SURPRISED WHEN OUR SEA MONSTER COMES KNOCKING.

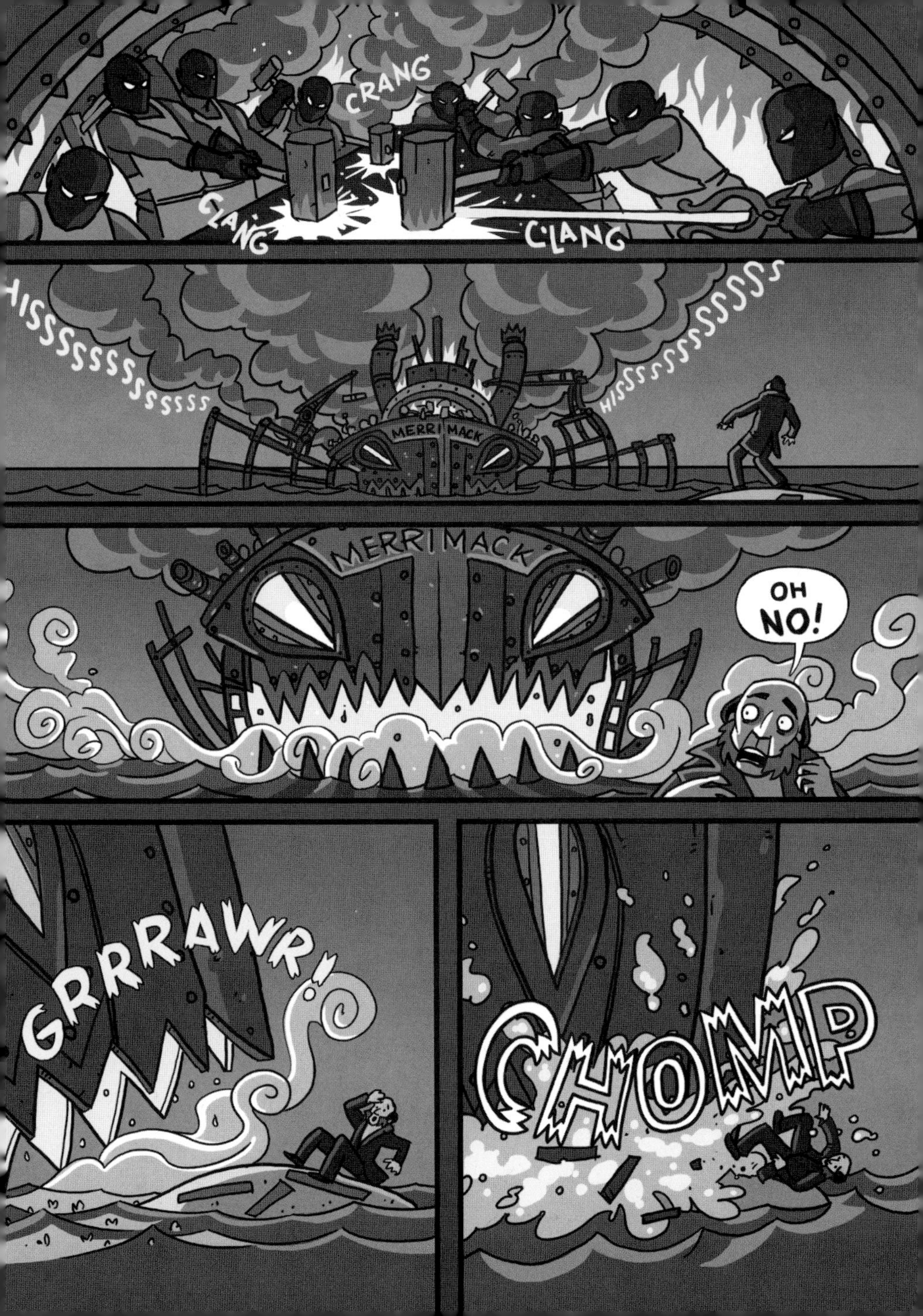
CRANG
CLANG
CLANG
HISSSSSSSSSSSSSS
HISSSSSSSSSSSSSSS
MERRIMACK
MERRIMACK
OH NO!
GRRRAWR!
CHOMP

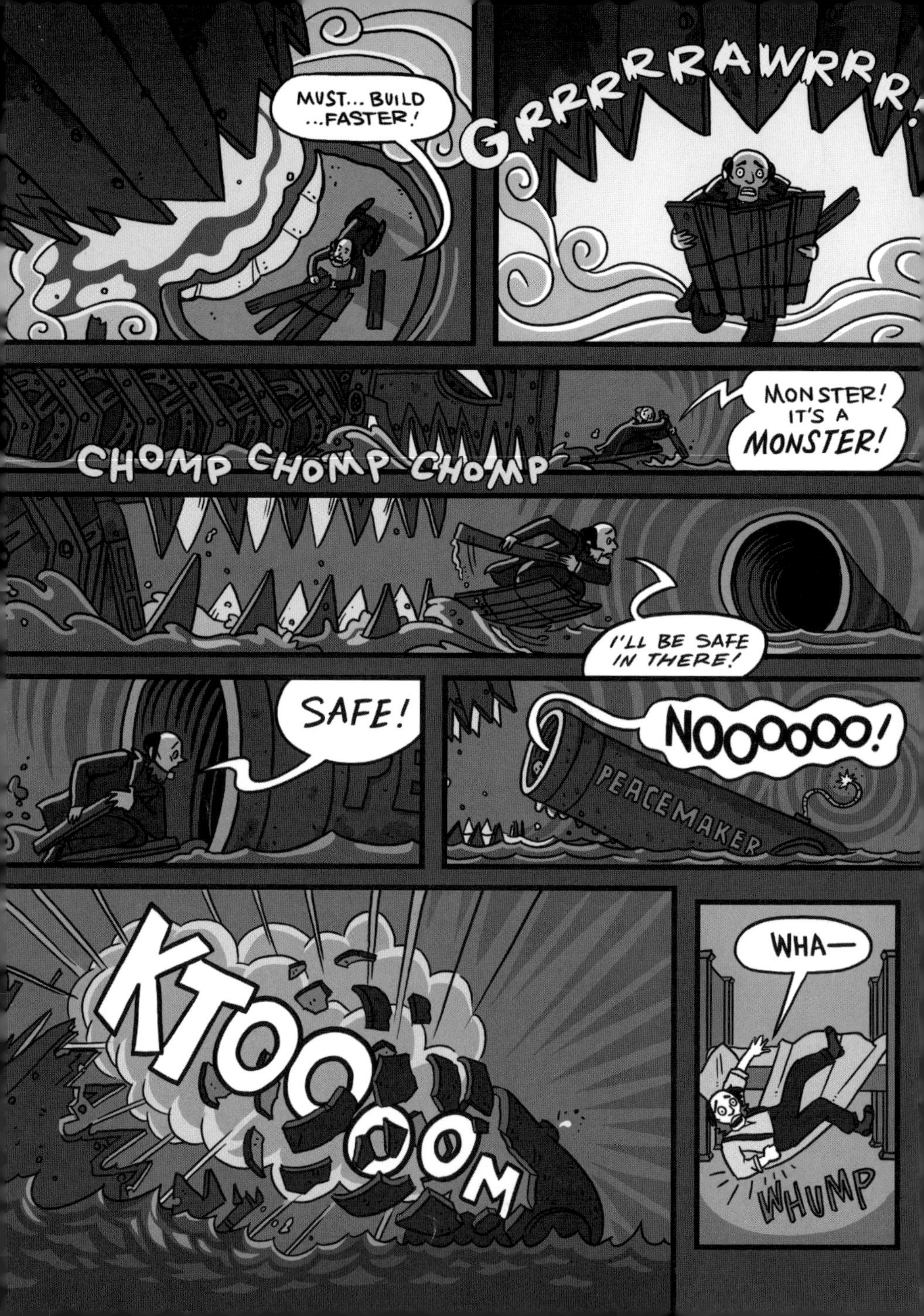
MUST... BUILD ...FASTER!
GRRRRRAWRRRR!
CHOMP CHOMP CHOMP
MONSTER! IT'S A MONSTER!
I'LL BE SAFE IN THERE!
SAFE!
PEACEMAKER
NOOOOOO!
KTOOOOOM
WHA—
WHUMP

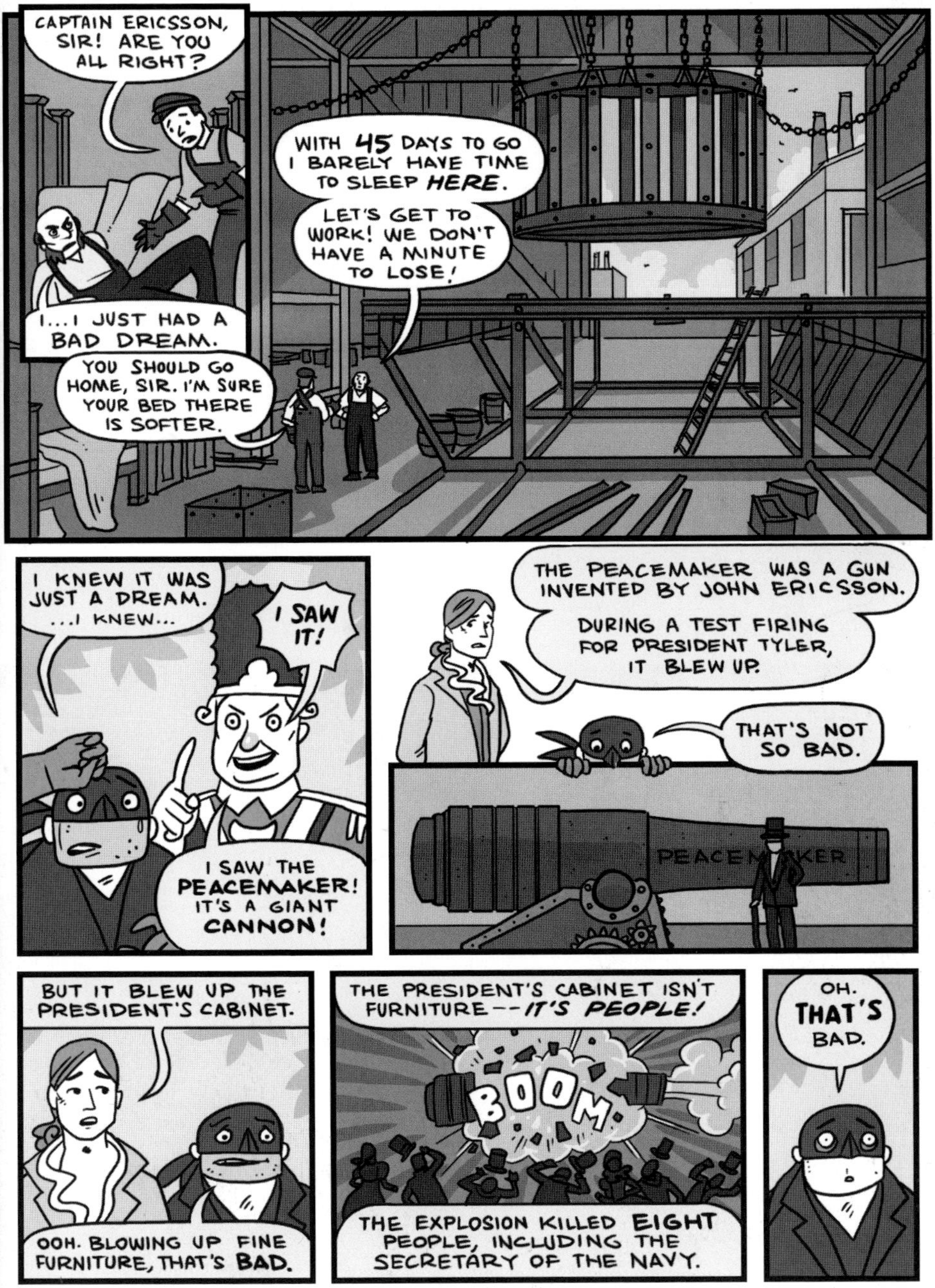
CAPTAIN ERICSSON, SIR! ARE YOU ALL RIGHT?
I... I JUST HAD A BAD DREAM.
YOU SHOULD GO HOME, SIR. I'M SURE YOUR BED THERE IS SOFTER.
WITH 45 DAYS TO GO I BARELY HAVE TIME TO SLEEP *HERE*.
LET'S GET TO WORK! WE DON'T HAVE A MINUTE TO LOSE!
I KNEW IT WAS JUST A DREAM. ...I KNEW...
I SAW IT!
I SAW THE **PEACEMAKER**! IT'S A GIANT **CANNON**!
THE PEACEMAKER WAS A GUN INVENTED BY JOHN ERICSSON.
DURING A TEST FIRING FOR PRESIDENT TYLER, IT BLEW UP.
THAT'S NOT SO BAD.
PEACEMAKER
BUT IT BLEW UP THE PRESIDENT'S CABINET.
OOH. BLOWING UP FINE FURNITURE, THAT'S **BAD**.
THE PRESIDENT'S CABINET ISN'T FURNITURE-- *IT'S PEOPLE!*
BOOM!
THE EXPLOSION KILLED **EIGHT** PEOPLE, INCLUDING THE SECRETARY OF THE NAVY.
OH. **THAT'S** BAD.

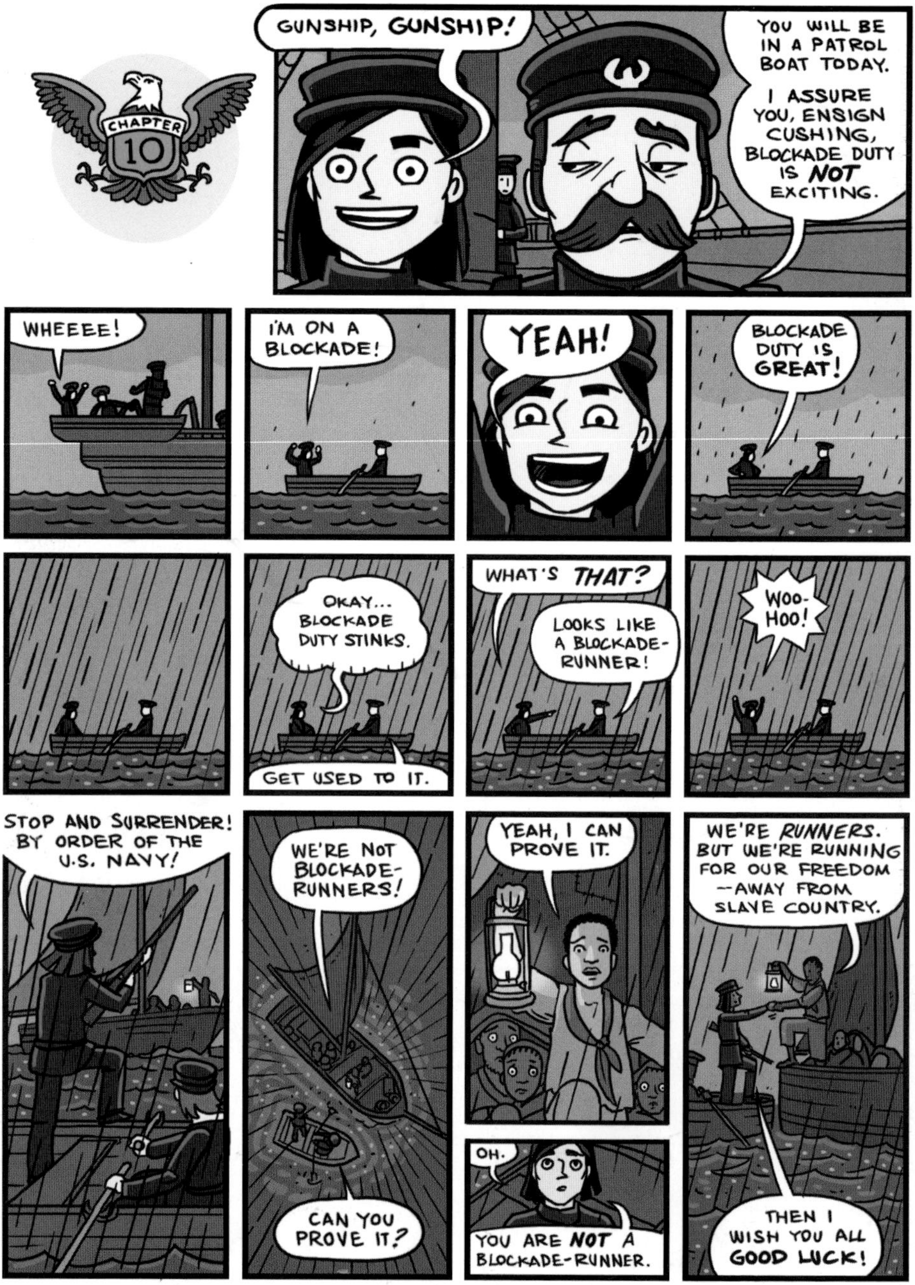
CHAPTER 10
GUNSHIP, GUNSHIP!
YOU WILL BE IN A PATROL BOAT TODAY.
I ASSURE YOU, ENSIGN CUSHING, BLOCKADE DUTY IS NOT EXCITING.
WHEEEEE!
I'M ON A BLOCKADE!
YEAH!
BLOCKADE DUTY IS GREAT!
OKAY... BLOCKADE DUTY STINKS.
GET USED TO IT.
WHAT'S THAT?
LOOKS LIKE A BLOCKADE-RUNNER!
WOO-HOO!
STOP AND SURRENDER! BY ORDER OF THE U.S. NAVY!
WE'RE NOT BLOCKADE-RUNNERS!
CAN YOU PROVE IT?
YEAH, I CAN PROVE IT.
OH.
YOU ARE NOT A BLOCKADE-RUNNER.
WE'RE RUNNERS. BUT WE'RE RUNNING FOR OUR FREEDOM --AWAY FROM SLAVE COUNTRY.
THEN I WISH YOU ALL GOOD LUCK!

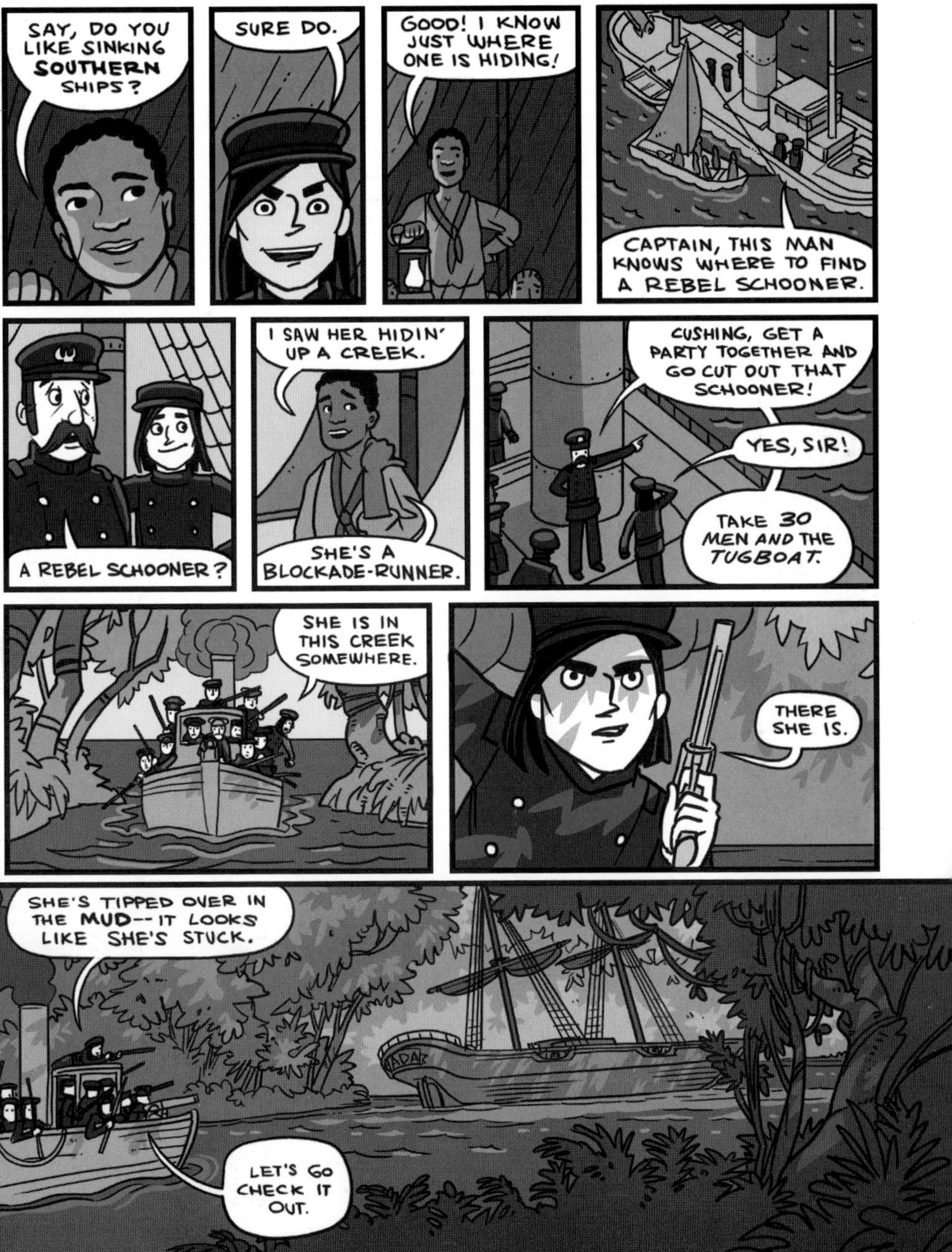
SAY, DO YOU LIKE SINKING **SOUTHERN** SHIPS?
SURE DO.
GOOD! I KNOW JUST WHERE ONE IS HIDING!
CAPTAIN, THIS MAN KNOWS WHERE TO FIND A REBEL SCHOONER.
A REBEL SCHOONER?
I SAW HER HIDIN' UP A CREEK.
SHE'S A BLOCKADE-RUNNER.
CUSHING, GET A PARTY TOGETHER AND GO CUT OUT THAT SCHOONER!
YES, SIR!
TAKE **30** MEN AND THE *TUGBOAT.*
SHE IS IN THIS CREEK SOMEWHERE.
THERE SHE IS.
SHE'S TIPPED OVER IN THE **MUD**-- IT LOOKS LIKE SHE'S STUCK.
LET'S GO CHECK IT OUT.

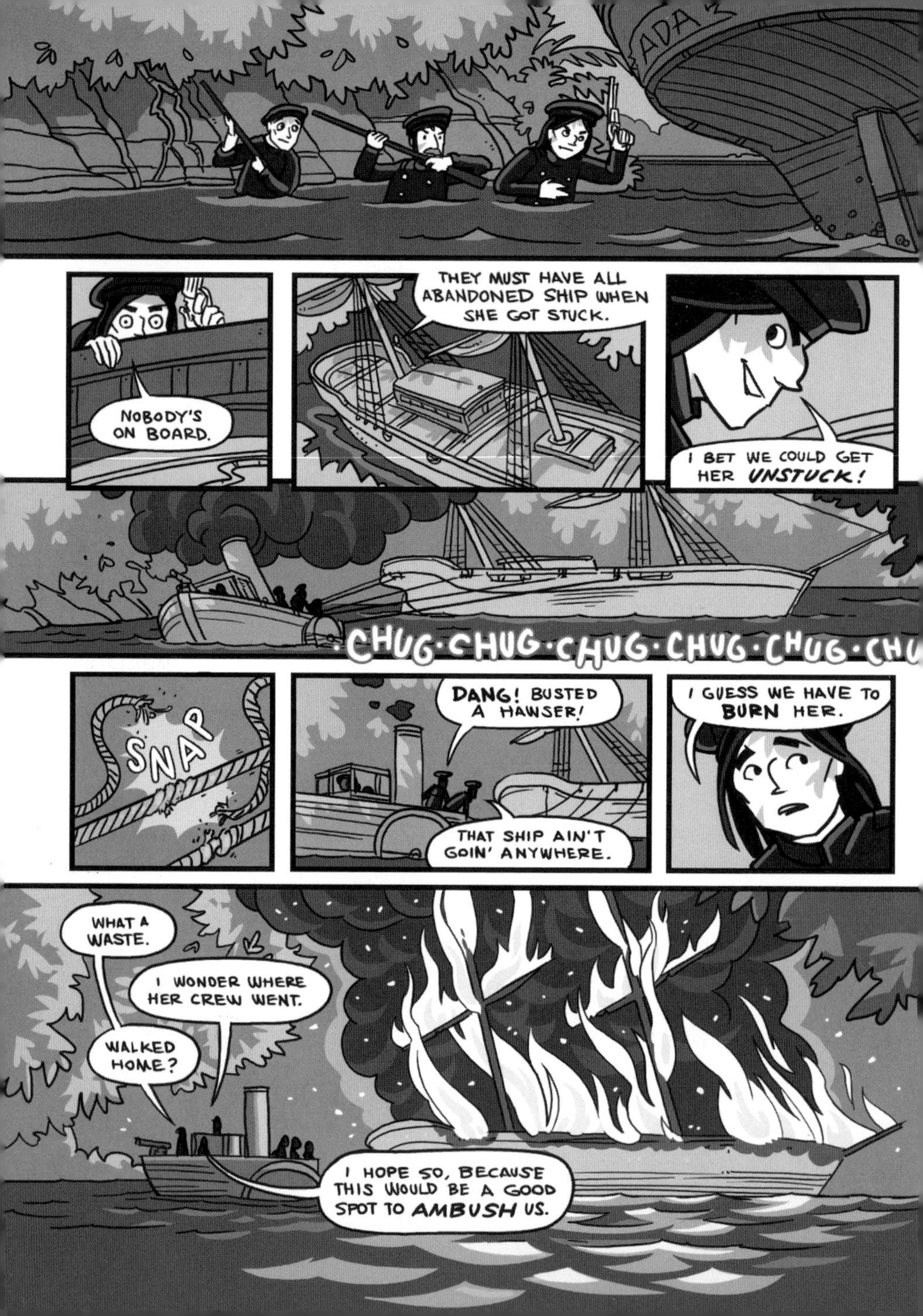
ADA
NOBODY'S ON BOARD.
THEY MUST HAVE ALL ABANDONED SHIP WHEN SHE GOT STUCK.
I BET WE COULD GET HER UNSTUCK!
CHUG·CHUG·CHUG·CHUG·CHUG·CHU
SNAP
DANG! BUSTED A HAWSER!
THAT SHIP AIN'T GOIN' ANYWHERE.
I GUESS WE HAVE TO BURN HER.
WHAT A WASTE.
I WONDER WHERE HER CREW WENT.
WALKED HOME?
I HOPE SO, BECAUSE THIS WOULD BE A GOOD SPOT TO AMBUSH US.

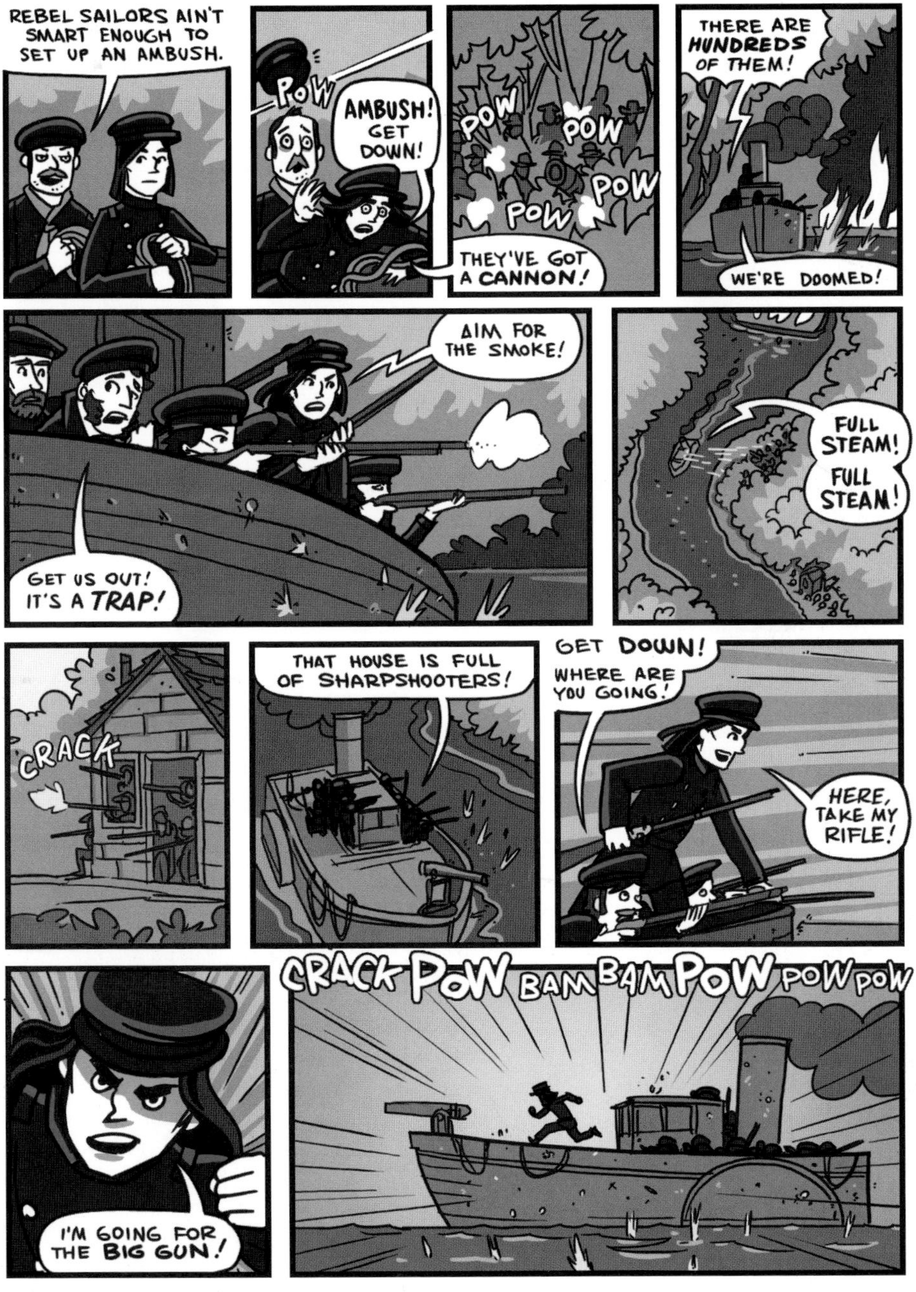

REBEL SAILORS AIN'T SMART ENOUGH TO SET UP AN AMBUSH.
POW
AMBUSH! GET DOWN!
POW
POW
POW
POW
THEY'VE GOT A CANNON!
THERE ARE HUNDREDS OF THEM!
WE'RE DOOMED!
AIM FOR THE SMOKE!
GET US OUT! IT'S A TRAP!
FULL STEAM!
FULL STEAM!
CRACK
THAT HOUSE IS FULL OF SHARPSHOOTERS!
GET DOWN!
WHERE ARE YOU GOING!
HERE, TAKE MY RIFLE!
I'M GOING FOR THE BIG GUN!
CRACK POW BAM BAM POW POW POW

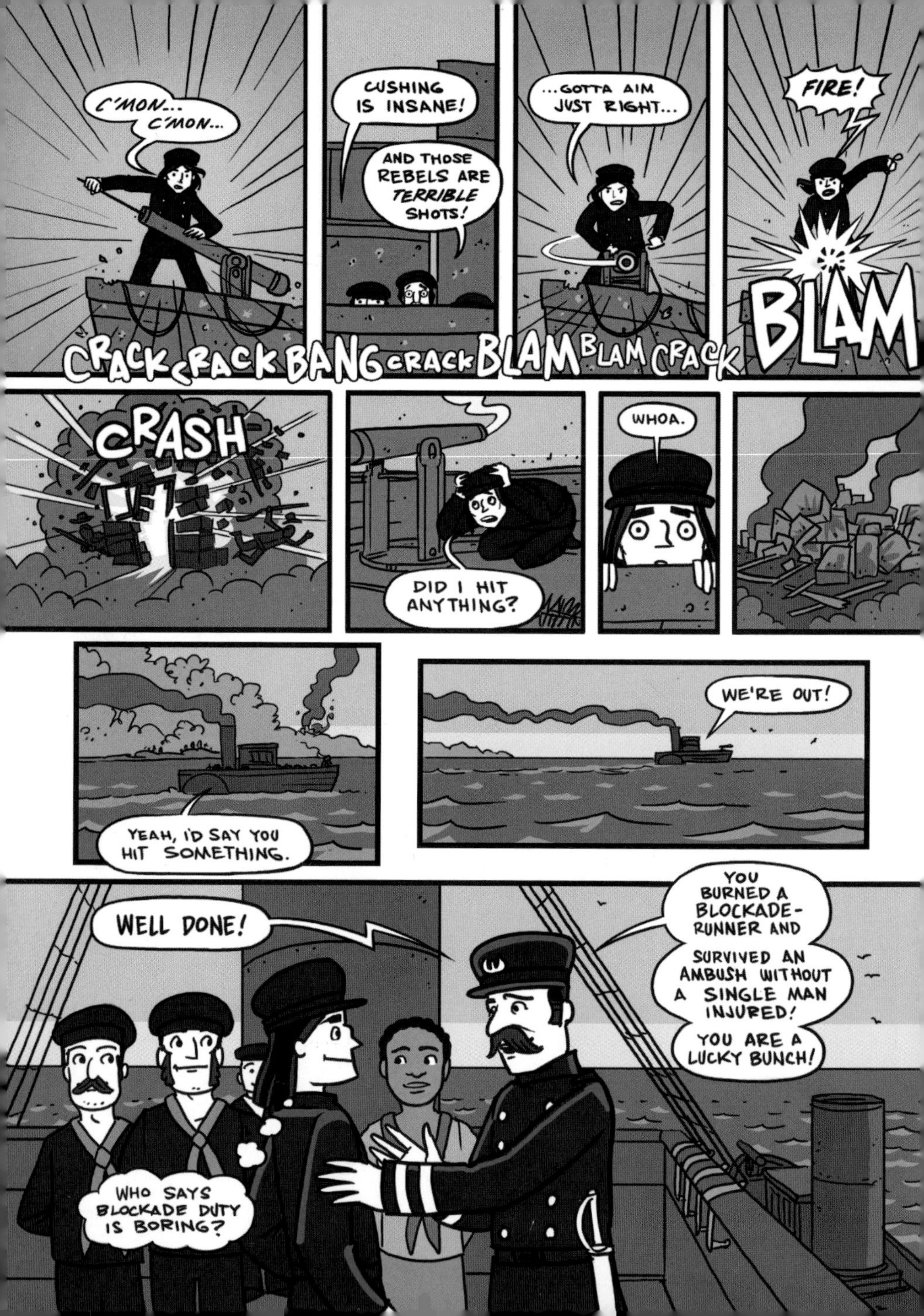
C'MON... C'MON...
CUSHING IS INSANE!
AND THOSE REBELS ARE TERRIBLE SHOTS!
...GOTTA AIM JUST RIGHT...
FIRE!
CRACK CRACK BANG CRACK BLAM BLAM CRACK BLAM
CRASH
DID I HIT ANYTHING?
WHOA.
YEAH, I'D SAY YOU HIT SOMETHING.
WE'RE OUT!
WELL DONE!
YOU BURNED A BLOCKADE-RUNNER AND
SURVIVED AN AMBUSH WITHOUT A SINGLE MAN INJURED!
YOU ARE A LUCKY BUNCH!
WHO SAYS BLOCKADE DUTY IS BORING?

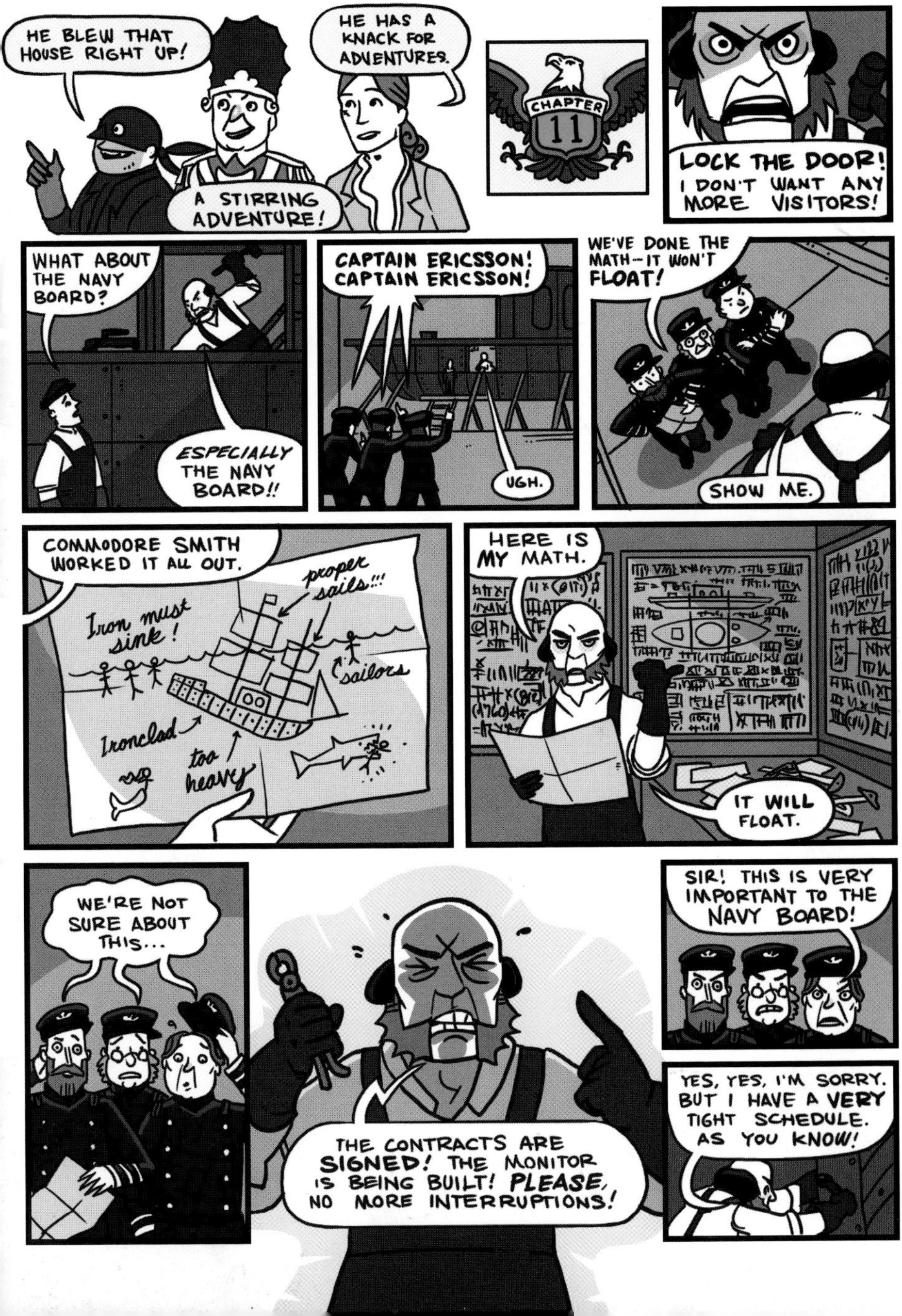

HE BLEW THAT HOUSE RIGHT UP!
A STIRRING ADVENTURE!
HE HAS A KNACK FOR ADVENTURES.
CHAPTER 11
LOCK THE DOOR! I DON'T WANT ANY MORE VISITORS!
WHAT ABOUT THE NAVY BOARD?
ESPECIALLY THE NAVY BOARD!!
CAPTAIN ERICSSON! CAPTAIN ERICSSON!
UGH.
WE'VE DONE THE MATH—IT WON'T FLOAT!
SHOW ME.
COMMODORE SMITH WORKED IT ALL OUT.
Iron must sink!
proper sails!!!
sailors
Ironclad
too heavy
HERE IS MY MATH.
IT WILL FLOAT.
WE'RE NOT SURE ABOUT THIS...
THE CONTRACTS ARE SIGNED! THE MONITOR IS BEING BUILT! PLEASE, NO MORE INTERRUPTIONS!
SIR! THIS IS VERY IMPORTANT TO THE NAVY BOARD!
YES, YES, I'M SORRY. BUT I HAVE A VERY TIGHT SCHEDULE. AS YOU KNOW!

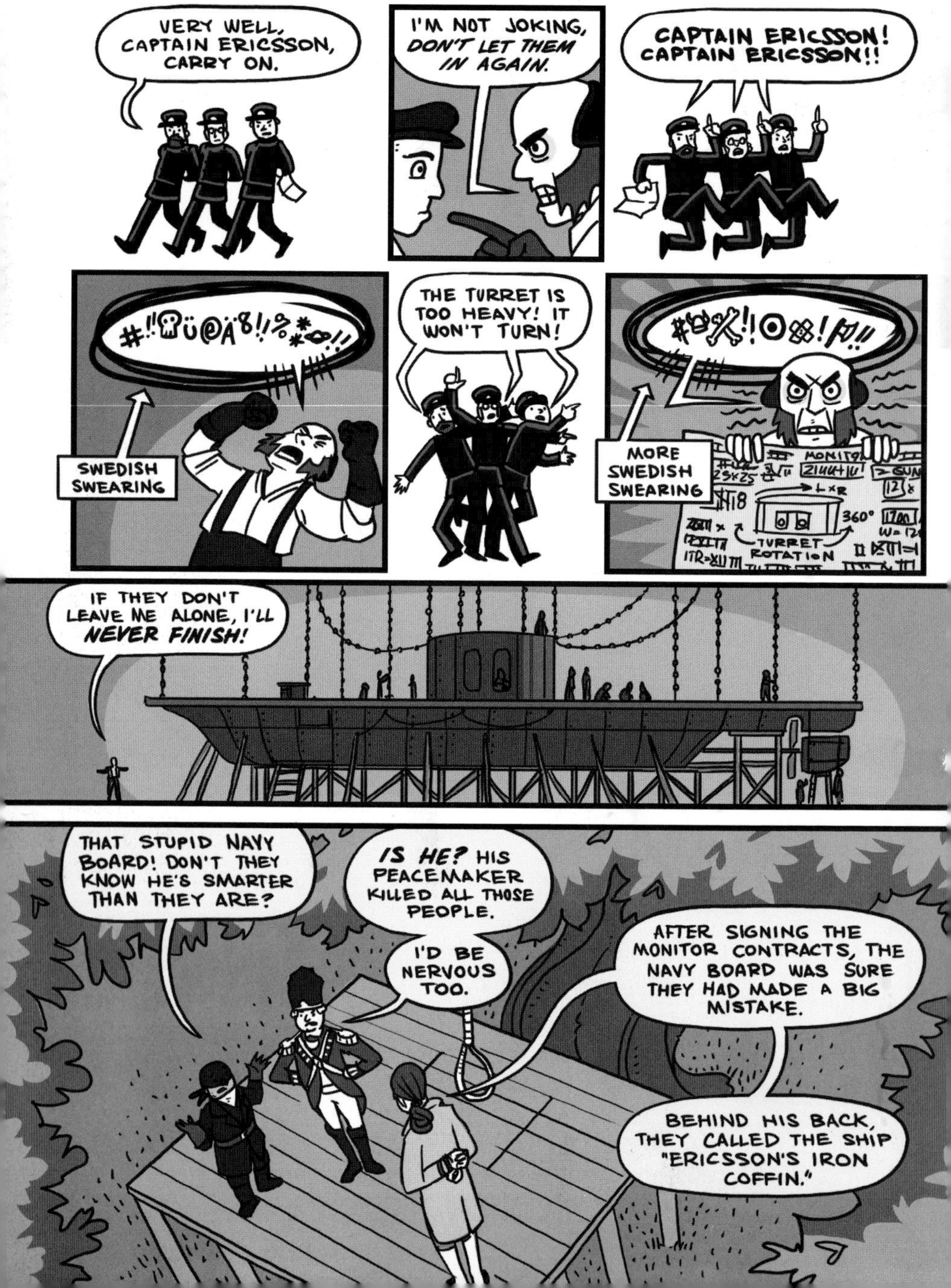
VERY WELL, CAPTAIN ERICSSON, CARRY ON.
I'M NOT JOKING, DON'T LET THEM IN AGAIN.
CAPTAIN ERICSSON! CAPTAIN ERICSSON!!
SWEDISH SWEARING
THE TURRET IS TOO HEAVY! IT WON'T TURN!
MORE SWEDISH SWEARING
360°
TURRET ROTATION
IF THEY DON'T LEAVE ME ALONE, I'LL NEVER FINISH!
THAT STUPID NAVY BOARD! DON'T THEY KNOW HE'S SMARTER THAN THEY ARE?
IS HE? HIS PEACEMAKER KILLED ALL THOSE PEOPLE.
I'D BE NERVOUS TOO.
AFTER SIGNING THE MONITOR CONTRACTS, THE NAVY BOARD WAS SURE THEY HAD MADE A BIG MISTAKE.
BEHIND HIS BACK, THEY CALLED THE SHIP "ERICSSON'S IRON COFFIN."

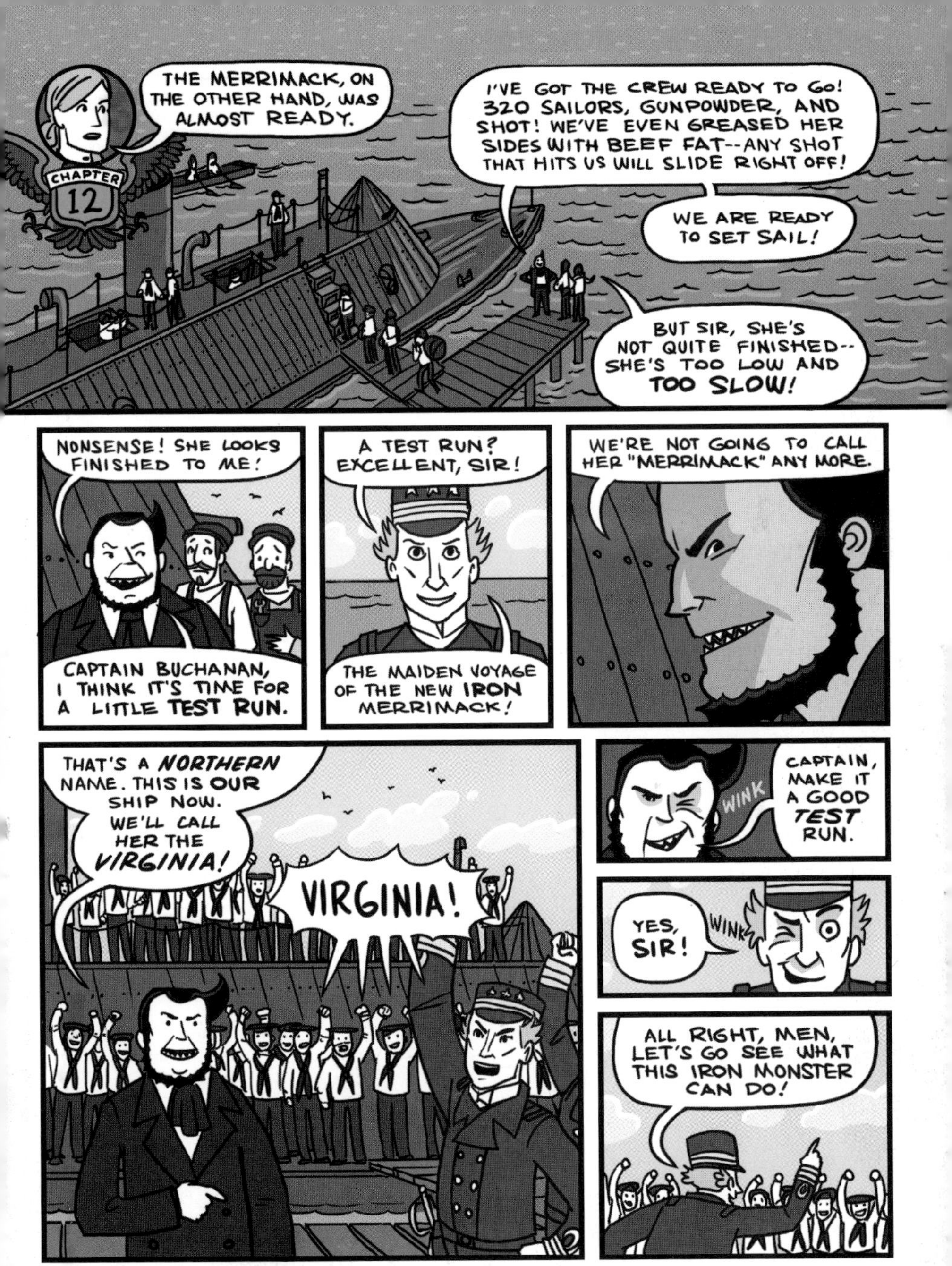
CHAPTER 12
THE MERRIMACK, ON THE OTHER HAND, WAS ALMOST READY.
I'VE GOT THE CREW READY TO GO! 320 SAILORS, GUNPOWDER, AND SHOT! WE'VE EVEN GREASED HER SIDES WITH BEEF FAT--ANY SHOT THAT HITS US WILL SLIDE RIGHT OFF!
WE ARE READY TO SET SAIL!
BUT SIR, SHE'S NOT QUITE FINISHED--SHE'S TOO LOW AND TOO SLOW!
NONSENSE! SHE LOOKS FINISHED TO ME!
CAPTAIN BUCHANAN, I THINK IT'S TIME FOR A LITTLE TEST RUN.
A TEST RUN? EXCELLENT, SIR!
THE MAIDEN VOYAGE OF THE NEW IRON MERRIMACK!
WE'RE NOT GOING TO CALL HER "MERRIMACK" ANY MORE.
THAT'S A NORTHERN NAME. THIS IS OUR SHIP NOW. WE'LL CALL HER THE VIRGINIA!
VIRGINIA!
WINK
CAPTAIN, MAKE IT A GOOD TEST RUN.
YES, SIR!
WINK
ALL RIGHT, MEN, LET'S GO SEE WHAT THIS IRON MONSTER CAN DO!

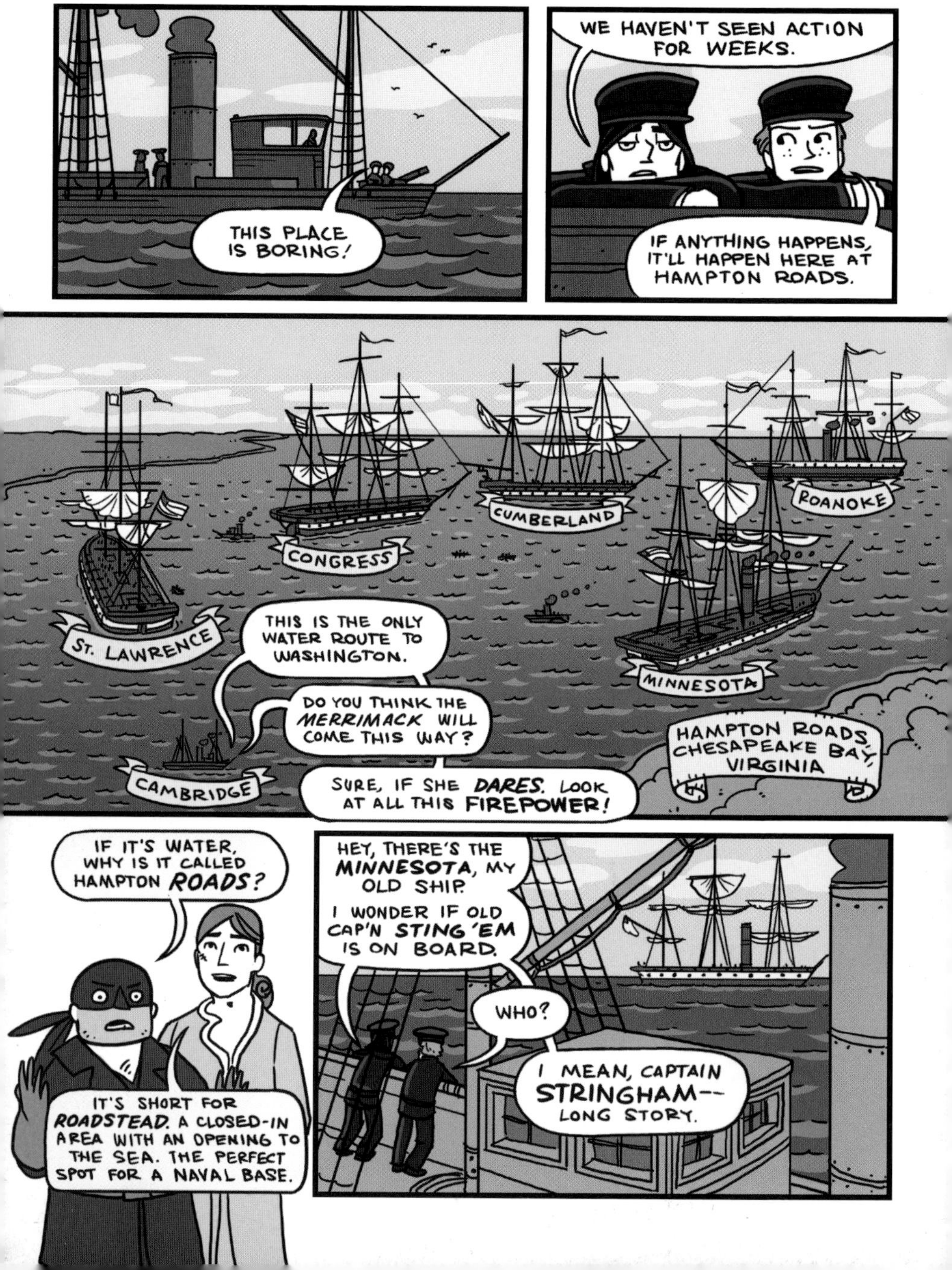
THIS PLACE IS BORING!
WE HAVEN'T SEEN ACTION FOR WEEKS.
IF ANYTHING HAPPENS, IT'LL HAPPEN HERE AT HAMPTON ROADS.
ST. LAWRENCE
CONGRESS
CUMBERLAND
ROANOKE
MINNESOTA
CAMBRIDGE
HAMPTON ROADS, CHESAPEAKE BAY, VIRGINIA
THIS IS THE ONLY WATER ROUTE TO WASHINGTON.
DO YOU THINK THE MERRIMACK WILL COME THIS WAY?
SURE, IF SHE DARES. LOOK AT ALL THIS FIREPOWER!
IF IT'S WATER, WHY IS IT CALLED HAMPTON ROADS?
IT'S SHORT FOR ROADSTEAD. A CLOSED-IN AREA WITH AN OPENING TO THE SEA. THE PERFECT SPOT FOR A NAVAL BASE.
HEY, THERE'S THE MINNESOTA, MY OLD SHIP.
I WONDER IF OLD CAP'N STING'EM IS ON BOARD.
WHO?
I MEAN, CAPTAIN STRINGHAM-- LONG STORY.

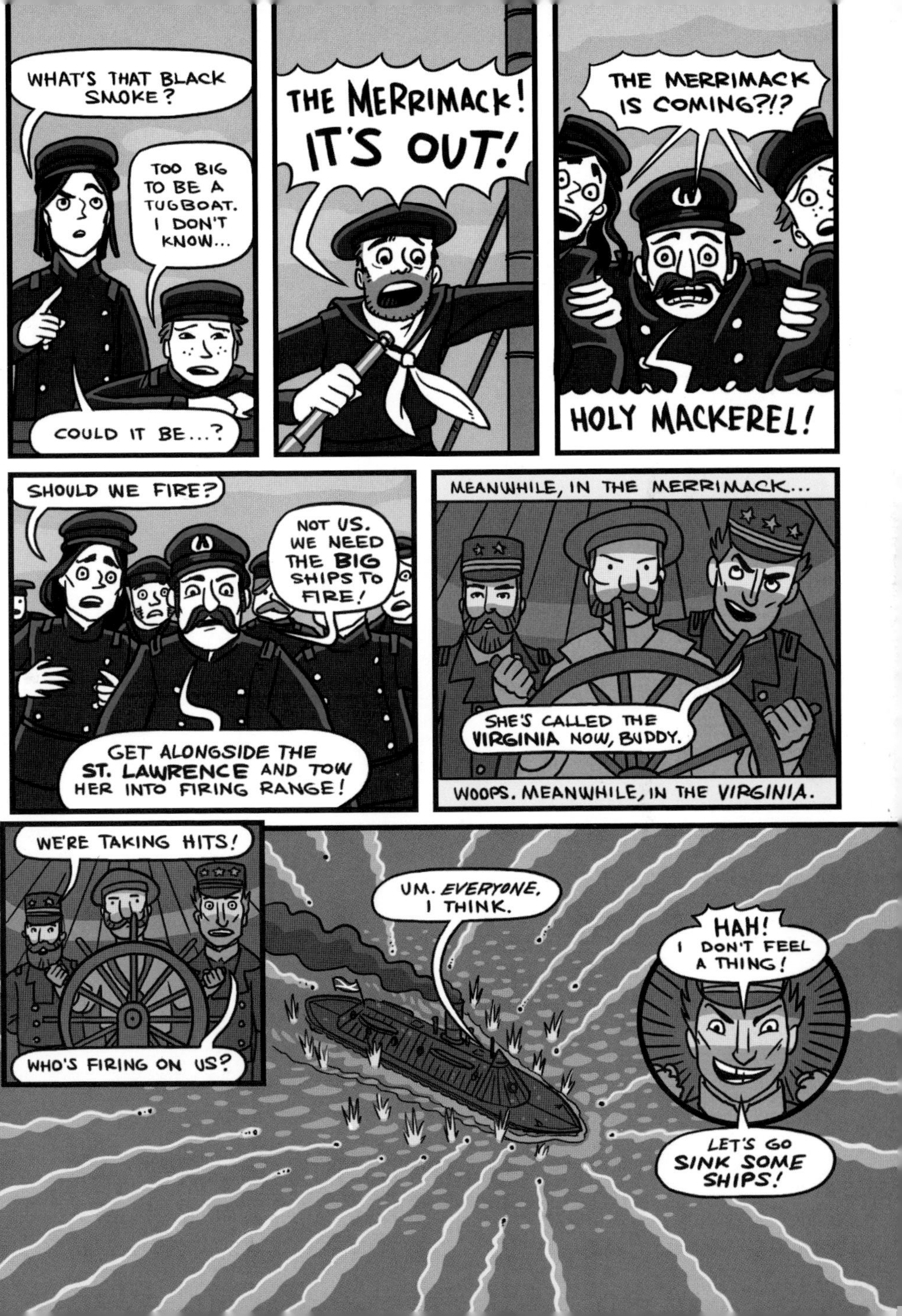
WHAT'S THAT BLACK SMOKE?
TOO BIG TO BE A TUGBOAT. I DON'T KNOW...
COULD IT BE...?
THE MERRIMACK! IT'S OUT!
THE MERRIMACK IS COMING?!?
HOLY MACKEREL!
SHOULD WE FIRE?
NOT US. WE NEED THE BIG SHIPS TO FIRE!
GET ALONGSIDE THE ST. LAWRENCE AND TOW HER INTO FIRING RANGE!
MEANWHILE, IN THE MERRIMACK...
SHE'S CALLED THE VIRGINIA NOW, BUDDY.
WOOPS. MEANWHILE, IN THE VIRGINIA.
WE'RE TAKING HITS!
WHO'S FIRING ON US?
UM. EVERYONE, I THINK.
HAH! I DON'T FEEL A THING!
LET'S GO SINK SOME SHIPS!

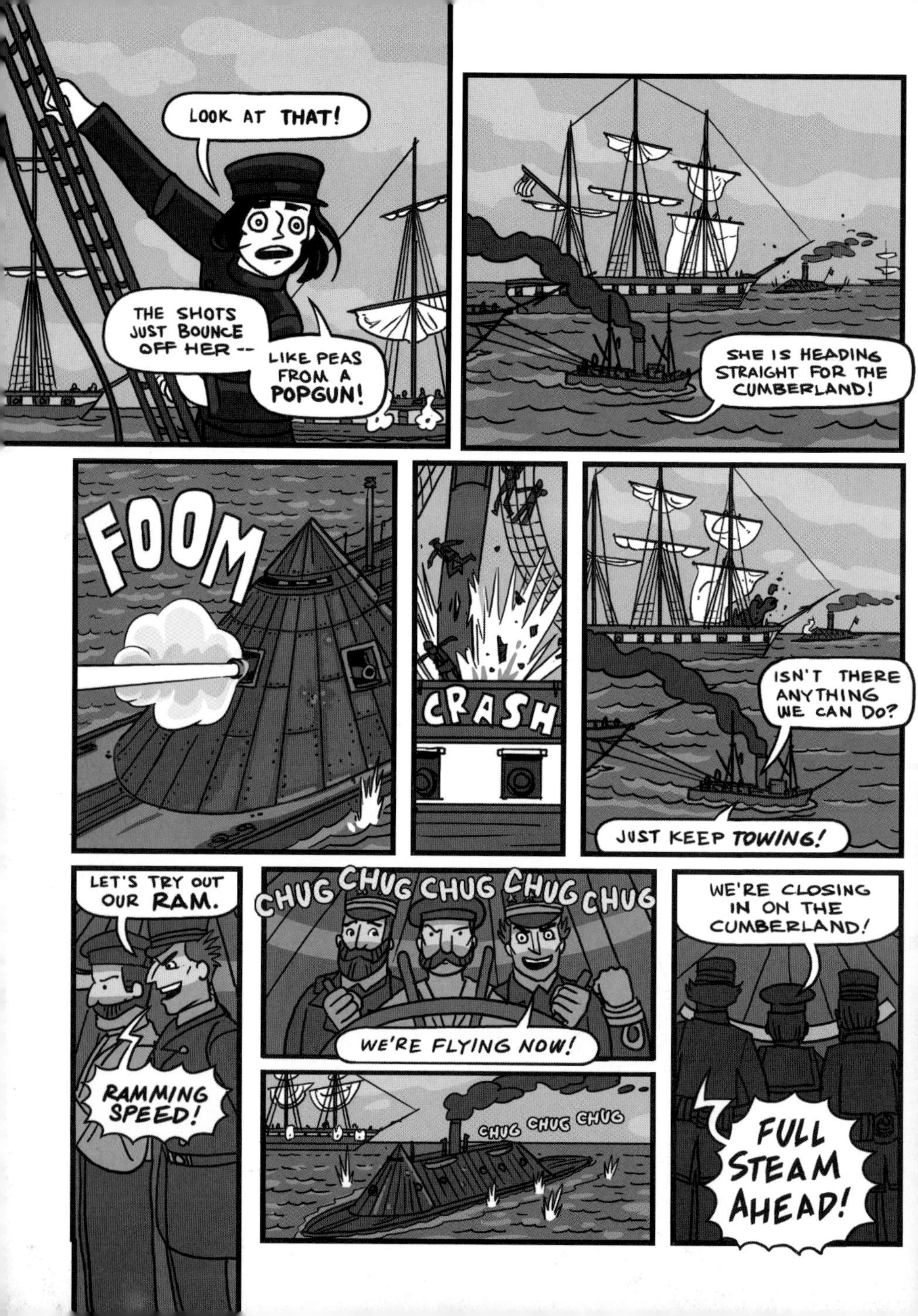
LOOK AT THAT!
THE SHOTS JUST BOUNCE OFF HER --
LIKE PEAS FROM A POPGUN!
SHE IS HEADING STRAIGHT FOR THE CUMBERLAND!
FOOM
CRASH
ISN'T THERE ANYTHING WE CAN DO?
JUST KEEP TOWING!
LET'S TRY OUT OUR RAM.
RAMMING SPEED!
CHUG CHUG CHUG CHUG CHUG
WE'RE FLYING NOW!
CHUG CHUG CHUG
WE'RE CLOSING IN ON THE CUMBERLAND!
FULL STEAM AHEAD!

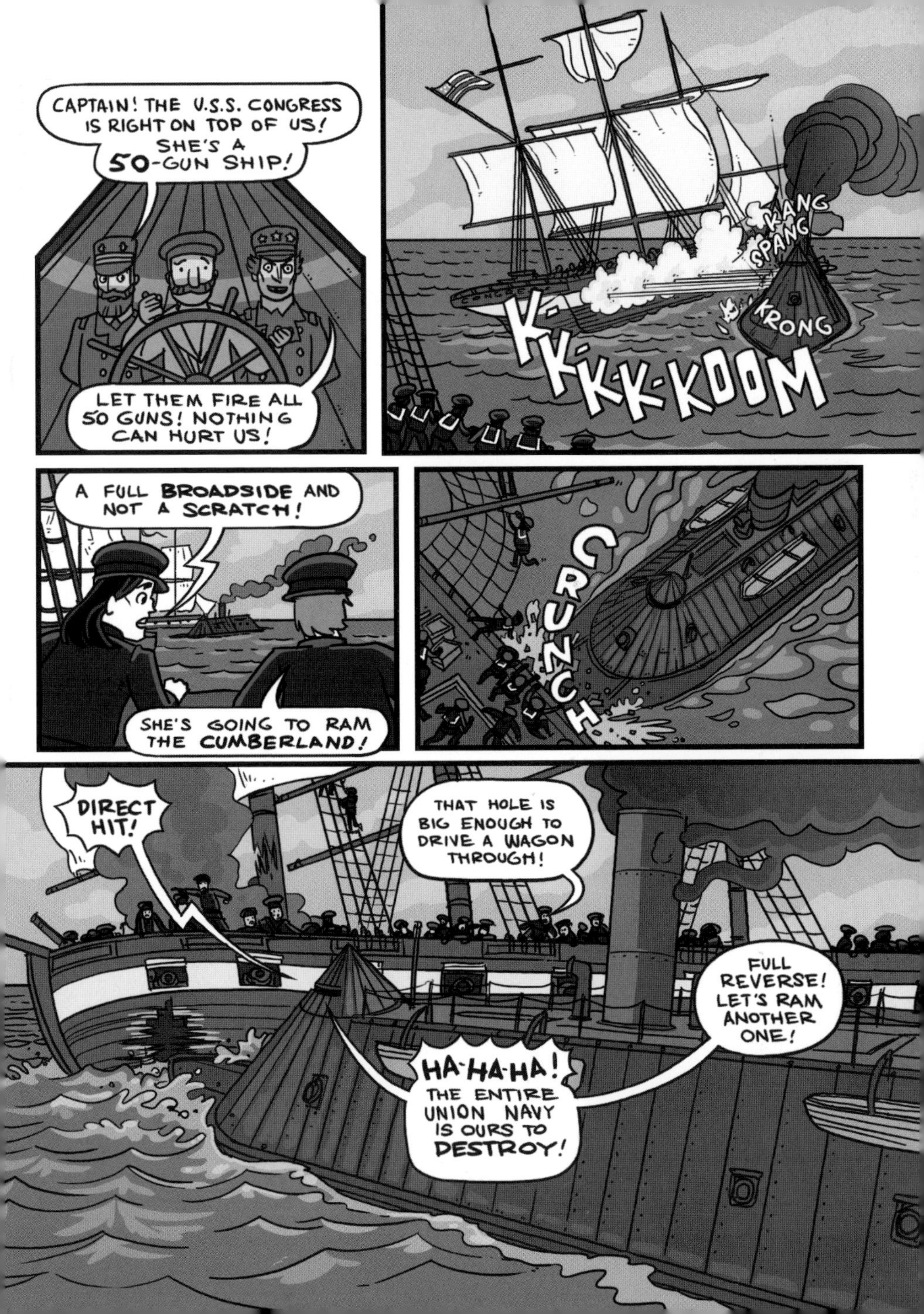
CAPTAIN! THE U.S.S. CONGRESS IS RIGHT ON TOP OF US! SHE'S A 50-GUN SHIP!
LET THEM FIRE ALL 50 GUNS! NOTHING CAN HURT US!
KANG
SPANG
KRONG
K-K-K-K-KOOM
A FULL BROADSIDE AND NOT A SCRATCH!
SHE'S GOING TO RAM THE CUMBERLAND!
CRUNCH
DIRECT HIT!
THAT HOLE IS BIG ENOUGH TO DRIVE A WAGON THROUGH!
HA-HA-HA! THE ENTIRE UNION NAVY IS OURS TO DESTROY!
FULL REVERSE! LET'S RAM ANOTHER ONE!

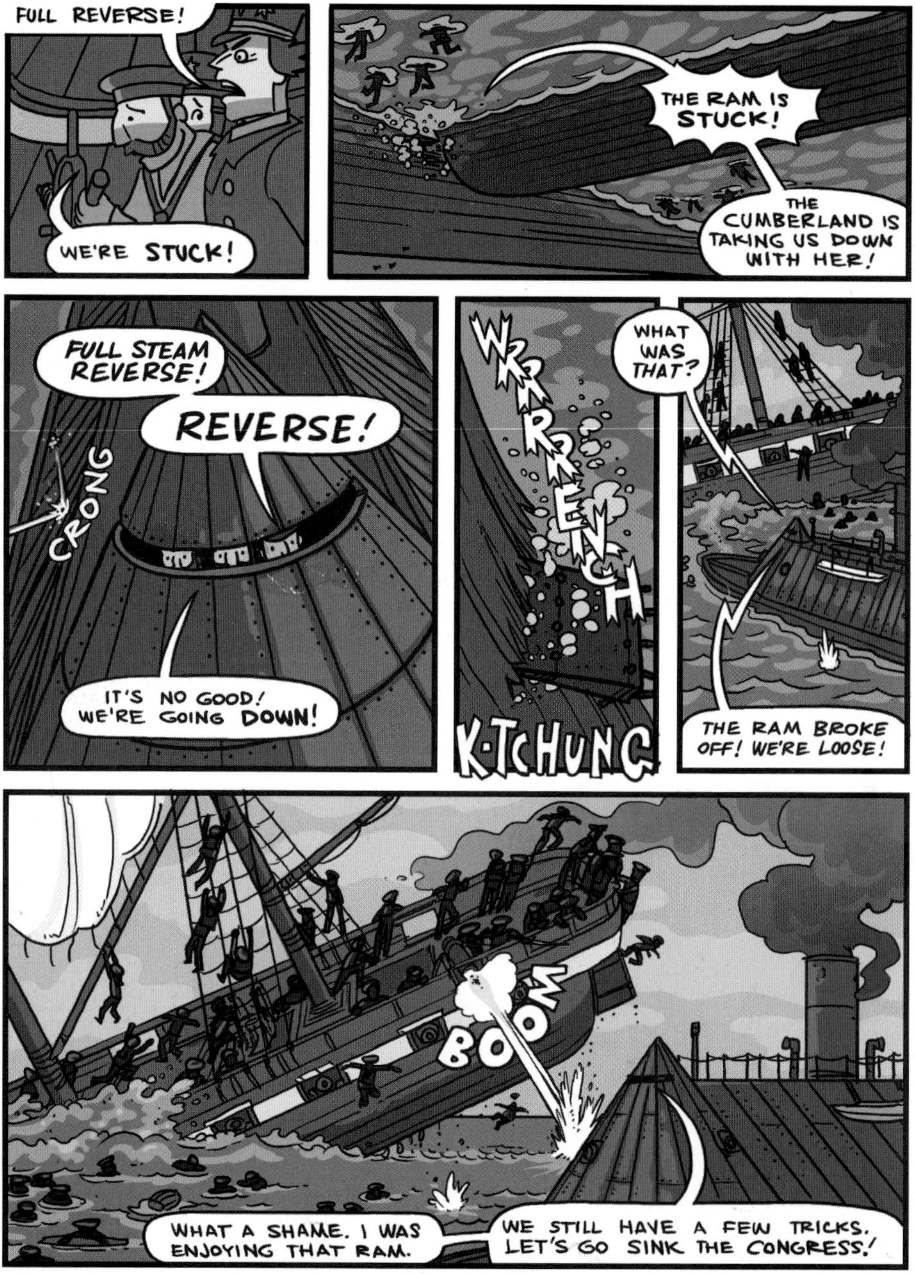
FULL REVERSE!
WE'RE STUCK!
THE RAM IS STUCK!
THE CUMBERLAND IS TAKING US DOWN WITH HER!
FULL STEAM REVERSE!
REVERSE!
CRONG
IT'S NO GOOD! WE'RE GOING DOWN!
WRRRENCH
K-TCHUNG
WHAT WAS THAT?
THE RAM BROKE OFF! WE'RE LOOSE!
BOOM
WHAT A SHAME. I WAS ENJOYING THAT RAM.
WE STILL HAVE A FEW TRICKS. LET'S GO SINK THE CONGRESS!

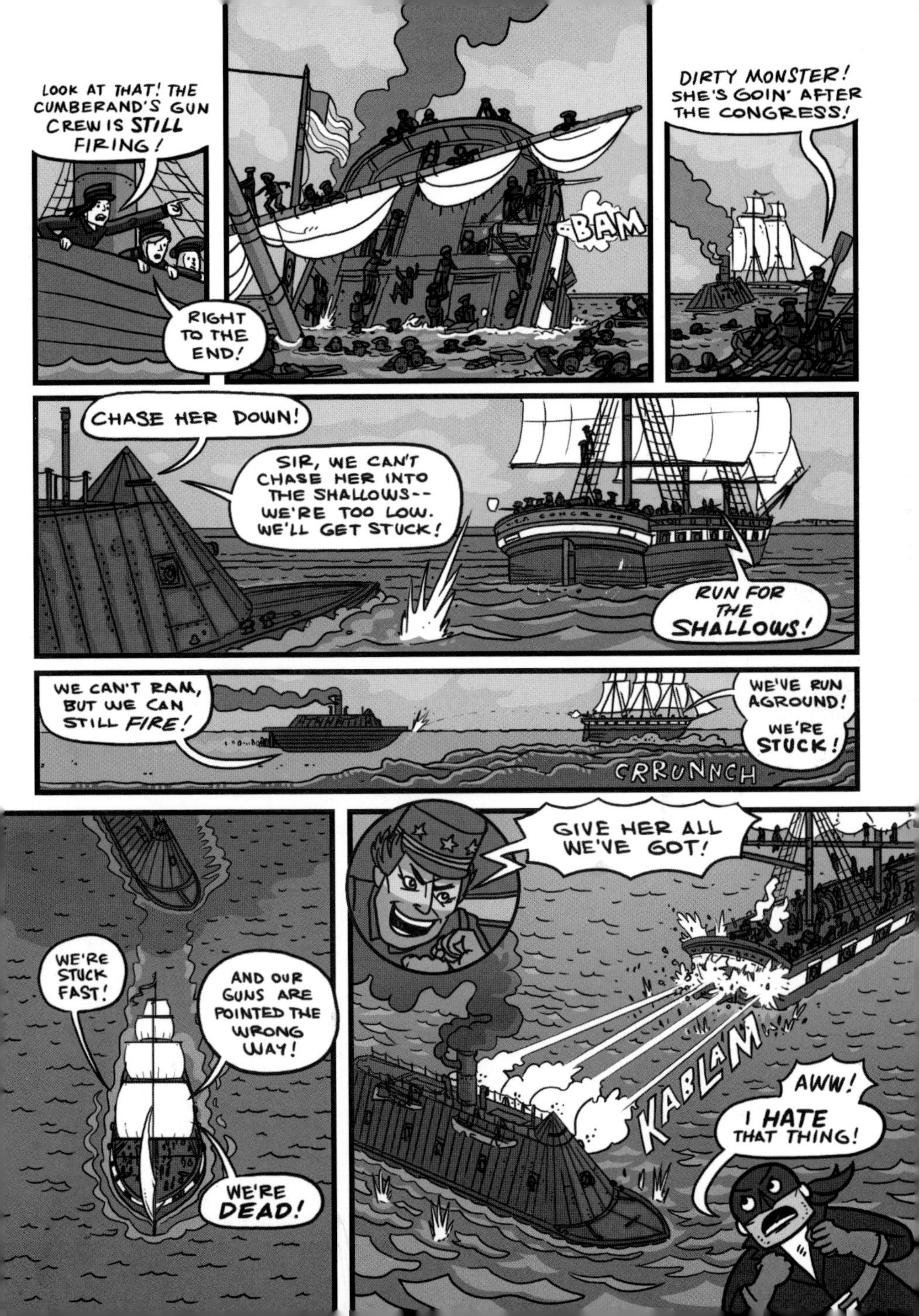
LOOK AT THAT! THE CUMBERAND'S GUN CREW IS STILL FIRING!
RIGHT TO THE END!
BAM
DIRTY MONSTER! SHE'S GOIN' AFTER THE CONGRESS!
CHASE HER DOWN!
SIR, WE CAN'T CHASE HER INTO THE SHALLOWS-- WE'RE TOO LOW. WE'LL GET STUCK!
RUN FOR THE SHALLOWS!
WE CAN'T RAM, BUT WE CAN STILL FIRE!
WE'VE RUN AGROUND!
WE'RE STUCK!
CRRUNNCH
WE'RE STUCK FAST!
AND OUR GUNS ARE POINTED THE WRONG WAY!
WE'RE DEAD!
GIVE HER ALL WE'VE GOT!
KABLAM
AWW!
I HATE THAT THING!

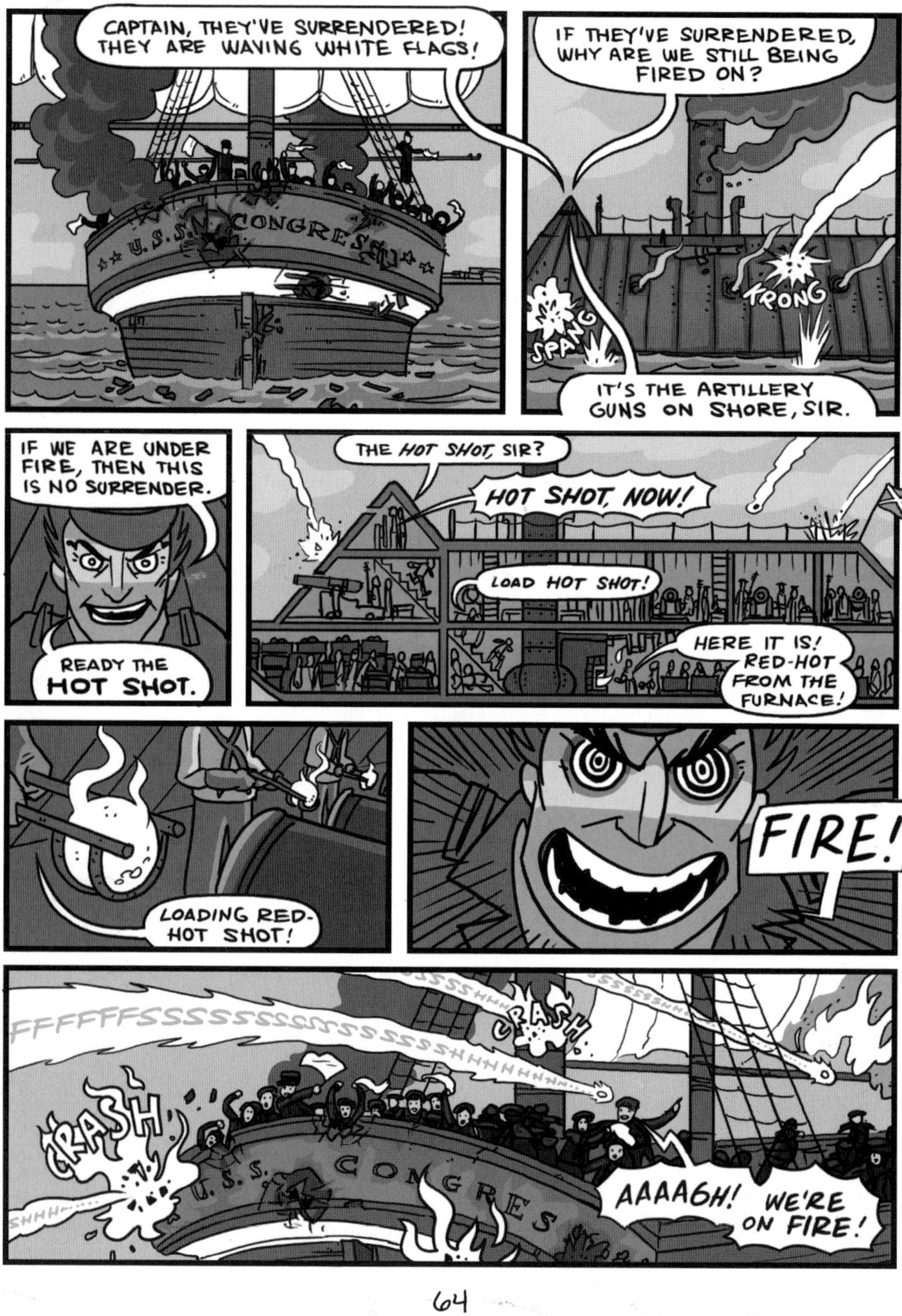
CAPTAIN, THEY'VE SURRENDERED! THEY ARE WAVING WHITE FLAGS!
U.S.S. CONGRESS
IF THEY'VE SURRENDERED, WHY ARE WE STILL BEING FIRED ON?
SPANG
KRONG
IT'S THE ARTILLERY GUNS ON SHORE, SIR.
IF WE ARE UNDER FIRE, THEN THIS IS NO SURRENDER.
READY THE HOT SHOT.
THE HOT SHOT, SIR?
HOT SHOT, NOW!
LOAD HOT SHOT!
HERE IT IS! RED-HOT FROM THE FURNACE!
LOADING RED-HOT SHOT!
FIRE!
FFFFFFSSSSSSSSSSSSSSSSSSSHHHHHHH
CRASH
CRASH
SHHHH
U.S.S. CONGRES
AAAAGH! WE'RE ON FIRE!

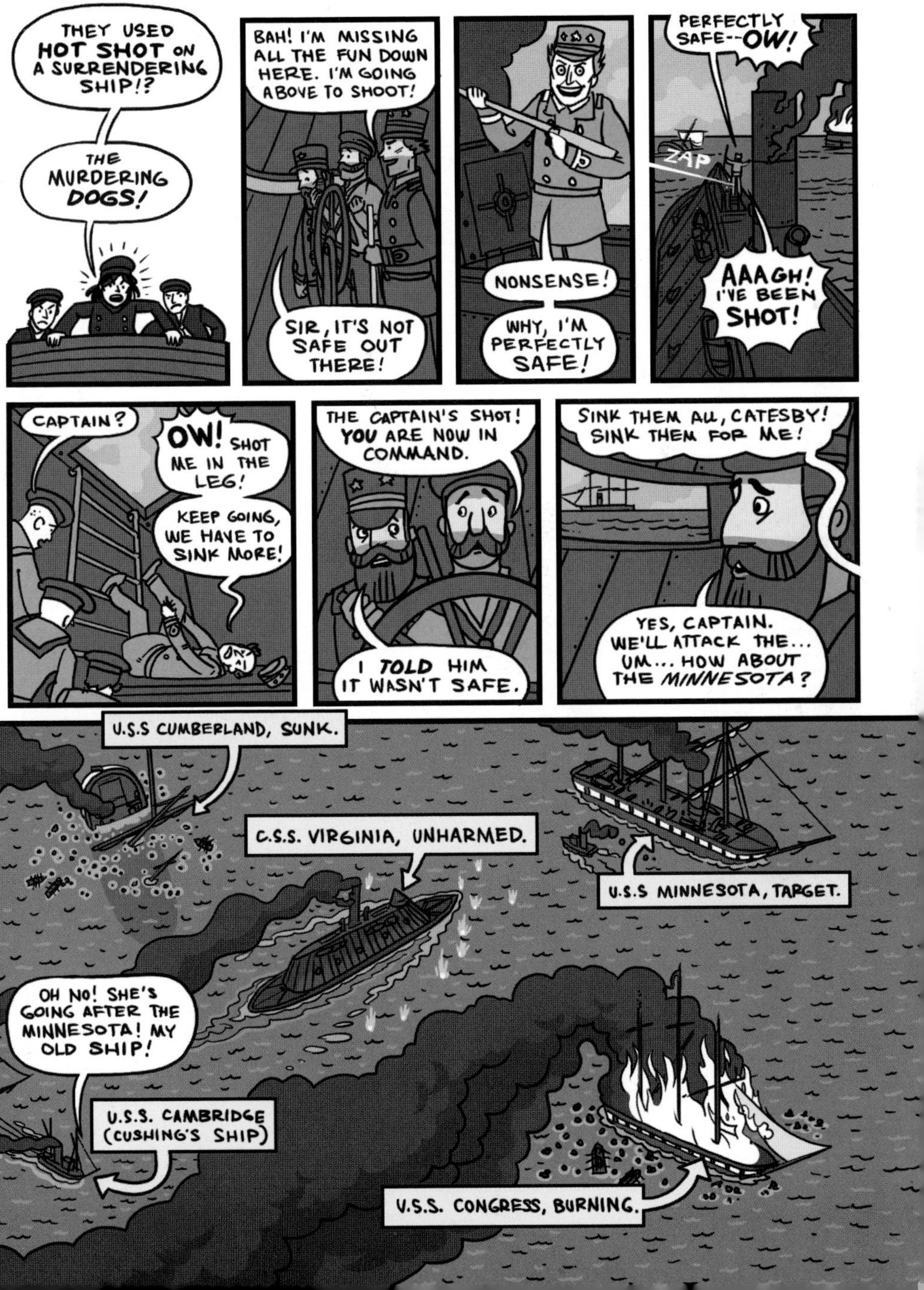
THEY USED HOT SHOT ON A SURRENDERING SHIP!?
THE MURDERING DOGS!
BAH! I'M MISSING ALL THE FUN DOWN HERE. I'M GOING ABOVE TO SHOOT!
SIR, IT'S NOT SAFE OUT THERE!
NONSENSE!
WHY, I'M PERFECTLY SAFE!
PERFECTLY SAFE--OW!
ZAP
AAAGH! I'VE BEEN SHOT!
CAPTAIN?
OW! SHOT ME IN THE LEG!
KEEP GOING, WE HAVE TO SINK MORE!
THE CAPTAIN'S SHOT! YOU ARE NOW IN COMMAND.
I TOLD HIM IT WASN'T SAFE.
SINK THEM ALL, CATESBY! SINK THEM FOR ME!
YES, CAPTAIN. WE'LL ATTACK THE... UM... HOW ABOUT THE MINNESOTA?
U.S.S CUMBERLAND, SUNK.
C.S.S. VIRGINIA, UNHARMED.
U.S.S MINNESOTA, TARGET.
OH NO! SHE'S GOING AFTER THE MINNESOTA! MY OLD SHIP!
U.S.S. CAMBRIDGE (CUSHING'S SHIP)
U.S.S. CONGRESS, BURNING.

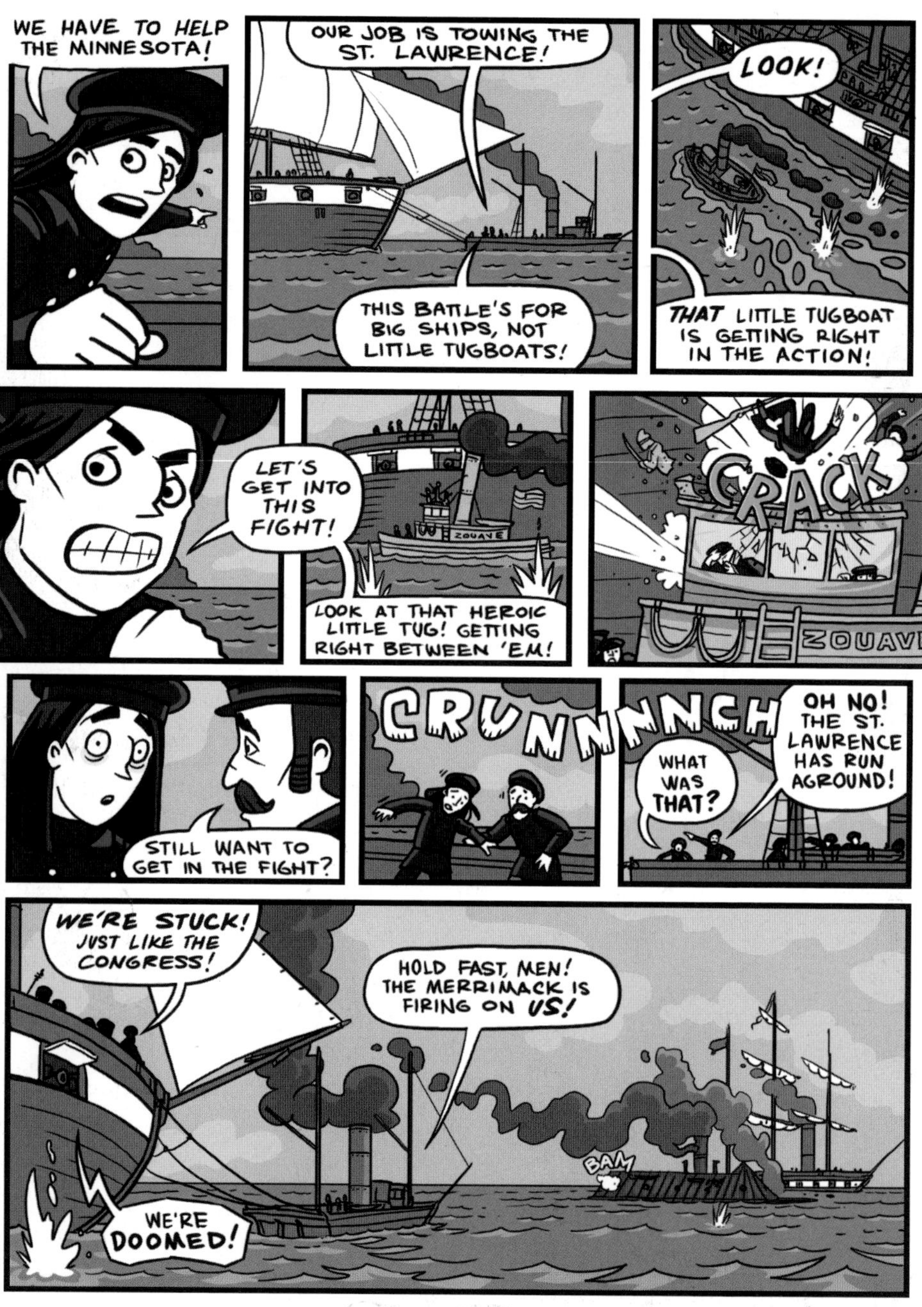

WE HAVE TO HELP THE MINNESOTA!
OUR JOB IS TOWING THE ST. LAWRENCE!
THIS BATTLE'S FOR BIG SHIPS, NOT LITTLE TUGBOATS!
LOOK!
THAT LITTLE TUGBOAT IS GETTING RIGHT IN THE ACTION!
LET'S GET INTO THIS FIGHT!
ZOUAVE
LOOK AT THAT HEROIC LITTLE TUG! GETTING RIGHT BETWEEN 'EM!
CRACK
ZOUAVE
STILL WANT TO GET IN THE FIGHT?
CRUNNNNCH
WHAT WAS THAT?
OH NO! THE ST. LAWRENCE HAS RUN AGROUND!
WE'RE STUCK! JUST LIKE THE CONGRESS!
HOLD FAST, MEN! THE MERRIMACK IS FIRING ON US!
BAM
WE'RE DOOMED!

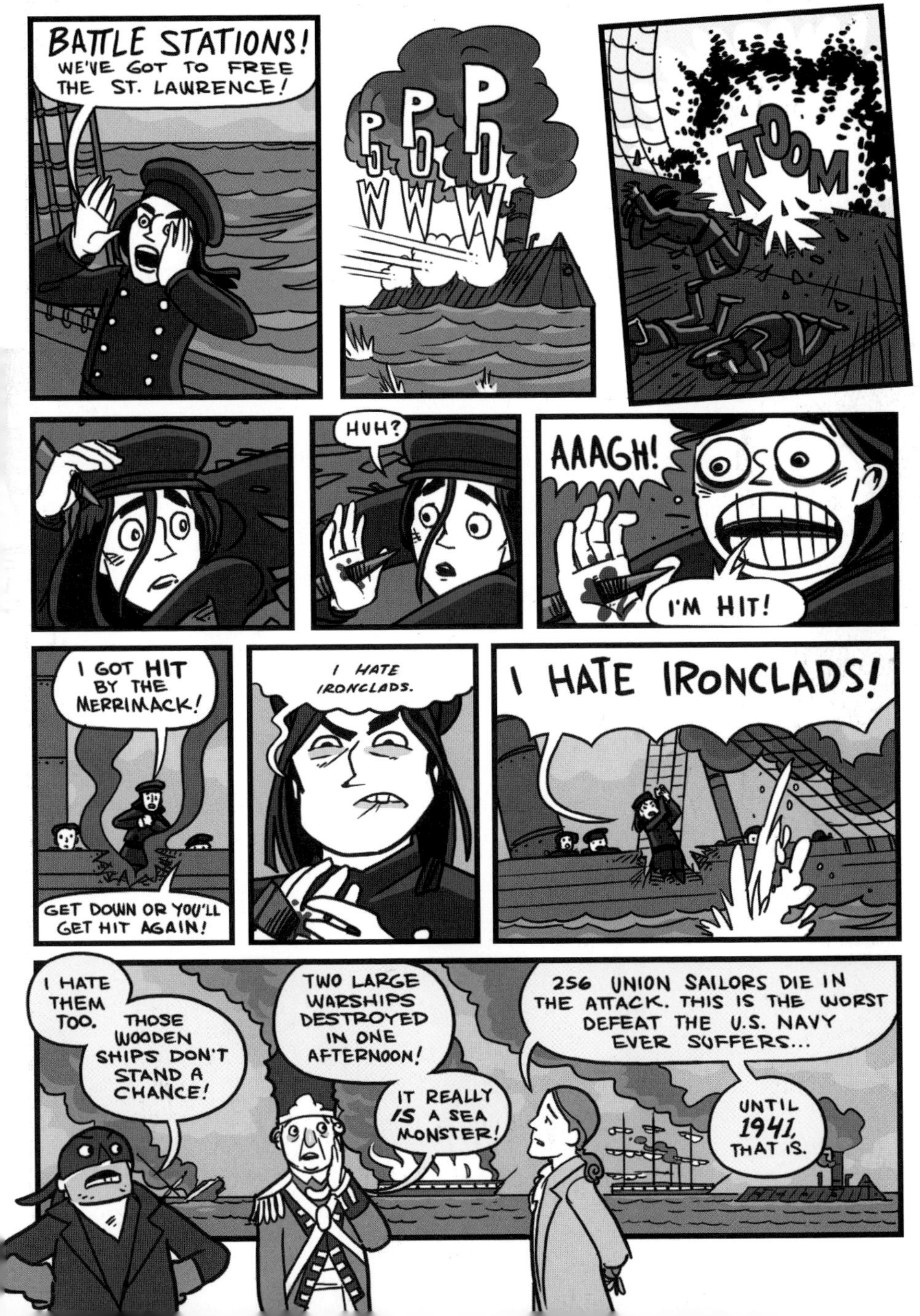

BATTLE STATIONS! WE'VE GOT TO FREE THE ST. LAWRENCE!
POOOWWW
KTOOM
HUH?
AAAGH!
I'M HIT!
I GOT HIT BY THE MERRIMACK!
GET DOWN OR YOU'LL GET HIT AGAIN!
I HATE IRONCLADS.
I HATE IRONCLADS!
I HATE THEM TOO.
THOSE WOODEN SHIPS DON'T STAND A CHANCE!
TWO LARGE WARSHIPS DESTROYED IN ONE AFTERNOON!
IT REALLY IS A SEA MONSTER!
256 UNION SAILORS DIE IN THE ATTACK. THIS IS THE WORST DEFEAT THE U.S. NAVY EVER SUFFERS...
UNTIL 1941, THAT IS.

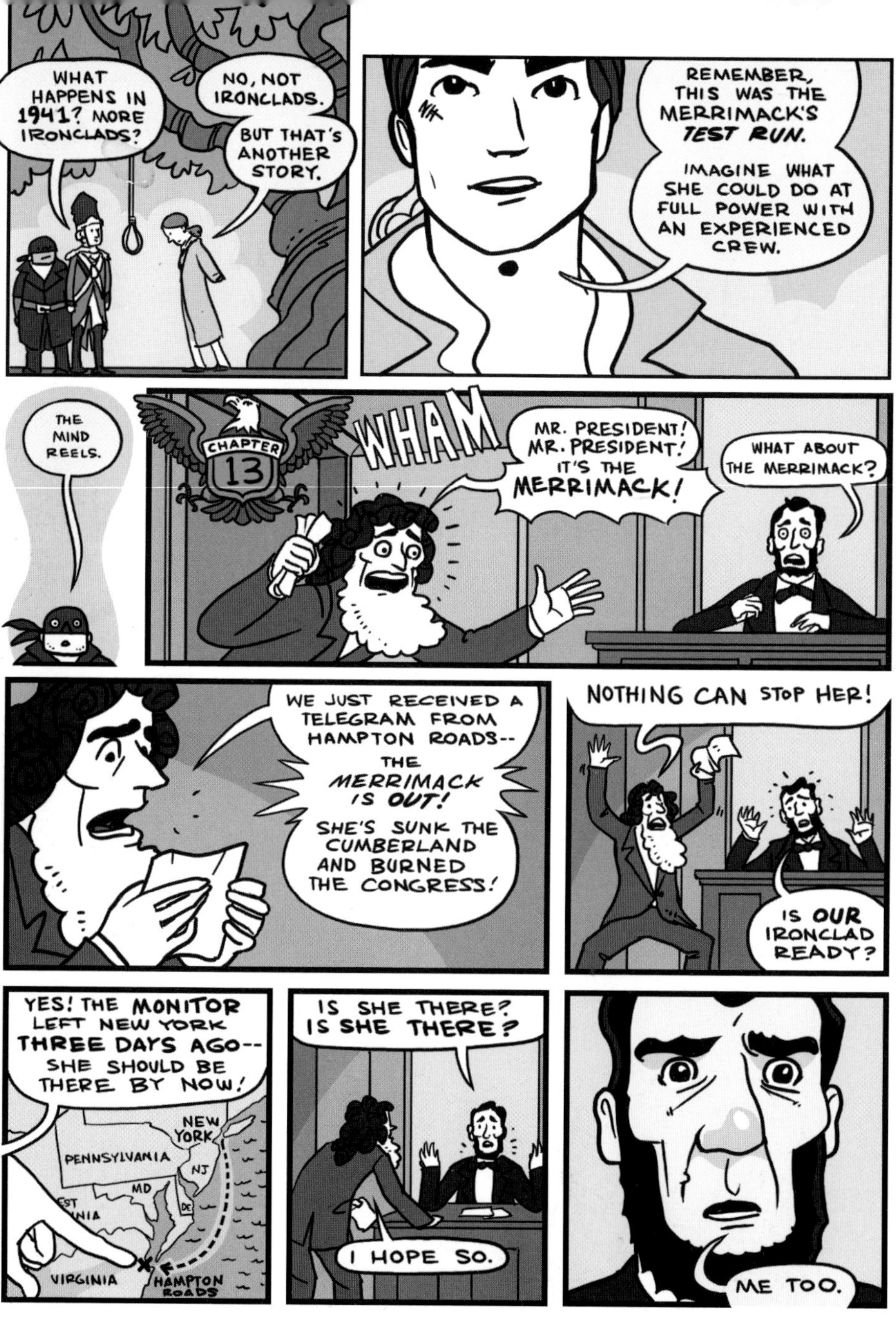
WHAT HAPPENS IN 1941? MORE IRONCLADS?
NO, NOT IRONCLADS.
BUT THAT'S ANOTHER STORY.
REMEMBER, THIS WAS THE MERRIMACK'S TEST RUN.
IMAGINE WHAT SHE COULD DO AT FULL POWER WITH AN EXPERIENCED CREW.
THE MIND REELS.
CHAPTER 13
WHAM
MR. PRESIDENT! MR. PRESIDENT! IT'S THE MERRIMACK!
WHAT ABOUT THE MERRIMACK?
WE JUST RECEIVED A TELEGRAM FROM HAMPTON ROADS--
THE MERRIMACK IS OUT!
SHE'S SUNK THE CUMBERLAND AND BURNED THE CONGRESS!
NOTHING CAN STOP HER!
IS OUR IRONCLAD READY?
YES! THE MONITOR LEFT NEW YORK THREE DAYS AGO-- SHE SHOULD BE THERE BY NOW!
NEW YORK
PENNSYLVANIA
NJ
MD
DE
VIRGINIA
HAMPTON ROADS
IS SHE THERE? IS SHE THERE?
I HOPE SO.
ME TOO.

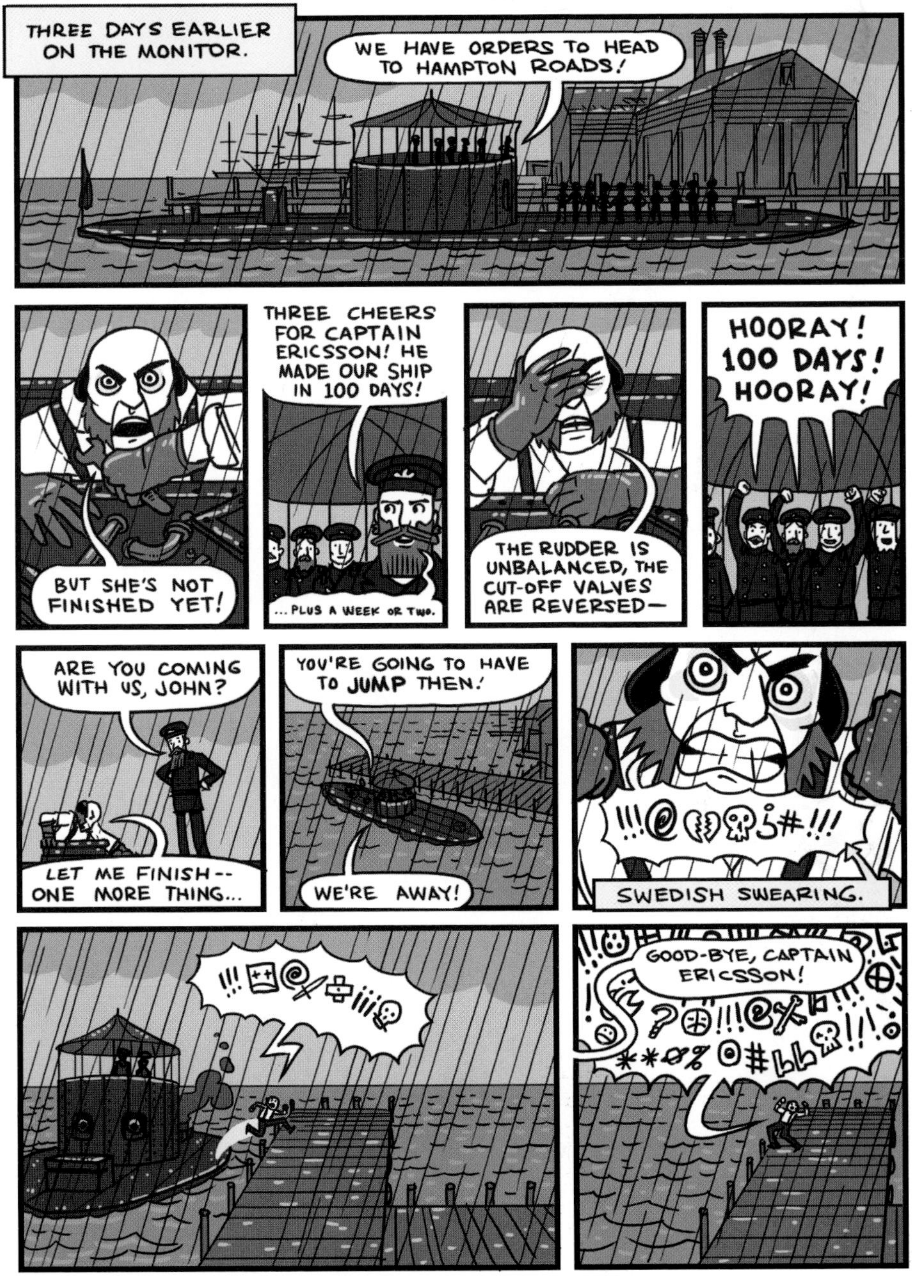
THREE DAYS EARLIER ON THE MONITOR.
WE HAVE ORDERS TO HEAD TO HAMPTON ROADS!
BUT SHE'S NOT FINISHED YET!
THREE CHEERS FOR CAPTAIN ERICSSON! HE MADE OUR SHIP IN 100 DAYS!
...PLUS A WEEK OR TWO.
THE RUDDER IS UNBALANCED, THE CUT-OFF VALVES ARE REVERSED—
HOORAY! 100 DAYS! HOORAY!
ARE YOU COMING WITH US, JOHN?
LET ME FINISH -- ONE MORE THING...
YOU'RE GOING TO HAVE TO JUMP THEN!
WE'RE AWAY!
SWEDISH SWEARING.
GOOD-BYE, CAPTAIN ERICSSON!

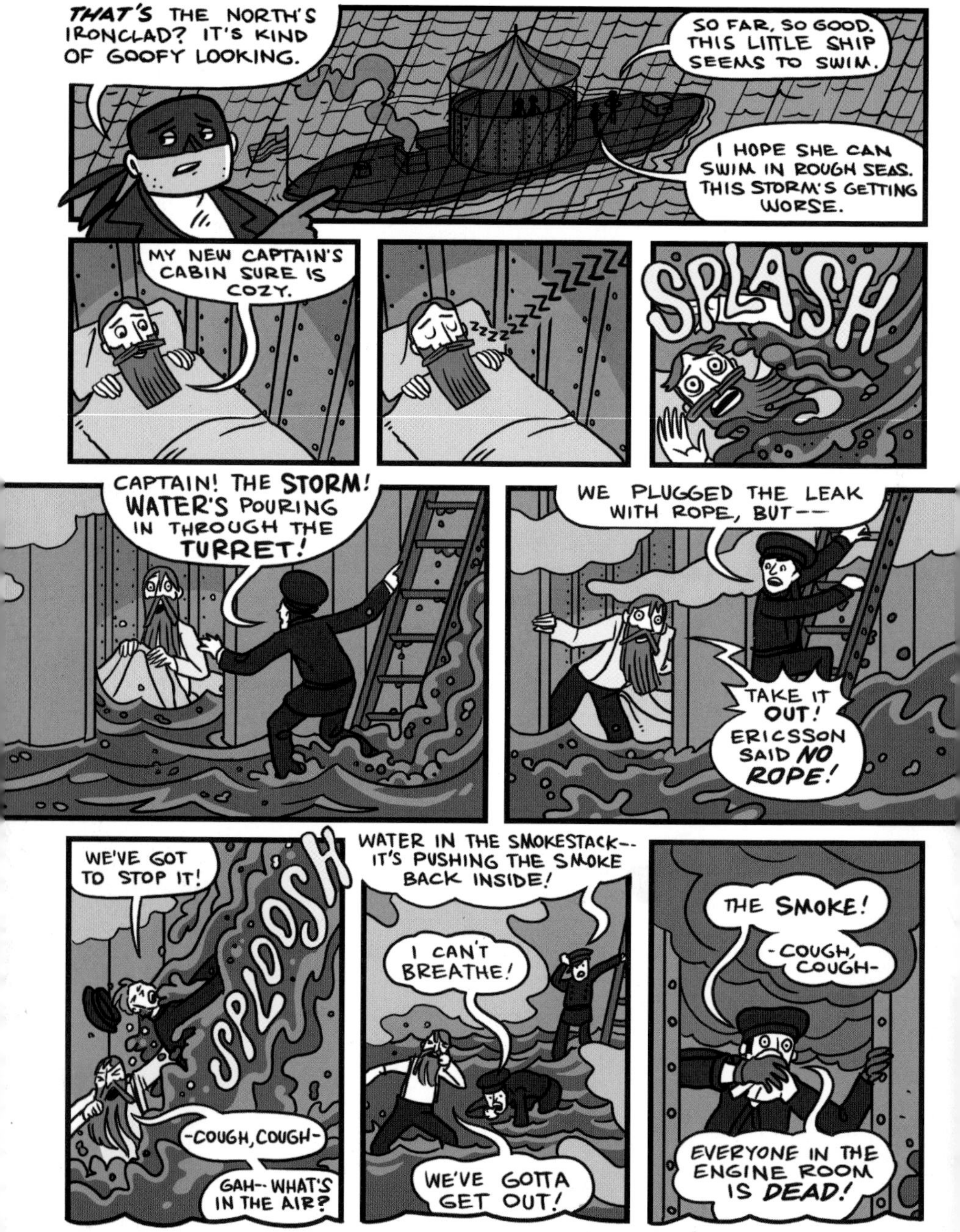

THAT'S THE NORTH'S IRONCLAD? IT'S KIND OF GOOFY LOOKING.
SO FAR, SO GOOD. THIS LITTLE SHIP SEEMS TO SWIM.
I HOPE SHE CAN SWIM IN ROUGH SEAS. THIS STORM'S GETTING WORSE.
MY NEW CAPTAIN'S CABIN SURE IS COZY.
ZZZZZZZZZZZZZ
SPLASH
CAPTAIN! THE STORM! WATER'S POURING IN THROUGH THE TURRET!
WE PLUGGED THE LEAK WITH ROPE, BUT--
TAKE IT OUT! ERICSSON SAID NO ROPE!
WE'VE GOT TO STOP IT!
SPLOOSH
-COUGH, COUGH-
GAH-- WHAT'S IN THE AIR?
WATER IN THE SMOKESTACK-- IT'S PUSHING THE SMOKE BACK INSIDE!
I CAN'T BREATHE!
WE'VE GOTTA GET OUT!
THE SMOKE!
-COUGH, COUGH-
EVERYONE IN THE ENGINE ROOM IS DEAD!

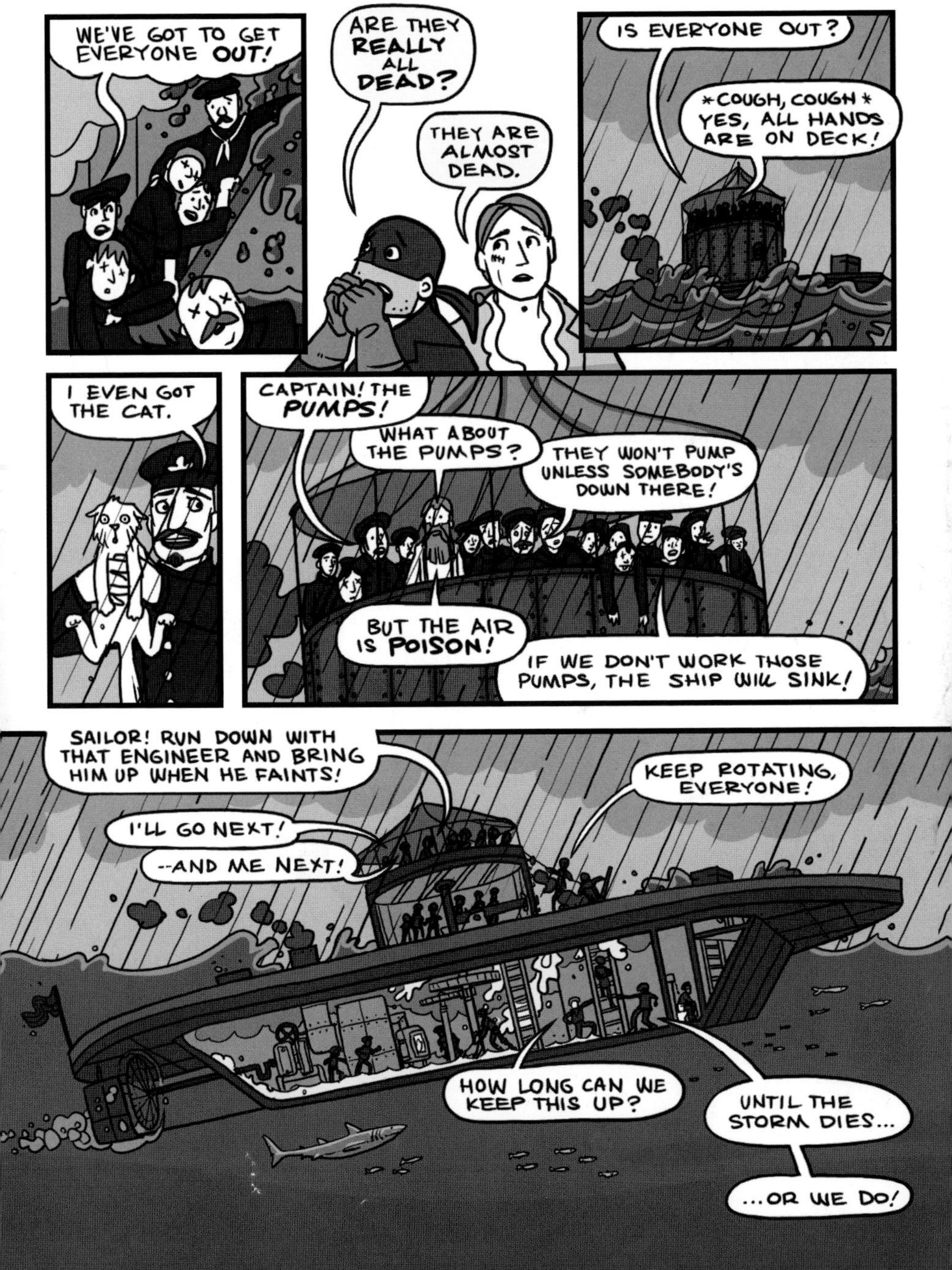
WE'VE GOT TO GET EVERYONE OUT!
ARE THEY REALLY ALL DEAD?
THEY ARE ALMOST DEAD.
IS EVERYONE OUT?
COUGH, COUGH YES, ALL HANDS ARE ON DECK!
I EVEN GOT THE CAT.
CAPTAIN! THE PUMPS!
WHAT ABOUT THE PUMPS?
THEY WON'T PUMP UNLESS SOMEBODY'S DOWN THERE!
BUT THE AIR IS POISON!
IF WE DON'T WORK THOSE PUMPS, THE SHIP WILL SINK!
SAILOR! RUN DOWN WITH THAT ENGINEER AND BRING HIM UP WHEN HE FAINTS!
KEEP ROTATING, EVERYONE!
I'LL GO NEXT!
--AND ME NEXT!
HOW LONG CAN WE KEEP THIS UP?
UNTIL THE STORM DIES...
...OR WE DO!

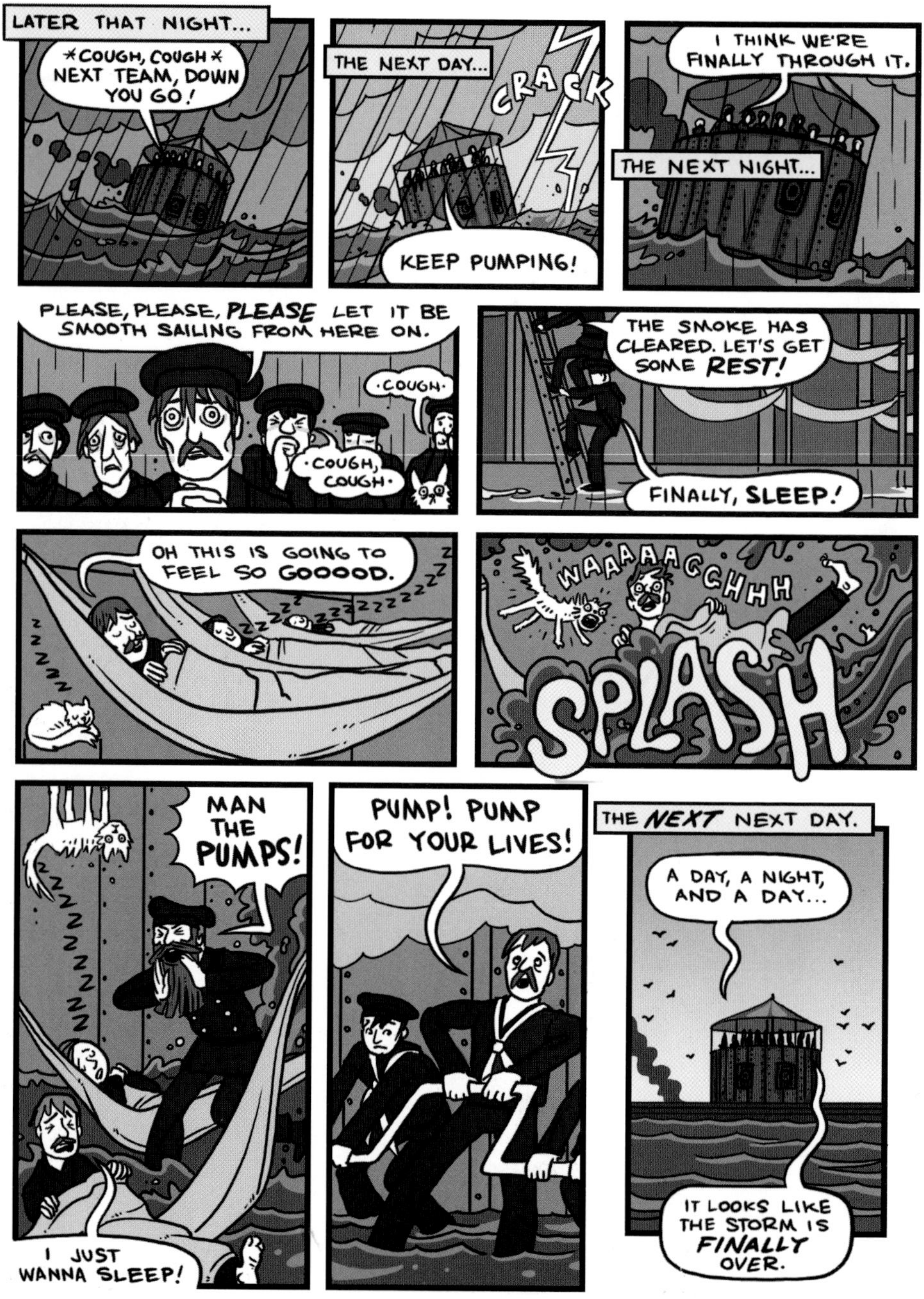
LATER THAT NIGHT...
COUGH, COUGH NEXT TEAM, DOWN YOU GO!
THE NEXT DAY...
CRACK
KEEP PUMPING!
I THINK WE'RE FINALLY THROUGH IT.
THE NEXT NIGHT...
PLEASE, PLEASE, PLEASE LET IT BE SMOOTH SAILING FROM HERE ON.
·COUGH·
·COUGH, COUGH·
THE SMOKE HAS CLEARED. LET'S GET SOME REST!
FINALLY, SLEEP!
OH THIS IS GOING TO FEEL SO GOOOOD.
WAAAAAGCHHHH
SPLASH
MAN THE PUMPS!
I JUST WANNA SLEEP!
PUMP! PUMP FOR YOUR LIVES!
THE NEXT NEXT DAY.
A DAY, A NIGHT, AND A DAY...
IT LOOKS LIKE THE STORM IS FINALLY OVER.

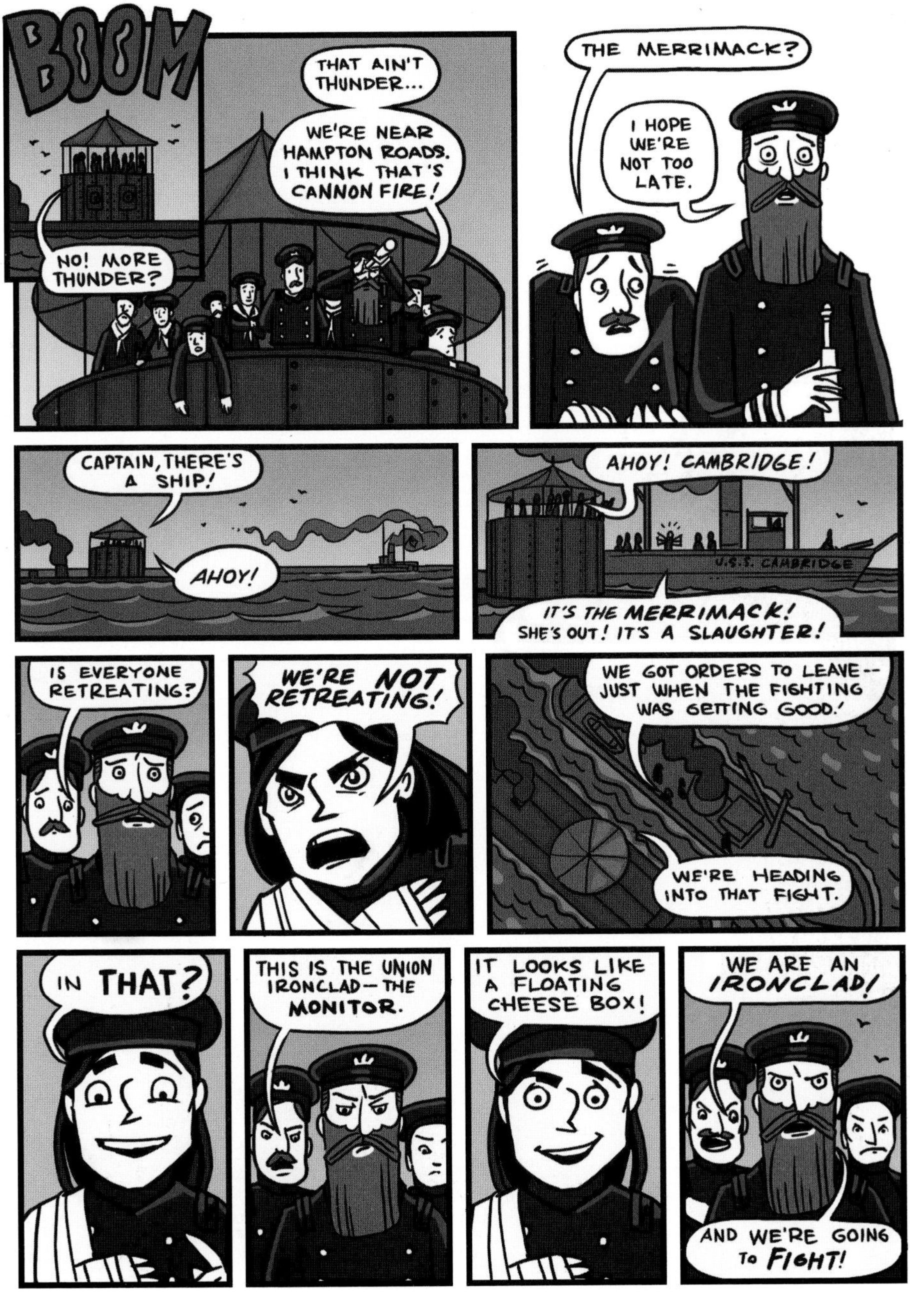
BOOM
NO! MORE THUNDER?
THAT AIN'T THUNDER...
WE'RE NEAR HAMPTON ROADS. I THINK THAT'S CANNON FIRE!
THE MERRIMACK?
I HOPE WE'RE NOT TOO LATE.
CAPTAIN, THERE'S A SHIP!
AHOY!
AHOY! CAMBRIDGE!
U.S.S. CAMBRIDGE
IT'S THE MERRIMACK! SHE'S OUT! IT'S A SLAUGHTER!
IS EVERYONE RETREATING?
WE'RE NOT RETREATING!
WE GOT ORDERS TO LEAVE-- JUST WHEN THE FIGHTING WAS GETTING GOOD!
WE'RE HEADING INTO THAT FIGHT.
IN THAT?
THIS IS THE UNION IRONCLAD—THE MONITOR.
IT LOOKS LIKE A FLOATING CHEESE BOX!
WE ARE AN IRONCLAD!
AND WE'RE GOING TO FIGHT!

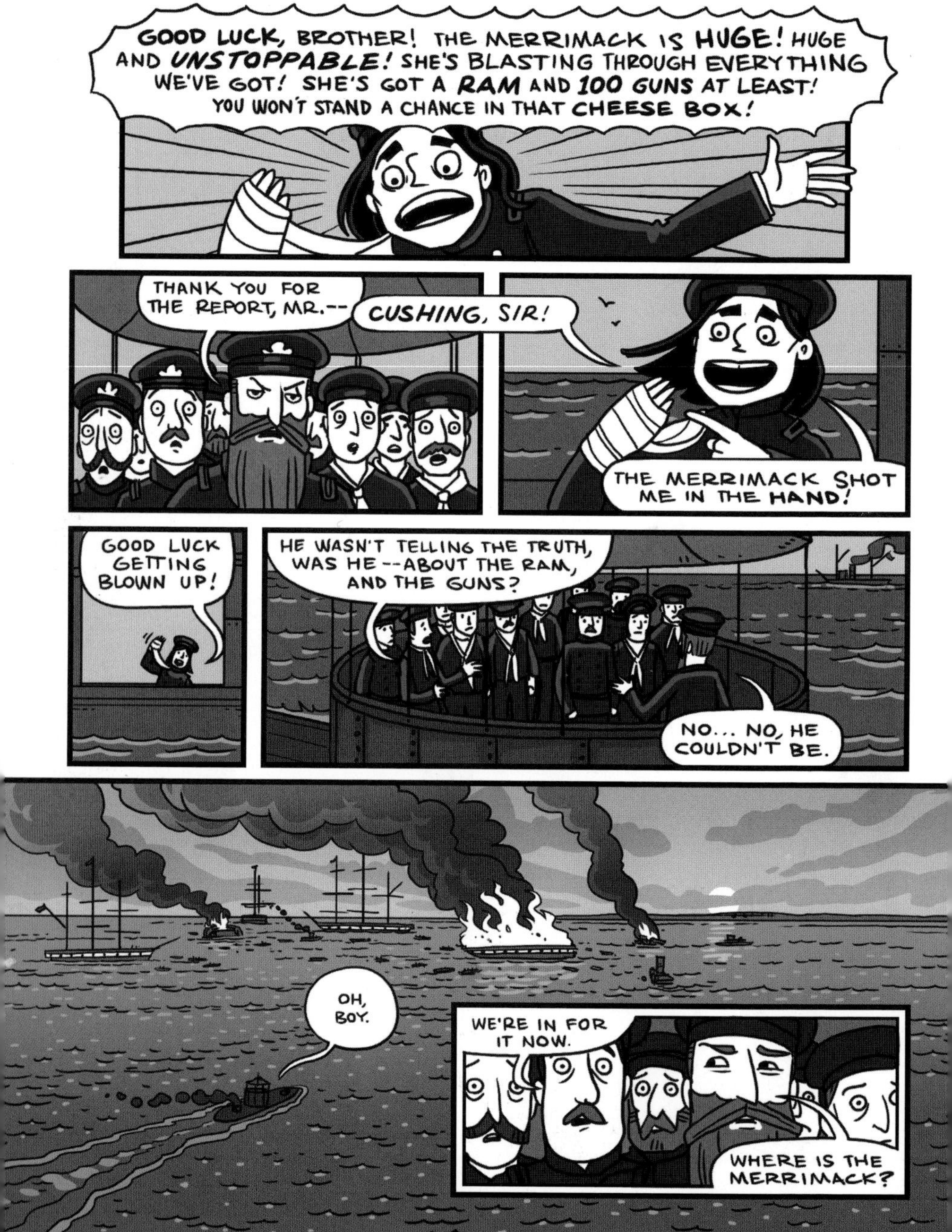
GOOD LUCK, BROTHER! THE MERRIMACK IS HUGE! HUGE AND UNSTOPPABLE! SHE'S BLASTING THROUGH EVERYTHING WE'VE GOT! SHE'S GOT A RAM AND 100 GUNS AT LEAST! YOU WON'T STAND A CHANCE IN THAT CHEESE BOX!
THANK YOU FOR THE REPORT, MR.--
CUSHING, SIR!
THE MERRIMACK SHOT ME IN THE HAND!
GOOD LUCK GETTING BLOWN UP!
HE WASN'T TELLING THE TRUTH, WAS HE--ABOUT THE RAM, AND THE GUNS?
NO... NO, HE COULDN'T BE.
OH, BOY.
WE'RE IN FOR IT NOW.
WHERE IS THE MERRIMACK?

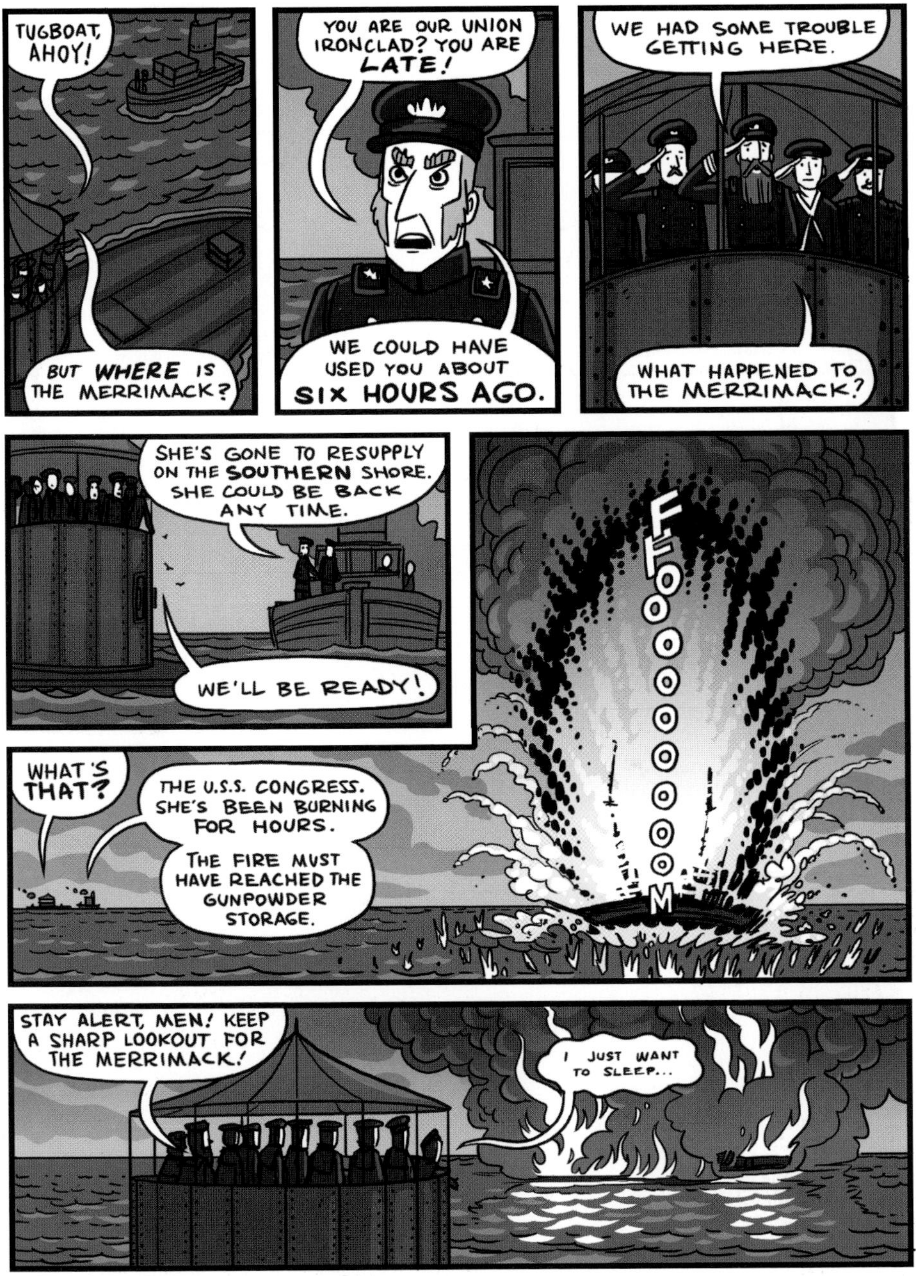
TUGBOAT, AHOY!
BUT WHERE IS THE MERRIMACK?
YOU ARE OUR UNION IRONCLAD? YOU ARE LATE!
WE COULD HAVE USED YOU ABOUT SIX HOURS AGO.
WE HAD SOME TROUBLE GETTING HERE.
WHAT HAPPENED TO THE MERRIMACK?
SHE'S GONE TO RESUPPLY ON THE SOUTHERN SHORE. SHE COULD BE BACK ANY TIME.
WE'LL BE READY!
FFOOOOOOOOOOM
WHAT'S THAT?
THE U.S.S. CONGRESS. SHE'S BEEN BURNING FOR HOURS.
THE FIRE MUST HAVE REACHED THE GUNPOWDER STORAGE.
STAY ALERT, MEN! KEEP A SHARP LOOKOUT FOR THE MERRIMACK!
I JUST WANT TO SLEEP...

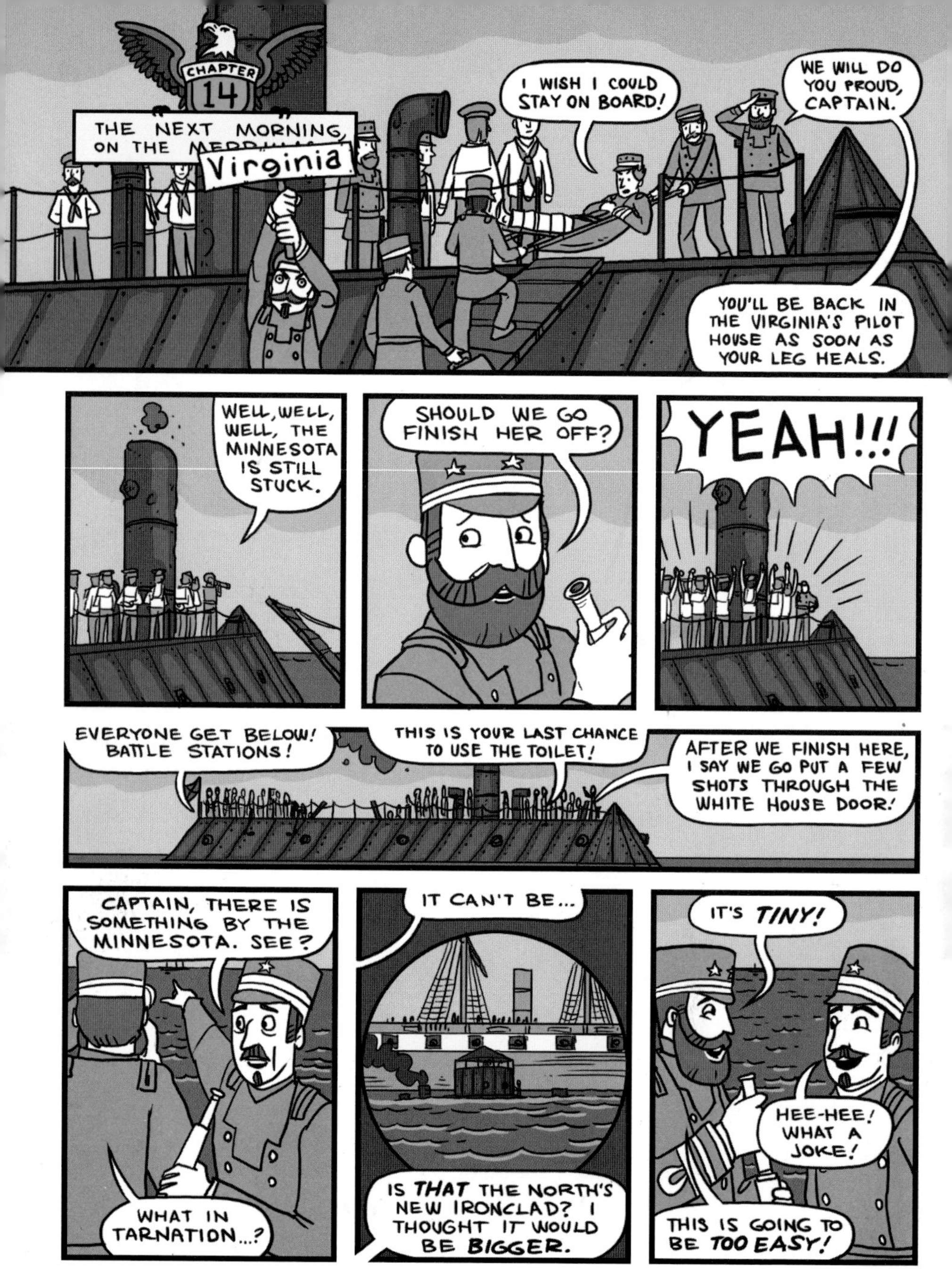
CHAPTER 14
THE NEXT MORNING, ON THE
Virginia
I WISH I COULD STAY ON BOARD!
WE WILL DO YOU PROUD, CAPTAIN.
YOU'LL BE BACK IN THE VIRGINIA'S PILOT HOUSE AS SOON AS YOUR LEG HEALS.
WELL, WELL, WELL, THE MINNESOTA IS STILL STUCK.
SHOULD WE GO FINISH HER OFF?
YEAH!!!
EVERYONE GET BELOW! BATTLE STATIONS!
THIS IS YOUR LAST CHANCE TO USE THE TOILET!
AFTER WE FINISH HERE, I SAY WE GO PUT A FEW SHOTS THROUGH THE WHITE HOUSE DOOR!
CAPTAIN, THERE IS SOMETHING BY THE MINNESOTA. SEE?
WHAT IN TARNATION...?
IT CAN'T BE...
IS *THAT* THE NORTH'S NEW IRONCLAD? I THOUGHT IT WOULD BE **BIGGER**.
IT'S *TINY!*
HEE-HEE! WHAT A JOKE!
THIS IS GOING TO BE *TOO EASY!*

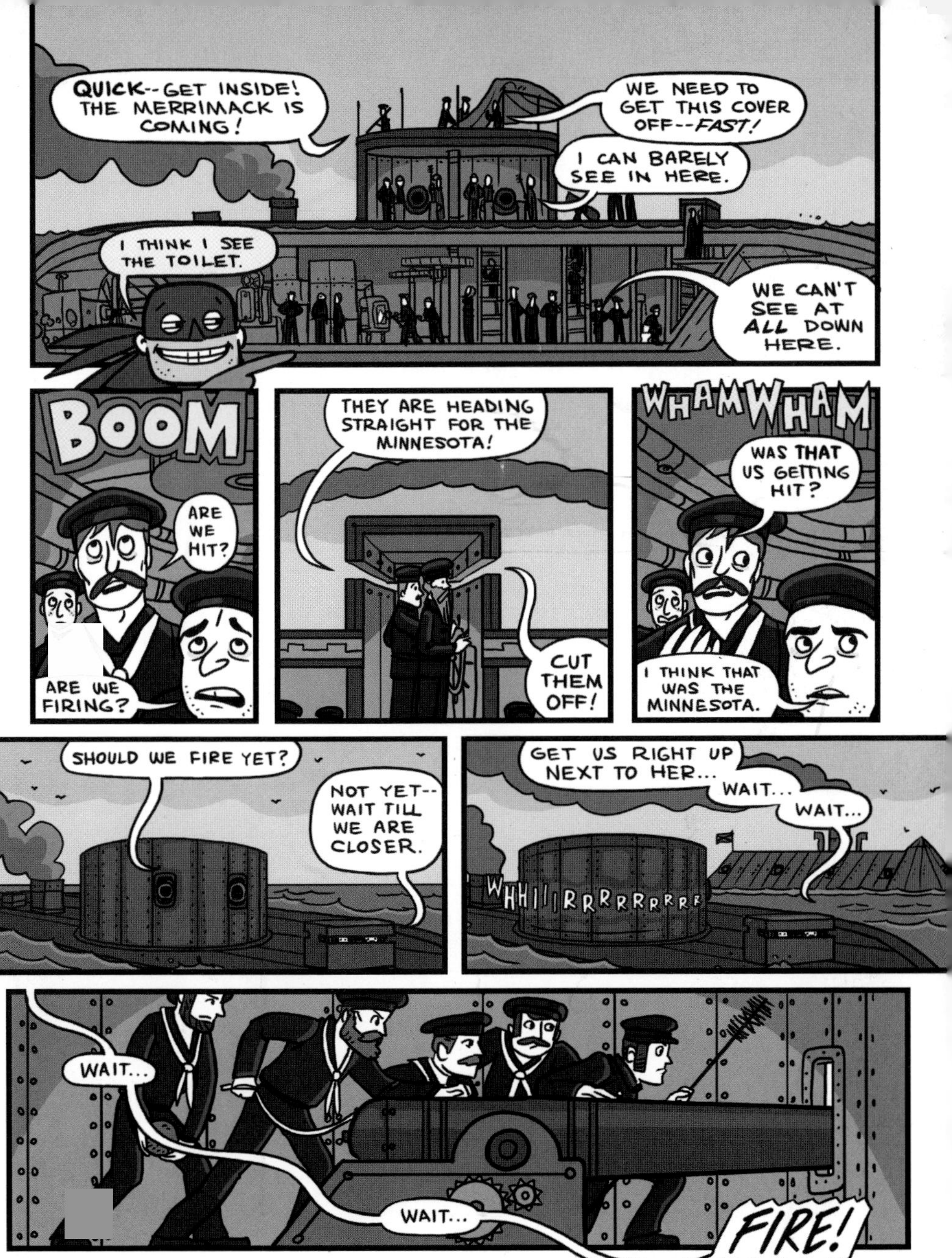
QUICK--GET INSIDE! THE MERRIMACK IS COMING!
WE NEED TO GET THIS COVER OFF--FAST!
I CAN BARELY SEE IN HERE.
I THINK I SEE THE TOILET.
WE CAN'T SEE AT ALL DOWN HERE.
BOOM
ARE WE HIT?
ARE WE FIRING?
THEY ARE HEADING STRAIGHT FOR THE MINNESOTA!
CUT THEM OFF!
WHAMWHAM
WAS THAT US GETTING HIT?
I THINK THAT WAS THE MINNESOTA.
SHOULD WE FIRE YET?
NOT YET--WAIT TILL WE ARE CLOSER.
GET US RIGHT UP NEXT TO HER...
WAIT...
WAIT...
WHHIIIRRRRRRRRR
WAIT...
WAIT...
FIRE!

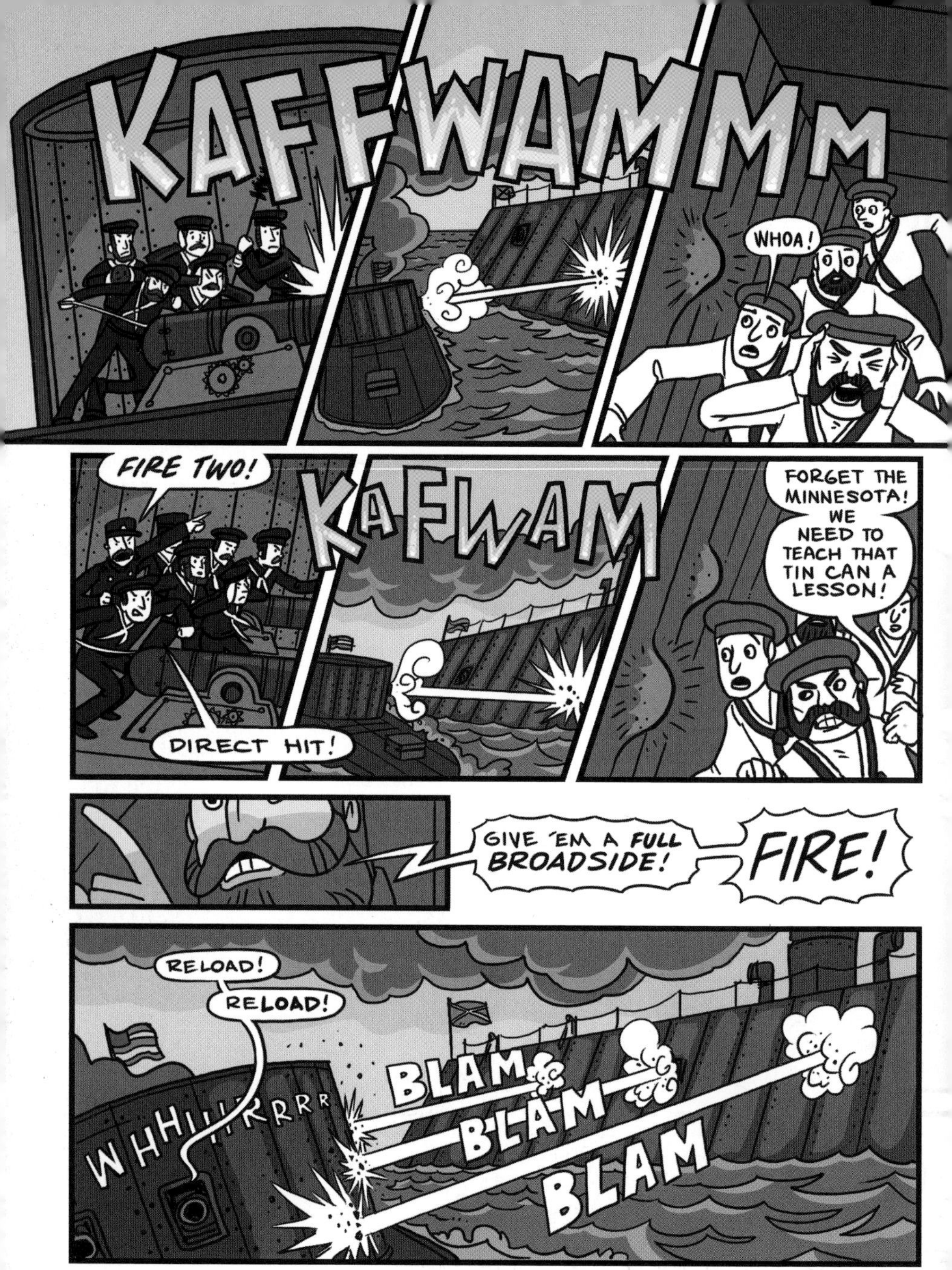
KAFFWAMMMm
WHOA!
FIRE TWO!
KAFWAM
DIRECT HIT!
FORGET THE MINNESOTA! WE NEED TO TEACH THAT TIN CAN A LESSON!
GIVE 'EM A FULL BROADSIDE!
FIRE!
RELOAD!
RELOAD!
WHHIIIRRRR
BLAM
BLAM
BLAM

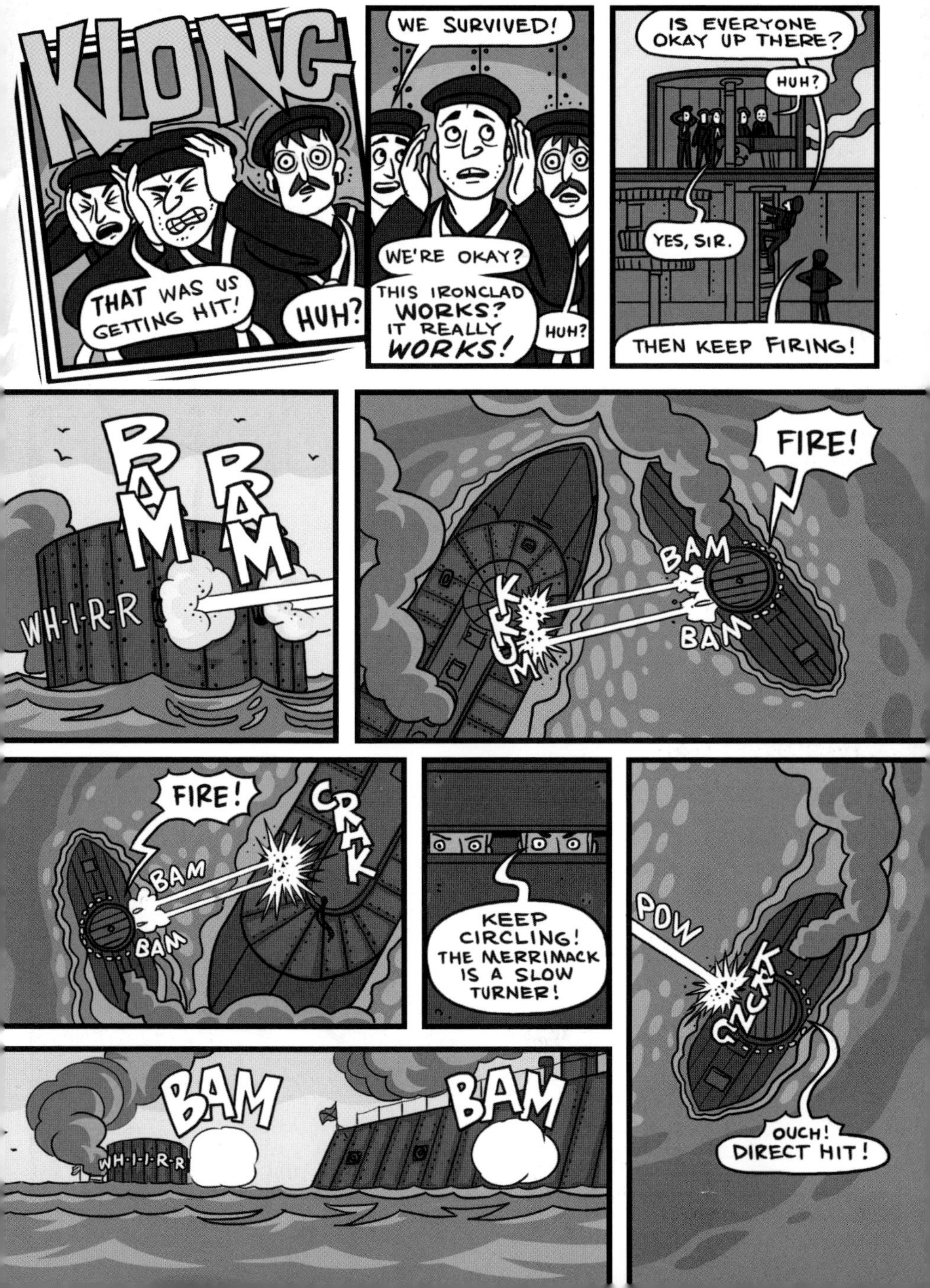
KLONG
THAT WAS US GETTING HIT!
HUH?
WE SURVIVED!
WE'RE OKAY?
THIS IRONCLAD WORKS? IT REALLY WORKS!
HUH?
IS EVERYONE OKAY UP THERE?
HUH?
YES, SIR.
THEN KEEP FIRING!
BAM BAM
WH-I-R-R
FIRE!
BAM
BAM
FIRE!
BAM
BAM
CRAK
KEEP CIRCLING! THE MERRIMACK IS A SLOW TURNER!
POW
OUCH! DIRECT HIT!
BAM
BAM
WH-I-I-R-R

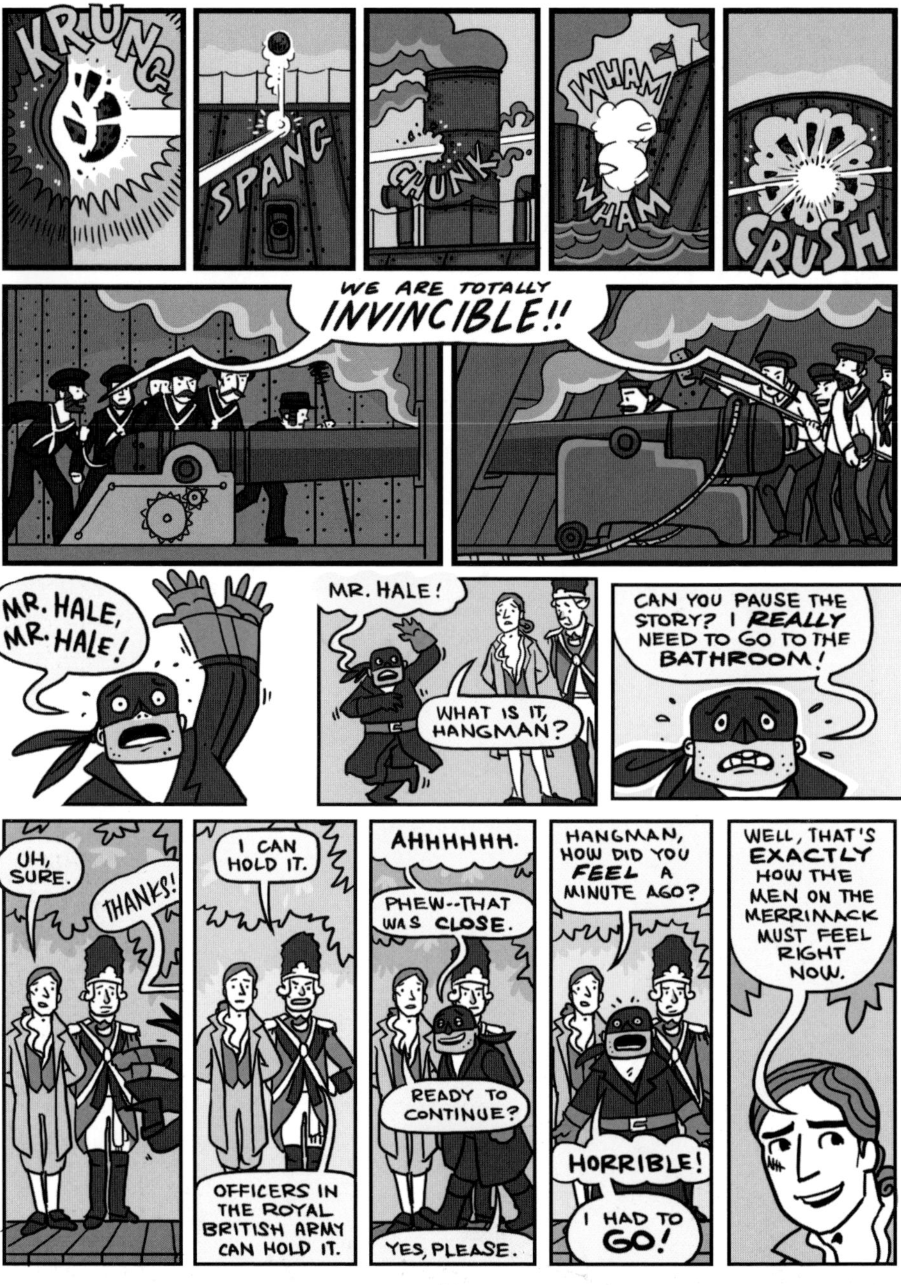
KRUNG
SPANG
CHUNK
WHAM
WHAM
CRUSH
WE ARE TOTALLY INVINCIBLE!!
MR. HALE, MR. HALE!
MR. HALE!
WHAT IS IT, HANGMAN?
CAN YOU PAUSE THE STORY? I REALLY NEED TO GO TO THE BATHROOM!
UH, SURE.
THANKS!
I CAN HOLD IT.
OFFICERS IN THE ROYAL BRITISH ARMY CAN HOLD IT.
AHHHHHH.
PHEW--THAT WAS CLOSE.
READY TO CONTINUE?
YES, PLEASE.
HANGMAN, HOW DID YOU FEEL A MINUTE AGO?
HORRIBLE!
I HAD TO GO!
WELL, THAT'S EXACTLY HOW THE MEN ON THE MERRIMACK MUST FEEL RIGHT NOW.

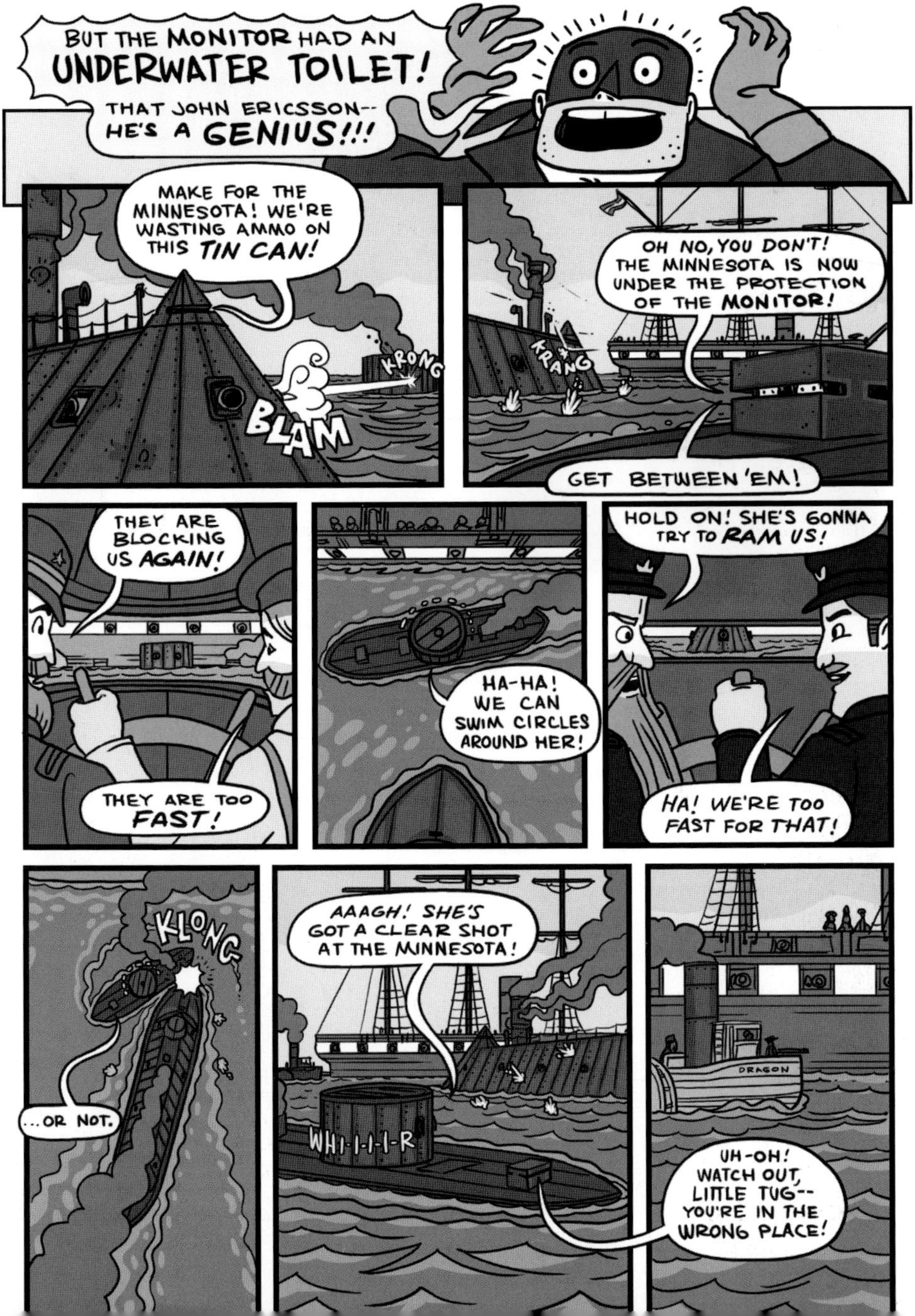
BUT THE MONITOR HAD AN UNDERWATER TOILET!
THAT JOHN ERICSSON--HE'S A GENIUS!!!
MAKE FOR THE MINNESOTA! WE'RE WASTING AMMO ON THIS TIN CAN!
KRONG
BLAM
OH NO, YOU DON'T! THE MINNESOTA IS NOW UNDER THE PROTECTION OF THE MONITOR!
KRANG
GET BETWEEN 'EM!
THEY ARE BLOCKING US AGAIN!
THEY ARE TOO FAST!
HA-HA! WE CAN SWIM CIRCLES AROUND HER!
HOLD ON! SHE'S GONNA TRY TO RAM US!
HA! WE'RE TOO FAST FOR THAT!
KLONG
...OR NOT.
AAAGH! SHE'S GOT A CLEAR SHOT AT THE MINNESOTA!
WHI-I-I-I-R
UH-OH! WATCH OUT, LITTLE TUG--YOU'RE IN THE WRONG PLACE!
DRAGON

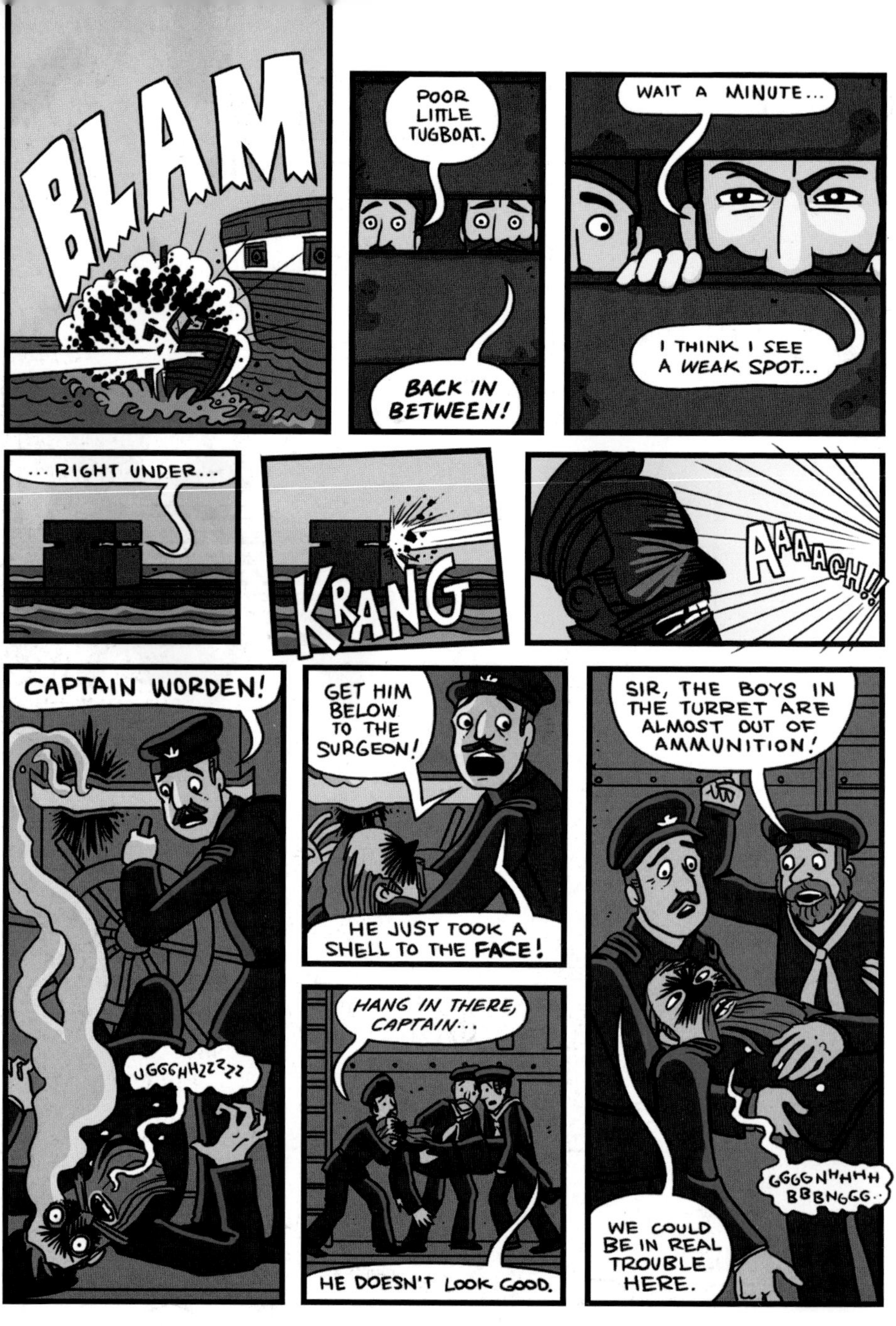
BLAM
POOR LITTLE TUGBOAT.
BACK IN BETWEEN!
WAIT A MINUTE...
I THINK I SEE A WEAK SPOT...
... RIGHT UNDER...
KRANG
AAAACH!!
CAPTAIN WORDEN!
UGGGHZZZZZ
GET HIM BELOW TO THE SURGEON!
HE JUST TOOK A SHELL TO THE FACE!
HANG IN THERE, CAPTAIN...
HE DOESN'T LOOK GOOD.
SIR, THE BOYS IN THE TURRET ARE ALMOST OUT OF AMMUNITION!
GGGGNHHHH BBBNGGG..
WE COULD BE IN REAL TROUBLE HERE.

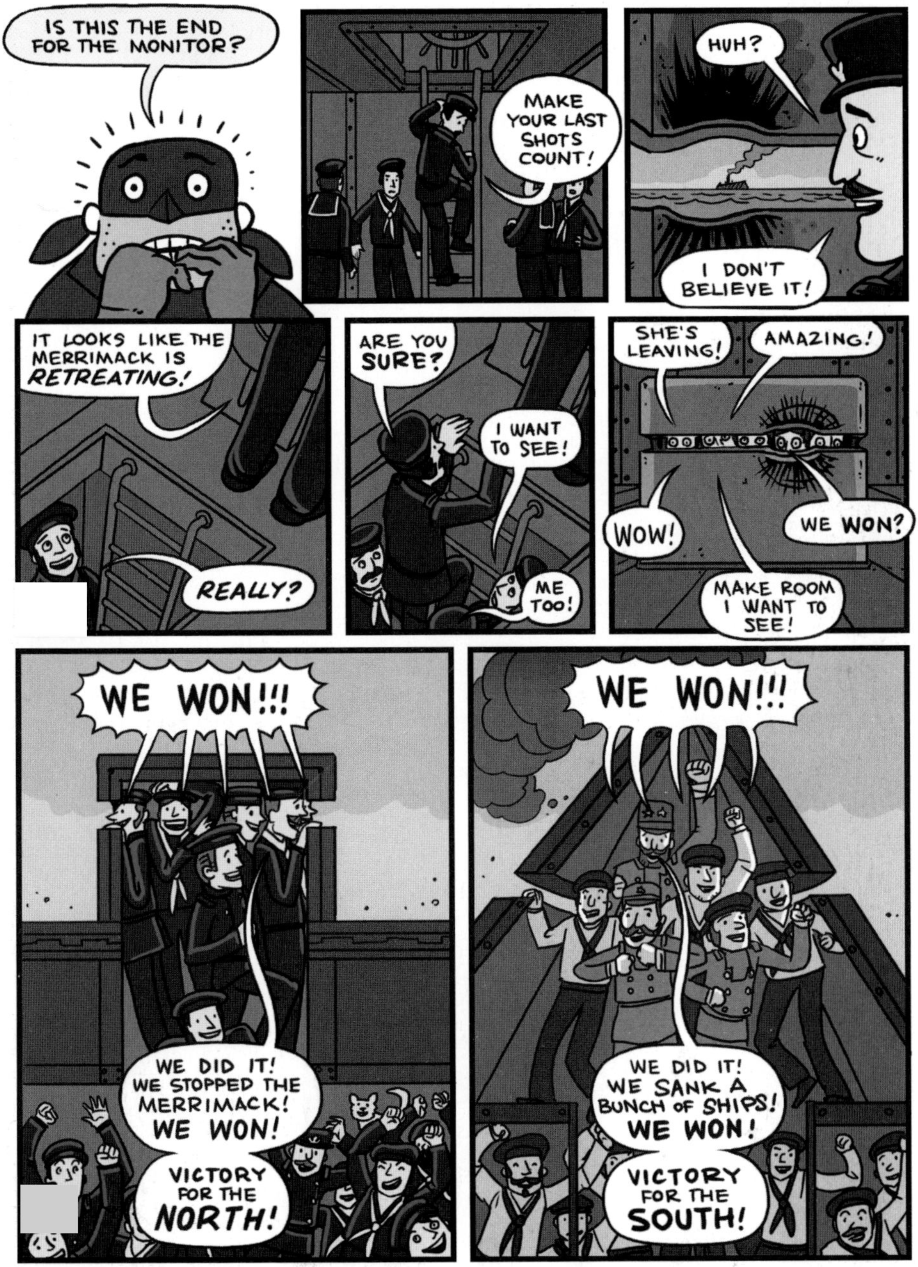

IS THIS THE END FOR THE MONITOR?
MAKE YOUR LAST SHOTS COUNT!
HUH?
I DON'T BELIEVE IT!
IT LOOKS LIKE THE MERRIMACK IS RETREATING!
REALLY?
ARE YOU SURE?
I WANT TO SEE!
ME TOO!
SHE'S LEAVING!
AMAZING!
WOW!
WE WON?
MAKE ROOM I WANT TO SEE!
WE WON!!!
WE DID IT! WE STOPPED THE MERRIMACK! WE WON!
VICTORY FOR THE NORTH!
WE WON!!!
WE DID IT! WE SANK A BUNCH OF SHIPS! WE WON!
VICTORY FOR THE SOUTH!

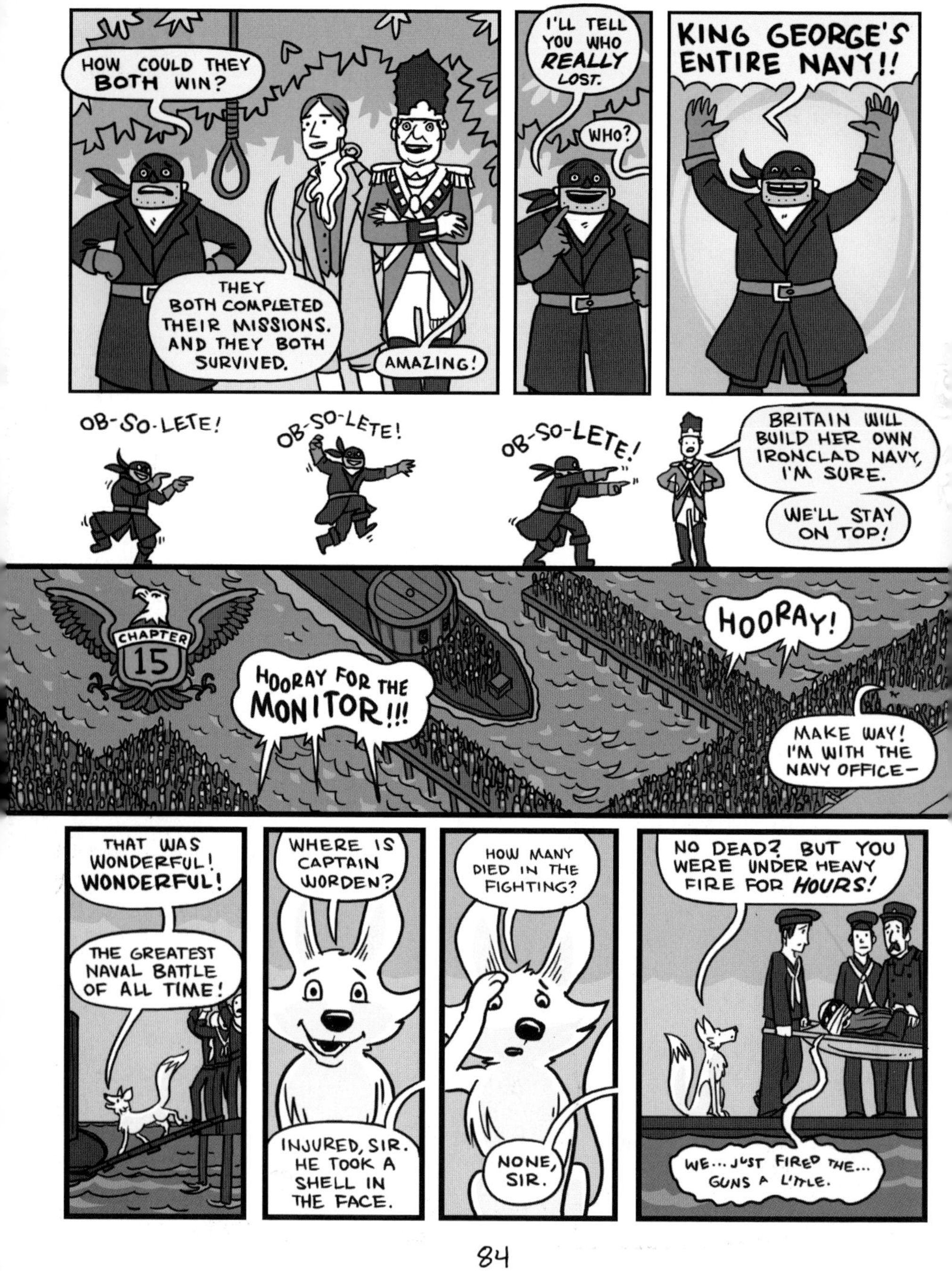
HOW COULD THEY BOTH WIN?
THEY BOTH COMPLETED THEIR MISSIONS. AND THEY BOTH SURVIVED.
AMAZING!
I'LL TELL YOU WHO REALLY LOST.
WHO?
KING GEORGE'S ENTIRE NAVY!!
OB-SO-LETE!
OB-SO-LETE!
OB-SO-LETE!
BRITAIN WILL BUILD HER OWN IRONCLAD NAVY, I'M SURE.
WE'LL STAY ON TOP!
CHAPTER 15
HOORAY FOR THE MONITOR!!!
HOORAY!
MAKE WAY! I'M WITH THE NAVY OFFICE—
THAT WAS WONDERFUL! WONDERFUL!
THE GREATEST NAVAL BATTLE OF ALL TIME!
WHERE IS CAPTAIN WORDEN?
INJURED, SIR. HE TOOK A SHELL IN THE FACE.
HOW MANY DIED IN THE FIGHTING?
NONE, SIR.
NO DEAD? BUT YOU WERE UNDER HEAVY FIRE FOR HOURS!
WE... JUST FIRED THE... GUNS A LITTLE.

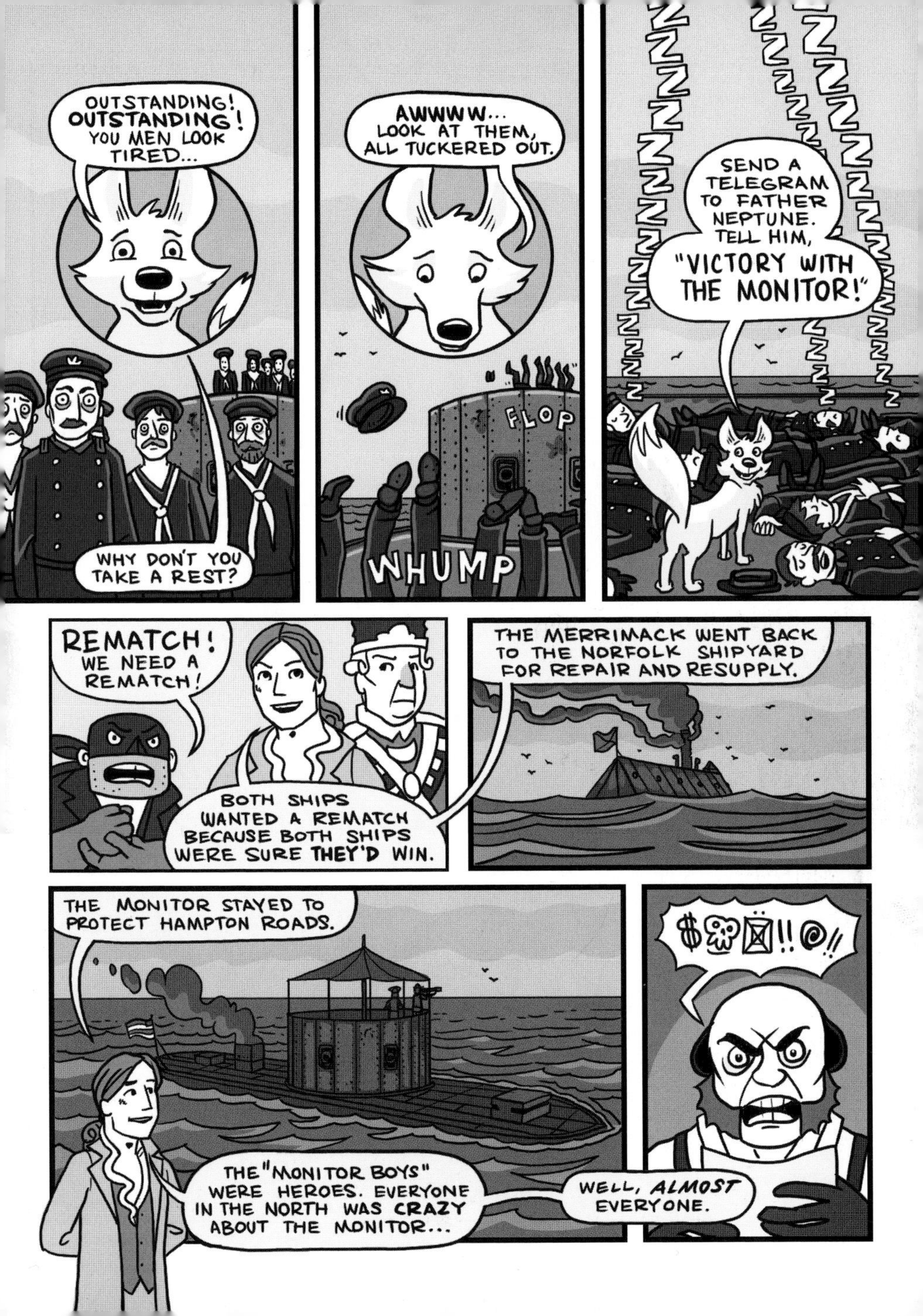

OUTSTANDING! OUTSTANDING! YOU MEN LOOK TIRED...
WHY DON'T YOU TAKE A REST?
AWWWW... LOOK AT THEM, ALL TUCKERED OUT.
FLOP
WHUMP
SEND A TELEGRAM TO FATHER NEPTUNE. TELL HIM, "VICTORY WITH THE MONITOR!"
REMATCH! WE NEED A REMATCH!
BOTH SHIPS WANTED A REMATCH BECAUSE BOTH SHIPS WERE SURE THEY'D WIN.
THE MERRIMACK WENT BACK TO THE NORFOLK SHIPYARD FOR REPAIR AND RESUPPLY.
THE MONITOR STAYED TO PROTECT HAMPTON ROADS.
THE "MONITOR BOYS" WERE HEROES. EVERYONE IN THE NORTH WAS CRAZY ABOUT THE MONITOR...
WELL, ALMOST EVERYONE.

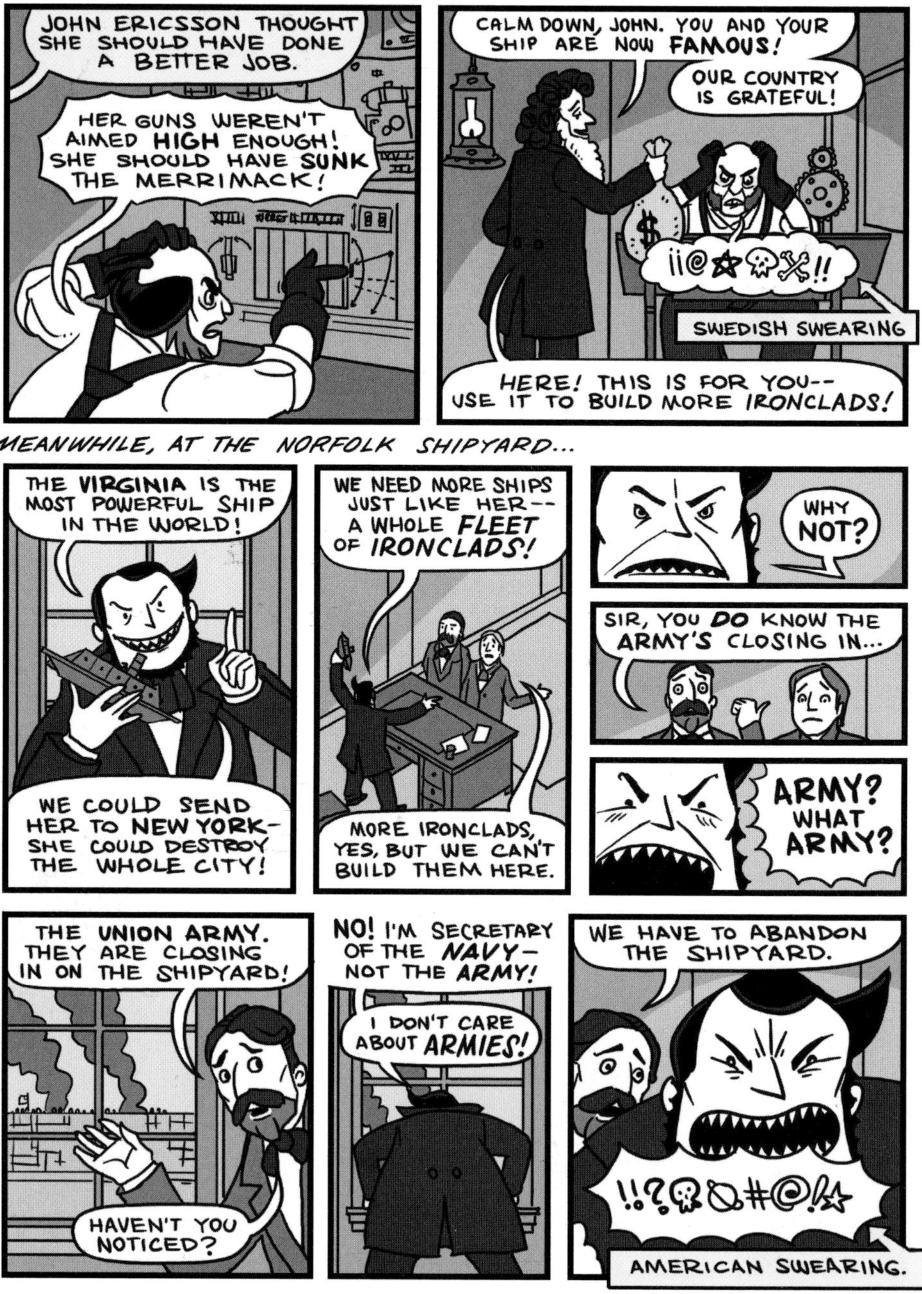
JOHN ERICSSON THOUGHT SHE SHOULD HAVE DONE A BETTER JOB.
HER GUNS WEREN'T AIMED HIGH ENOUGH! SHE SHOULD HAVE SUNK THE MERRIMACK!
CALM DOWN, JOHN. YOU AND YOUR SHIP ARE NOW FAMOUS!
OUR COUNTRY IS GRATEFUL!
SWEDISH SWEARING
HERE! THIS IS FOR YOU-- USE IT TO BUILD MORE IRONCLADS!
MEANWHILE, AT THE NORFOLK SHIPYARD...
THE VIRGINIA IS THE MOST POWERFUL SHIP IN THE WORLD!
WE COULD SEND HER TO NEW YORK- SHE COULD DESTROY THE WHOLE CITY!
WE NEED MORE SHIPS JUST LIKE HER-- A WHOLE FLEET OF IRONCLADS!
MORE IRONCLADS, YES, BUT WE CAN'T BUILD THEM HERE.
WHY NOT?
SIR, YOU DO KNOW THE ARMY'S CLOSING IN...
ARMY? WHAT ARMY?
THE UNION ARMY. THEY ARE CLOSING IN ON THE SHIPYARD!
HAVEN'T YOU NOTICED?
NO! I'M SECRETARY OF THE NAVY— NOT THE ARMY!
I DON'T CARE ABOUT ARMIES!
WE HAVE TO ABANDON THE SHIPYARD.
AMERICAN SWEARING.

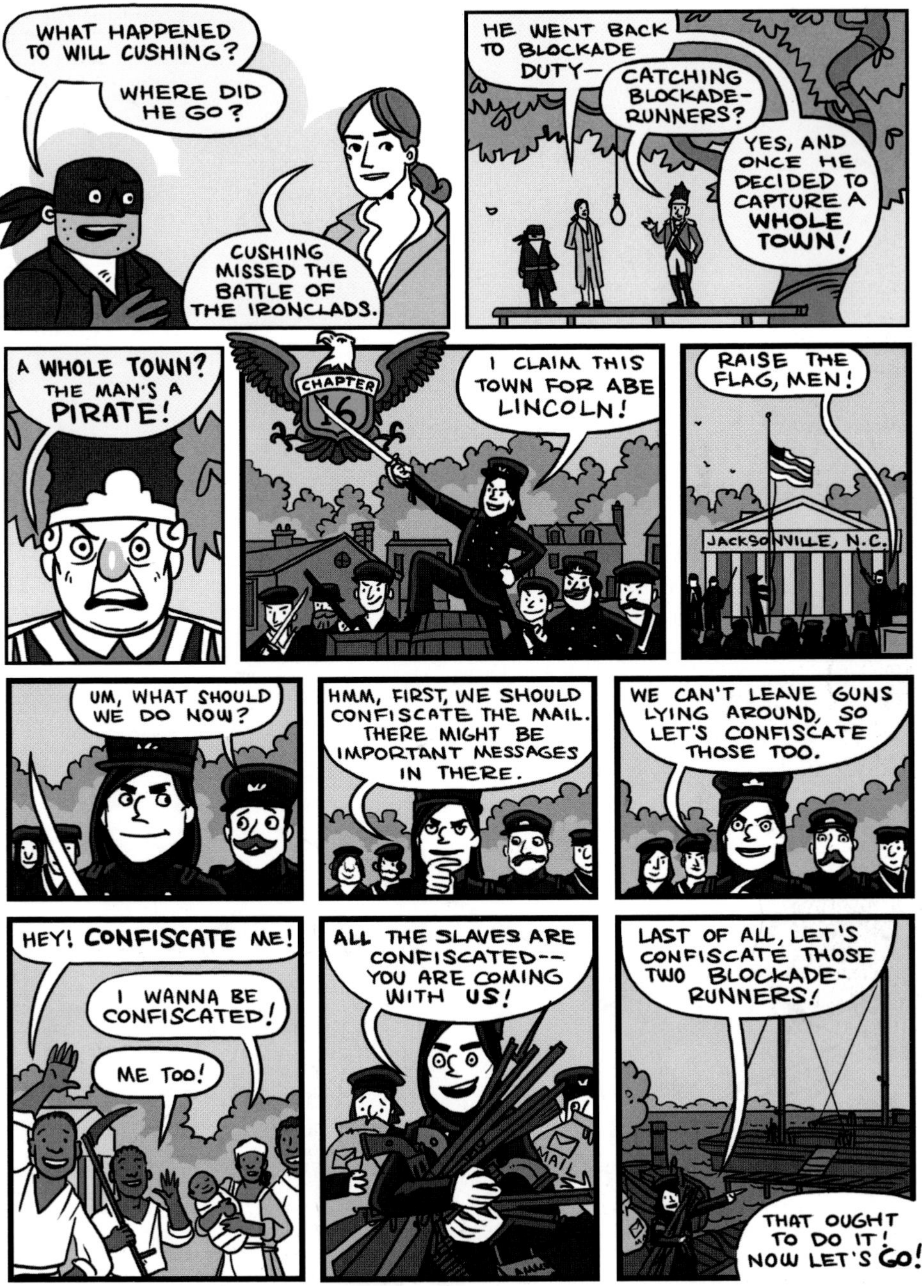
WHAT HAPPENED TO WILL CUSHING?
WHERE DID HE GO?
CUSHING MISSED THE BATTLE OF THE IRONCLADS.
HE WENT BACK TO BLOCKADE DUTY—
CATCHING BLOCKADE-RUNNERS?
YES, AND ONCE HE DECIDED TO CAPTURE A WHOLE TOWN!
A WHOLE TOWN? THE MAN'S A PIRATE!
CHAPTER
16
I CLAIM THIS TOWN FOR ABE LINCOLN!
RAISE THE FLAG, MEN!
JACKSONVILLE, N.C.
UM, WHAT SHOULD WE DO NOW?
HMM, FIRST, WE SHOULD CONFISCATE THE MAIL. THERE MIGHT BE IMPORTANT MESSAGES IN THERE.
WE CAN'T LEAVE GUNS LYING AROUND, SO LET'S CONFISCATE THOSE TOO.
HEY! CONFISCATE ME!
I WANNA BE CONFISCATED!
ME TOO!
ALL THE SLAVES ARE CONFISCATED-- YOU ARE COMING WITH US!
MAIL
LAST OF ALL, LET'S CONFISCATE THOSE TWO BLOCKADE-RUNNERS!
THAT OUGHT TO DO IT! NOW LET'S GO!

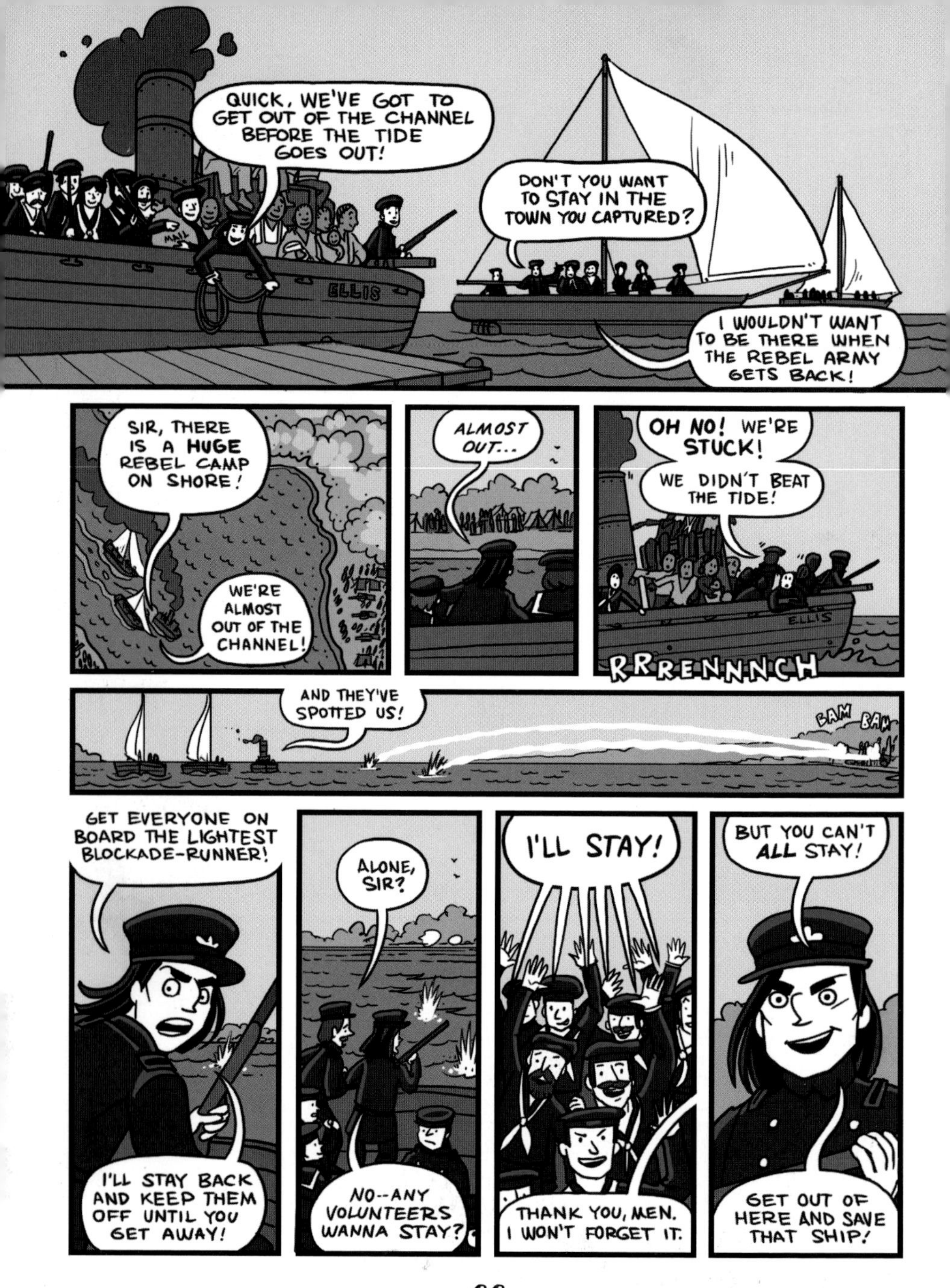

QUICK, WE'VE GOT TO GET OUT OF THE CHANNEL BEFORE THE TIDE GOES OUT!
MAIL
ELLIS
DON'T YOU WANT TO STAY IN THE TOWN YOU CAPTURED?
I WOULDN'T WANT TO BE THERE WHEN THE REBEL ARMY GETS BACK!
SIR, THERE IS A HUGE REBEL CAMP ON SHORE!
WE'RE ALMOST OUT OF THE CHANNEL!
ALMOST OUT...
OH NO! WE'RE STUCK!
WE DIDN'T BEAT THE TIDE!
ELLIS
RRRENNNCH
AND THEY'VE SPOTTED US!
BAM BAM
GET EVERYONE ON BOARD THE LIGHTEST BLOCKADE-RUNNER!
I'LL STAY BACK AND KEEP THEM OFF UNTIL YOU GET AWAY!
ALONE, SIR?
NO--ANY VOLUNTEERS WANNA STAY?
I'LL STAY!
THANK YOU, MEN. I WON'T FORGET IT.
BUT YOU CAN'T ALL STAY!
GET OUT OF HERE AND SAVE THAT SHIP!

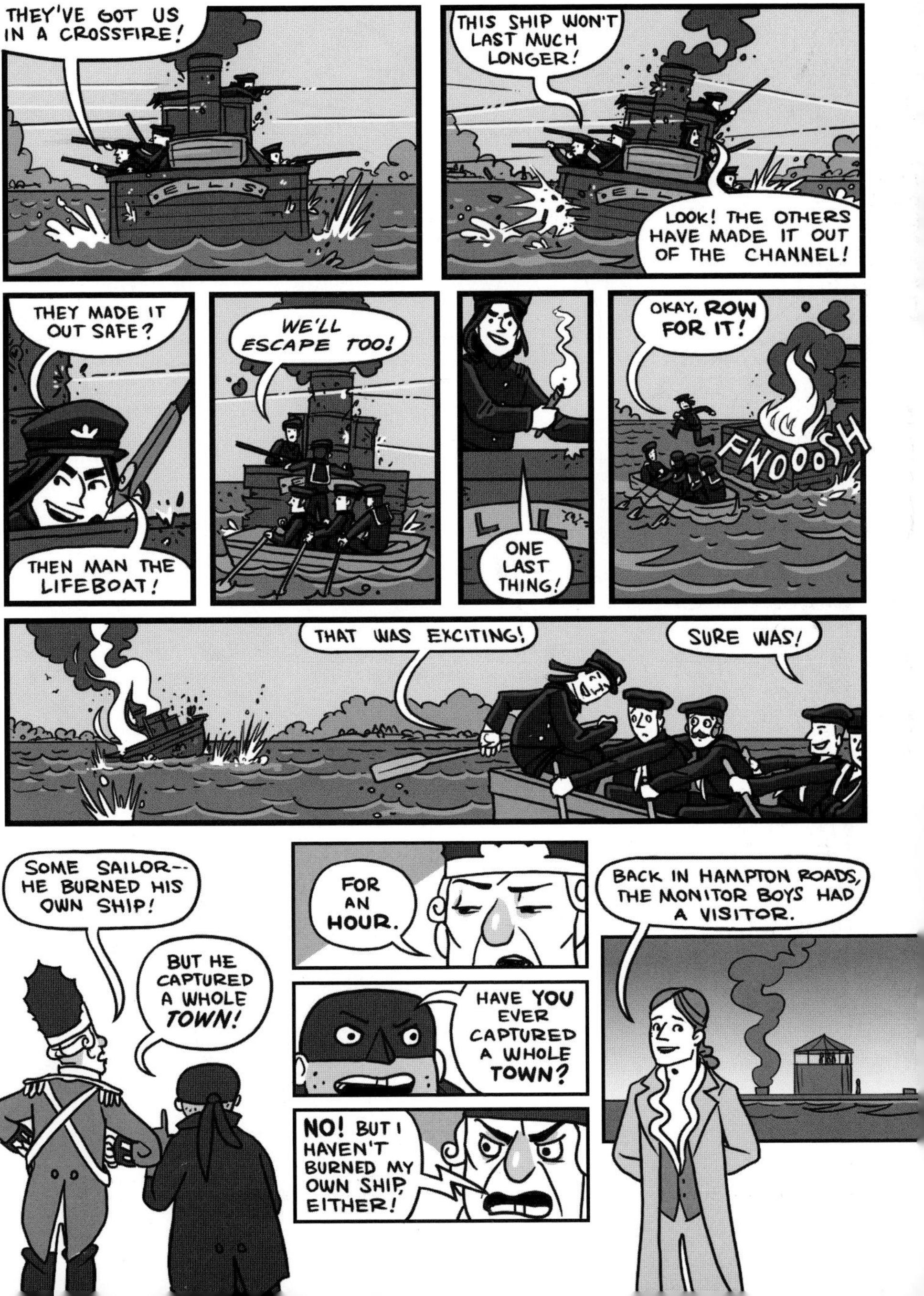
THEY'VE GOT US IN A CROSSFIRE!
ELLIS
THIS SHIP WON'T LAST MUCH LONGER!
LOOK! THE OTHERS HAVE MADE IT OUT OF THE CHANNEL!
THEY MADE IT OUT SAFE?
THEN MAN THE LIFEBOAT!
WE'LL ESCAPE TOO!
ONE LAST THING!
OKAY, ROW FOR IT!
FWOOOSH
THAT WAS EXCITING!
SURE WAS!
SOME SAILOR-- HE BURNED HIS OWN SHIP!
BUT HE CAPTURED A WHOLE TOWN!
FOR AN HOUR.
HAVE YOU EVER CAPTURED A WHOLE TOWN?
NO! BUT I HAVEN'T BURNED MY OWN SHIP, EITHER!
BACK IN HAMPTON ROADS, THE MONITOR BOYS HAD A VISITOR.

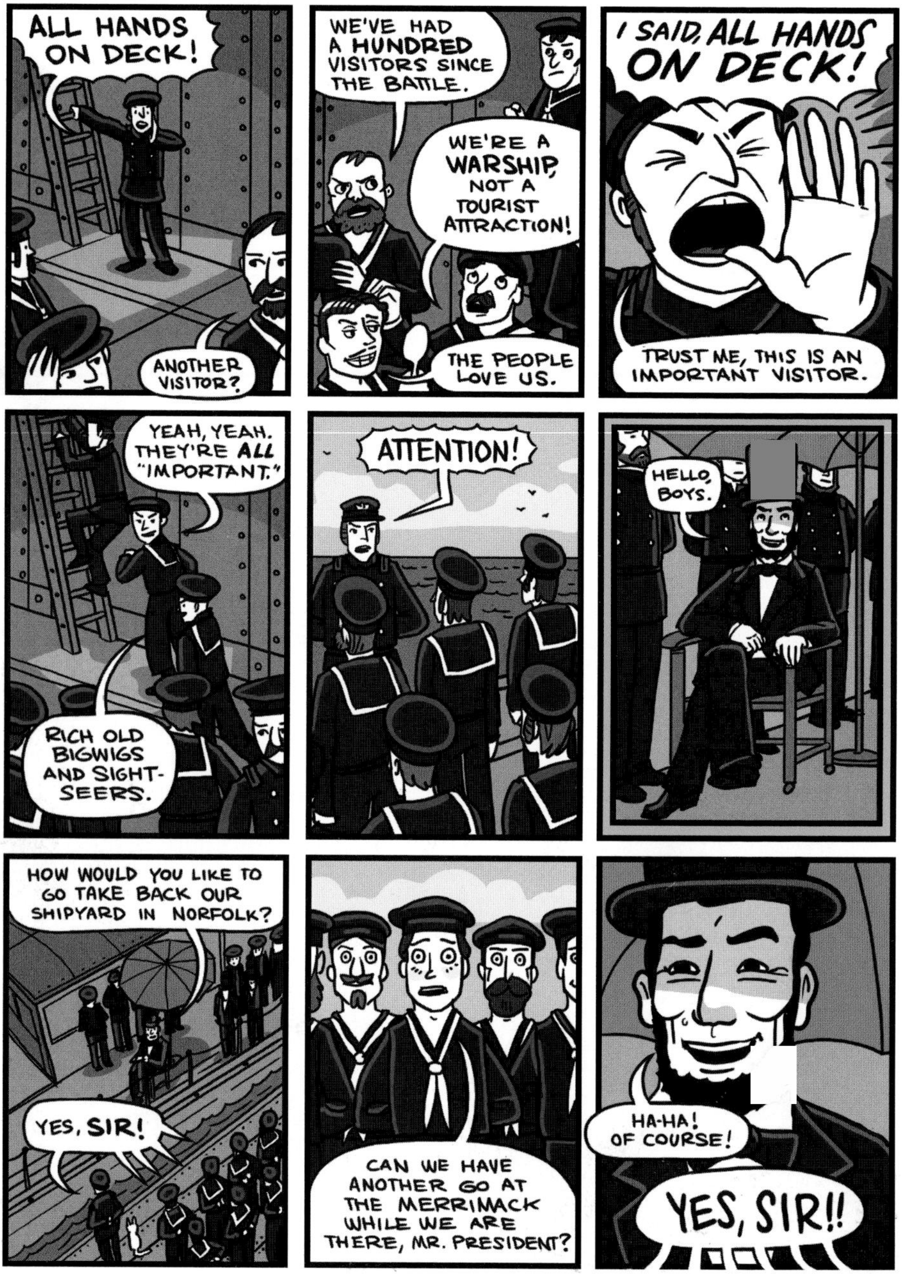
ALL HANDS ON DECK!
ANOTHER VISITOR?
WE'VE HAD A HUNDRED VISITORS SINCE THE BATTLE.
WE'RE A WARSHIP, NOT A TOURIST ATTRACTION!
THE PEOPLE LOVE US.
I SAID, ALL HANDS ON DECK!
TRUST ME, THIS IS AN IMPORTANT VISITOR.
YEAH, YEAH. THEY'RE ALL "IMPORTANT."
RICH OLD BIGWIGS AND SIGHT-SEERS.
ATTENTION!
HELLO, BOYS.
HOW WOULD YOU LIKE TO GO TAKE BACK OUR SHIPYARD IN NORFOLK?
YES, SIR!
CAN WE HAVE ANOTHER GO AT THE MERRIMACK WHILE WE ARE THERE, MR. PRESIDENT?
HA-HA! OF COURSE!
YES, SIR!!

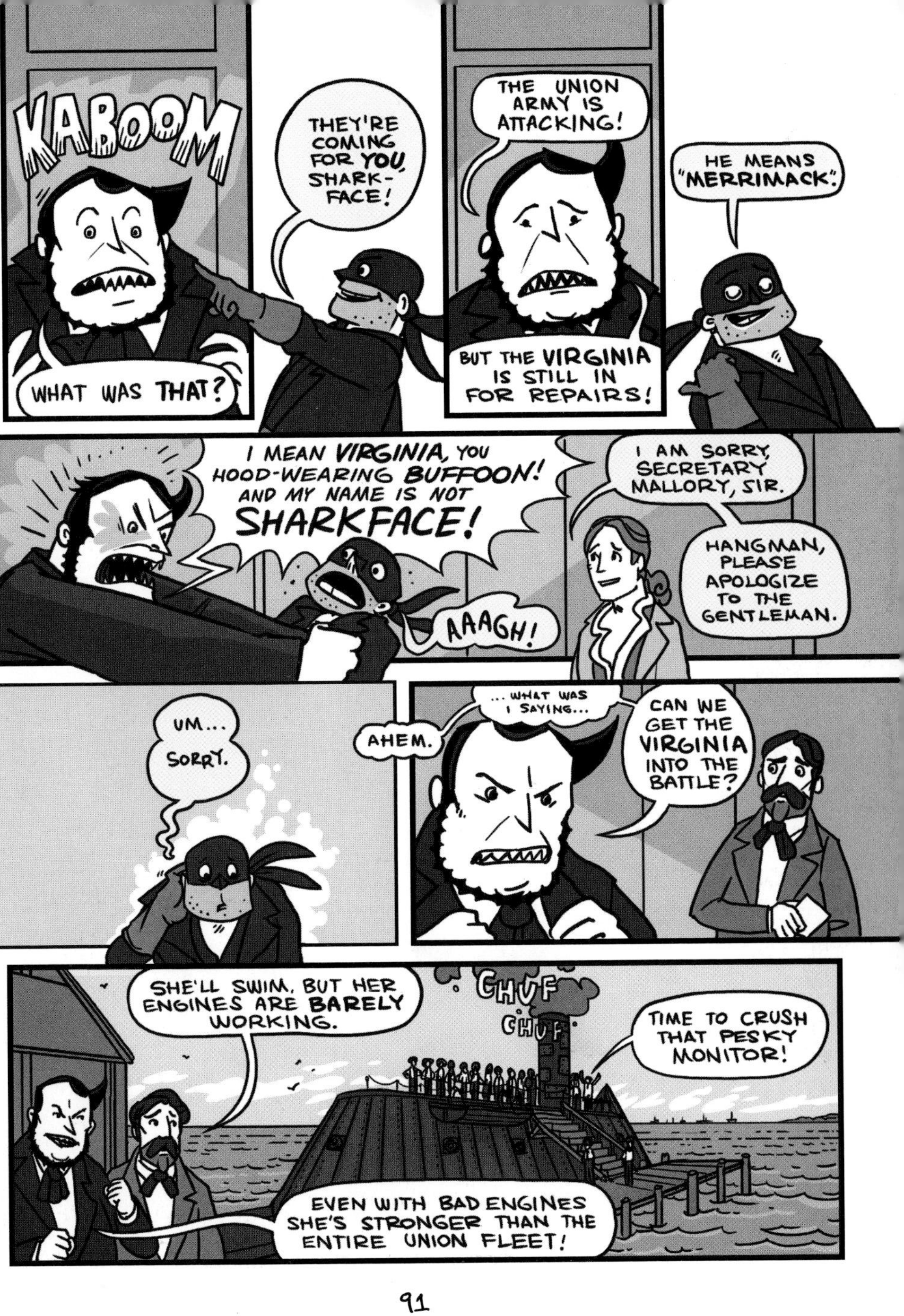
KABOOM
WHAT WAS THAT?
THEY'RE COMING FOR YOU, SHARK-FACE!
THE UNION ARMY IS ATTACKING!
BUT THE VIRGINIA IS STILL IN FOR REPAIRS!
HE MEANS "MERRIMACK".
I MEAN VIRGINIA, YOU HOOD-WEARING BUFFOON! AND MY NAME IS NOT SHARKFACE!
AAAGH!
I AM SORRY, SECRETARY MALLORY, SIR.
HANGMAN, PLEASE APOLOGIZE TO THE GENTLEMAN.
UM... SORRY.
AHEM.
...WHAT WAS I SAYING...
CAN WE GET THE VIRGINIA INTO THE BATTLE?
SHE'LL SWIM, BUT HER ENGINES ARE BARELY WORKING.
CHUF
CHUF
TIME TO CRUSH THAT PESKY MONITOR!
EVEN WITH BAD ENGINES SHE'S STRONGER THAN THE ENTIRE UNION FLEET!

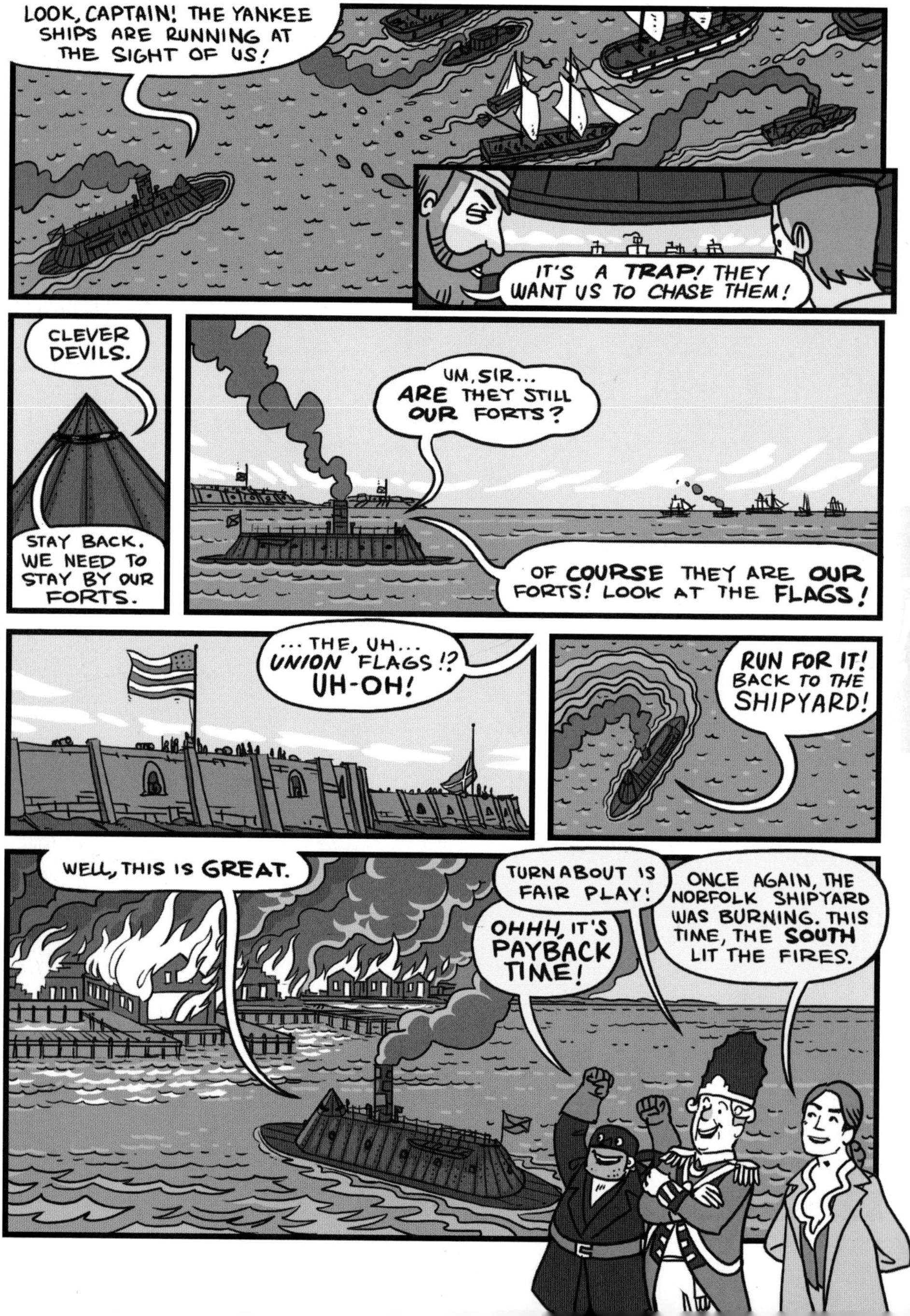
LOOK, CAPTAIN! THE YANKEE SHIPS ARE RUNNING AT THE SIGHT OF US!
IT'S A TRAP! THEY WANT US TO CHASE THEM!
CLEVER DEVILS.
STAY BACK. WE NEED TO STAY BY OUR FORTS.
UM, SIR... ARE THEY STILL OUR FORTS?
OF COURSE THEY ARE OUR FORTS! LOOK AT THE FLAGS!
... THE, UH... UNION FLAGS!? UH-OH!
RUN FOR IT! BACK TO THE SHIPYARD!
WELL, THIS IS GREAT.
TURNABOUT IS FAIR PLAY!
OHHH, IT'S PAYBACK TIME!
ONCE AGAIN, THE NORFOLK SHIPYARD WAS BURNING. THIS TIME, THE SOUTH LIT THE FIRES.

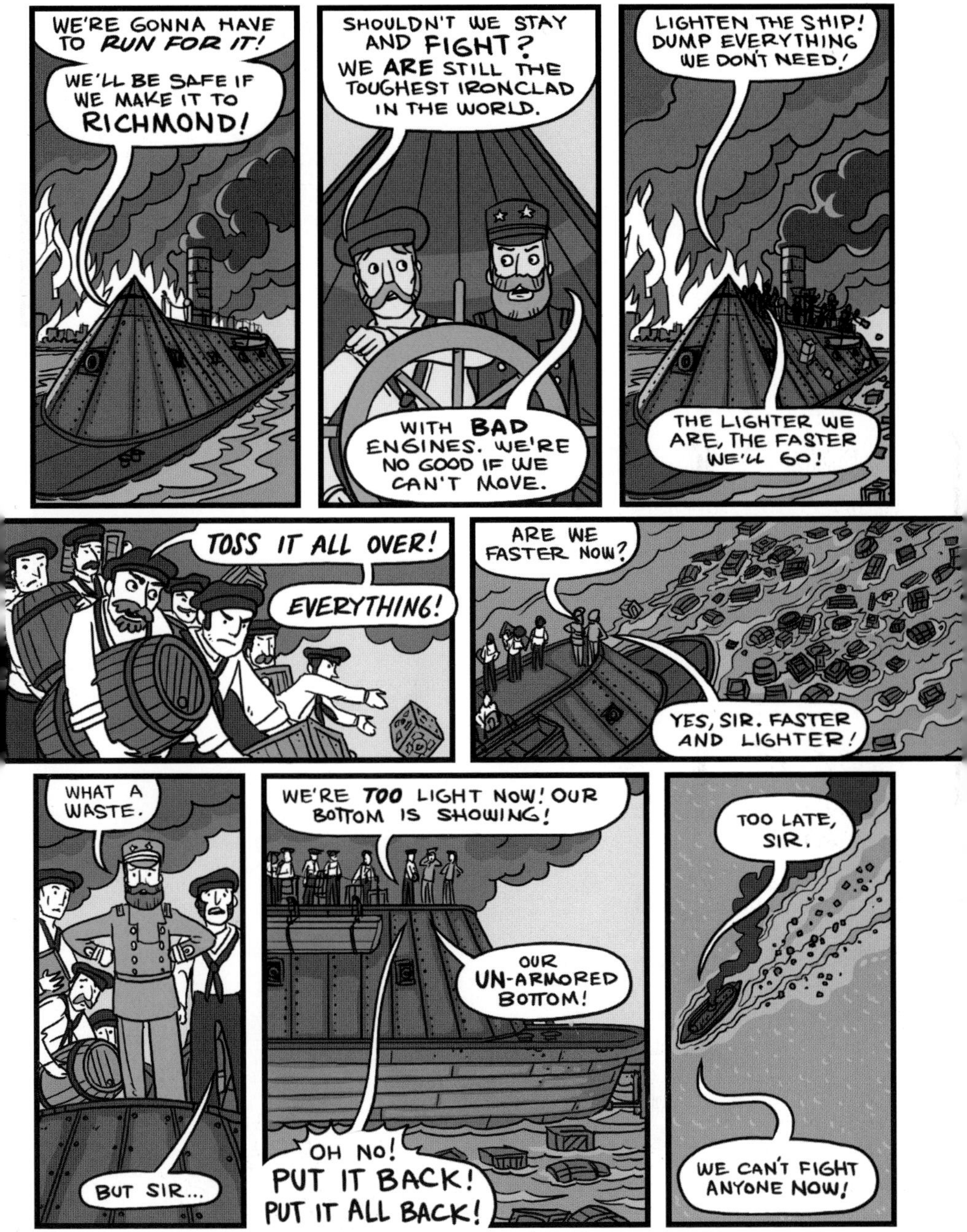
WE'RE GONNA HAVE TO RUN FOR IT!
WE'LL BE SAFE IF WE MAKE IT TO RICHMOND!
SHOULDN'T WE STAY AND FIGHT? WE ARE STILL THE TOUGHEST IRONCLAD IN THE WORLD.
WITH BAD ENGINES. WE'RE NO GOOD IF WE CAN'T MOVE.
LIGHTEN THE SHIP! DUMP EVERYTHING WE DON'T NEED!
THE LIGHTER WE ARE, THE FASTER WE'LL GO!
TOSS IT ALL OVER!
EVERYTHING!
ARE WE FASTER NOW?
YES, SIR. FASTER AND LIGHTER!
WHAT A WASTE.
BUT SIR...
WE'RE TOO LIGHT NOW! OUR BOTTOM IS SHOWING!
OUR UN-ARMORED BOTTOM!
OH NO! PUT IT BACK! PUT IT ALL BACK!
TOO LATE, SIR.
WE CAN'T FIGHT ANYONE NOW!

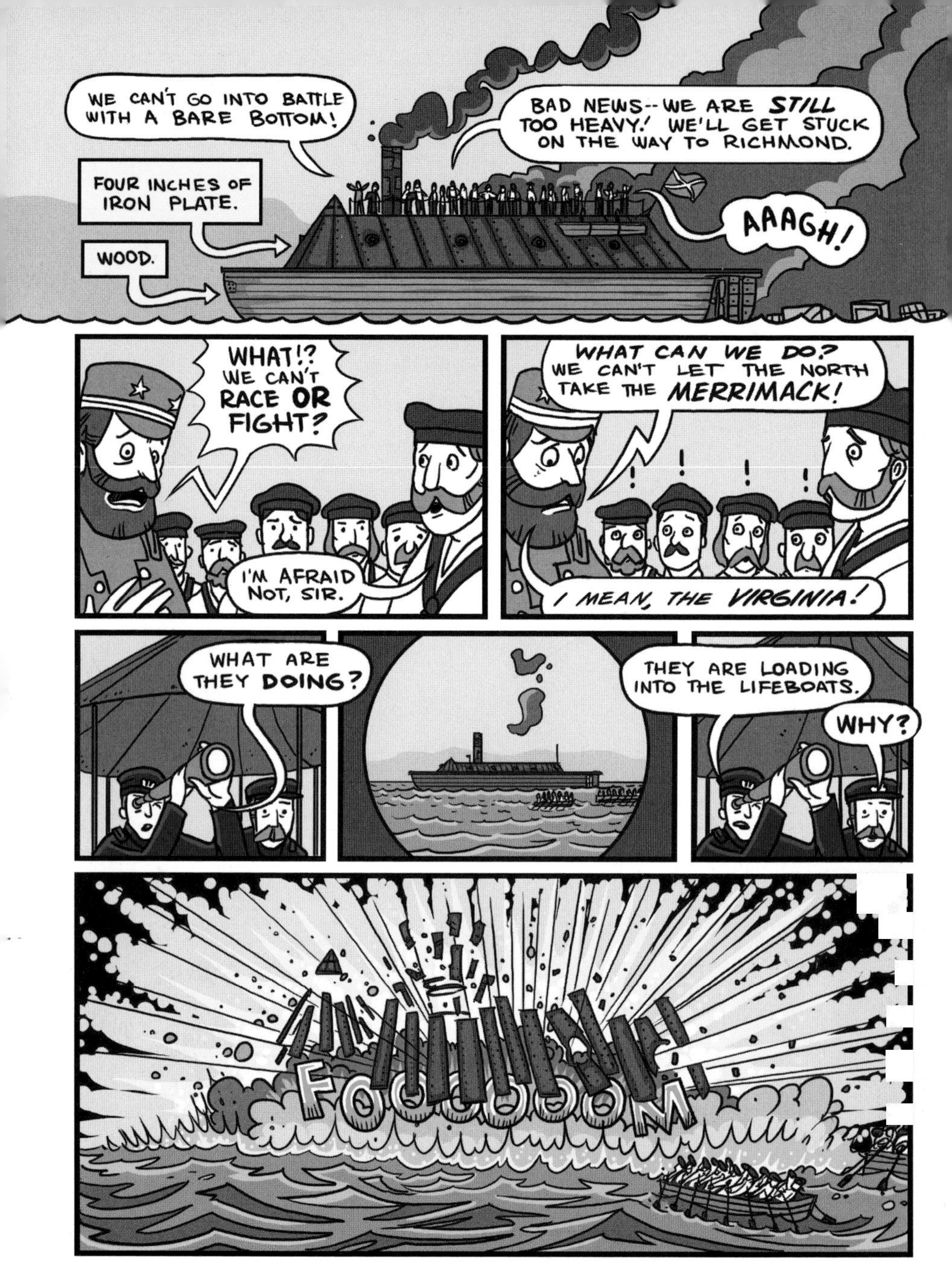

WE CAN'T GO INTO BATTLE WITH A BARE BOTTOM!
BAD NEWS-- WE ARE STILL TOO HEAVY! WE'LL GET STUCK ON THE WAY TO RICHMOND.
FOUR INCHES OF IRON PLATE.
WOOD.
AAAGH!
WHAT!? WE CAN'T RACE OR FIGHT?
I'M AFRAID NOT, SIR.
WHAT CAN WE DO? WE CAN'T LET THE NORTH TAKE THE MERRIMACK!
I MEAN, THE VIRGINIA!
WHAT ARE THEY DOING?
THEY ARE LOADING INTO THE LIFEBOATS.
WHY?
FOOOOOOOM

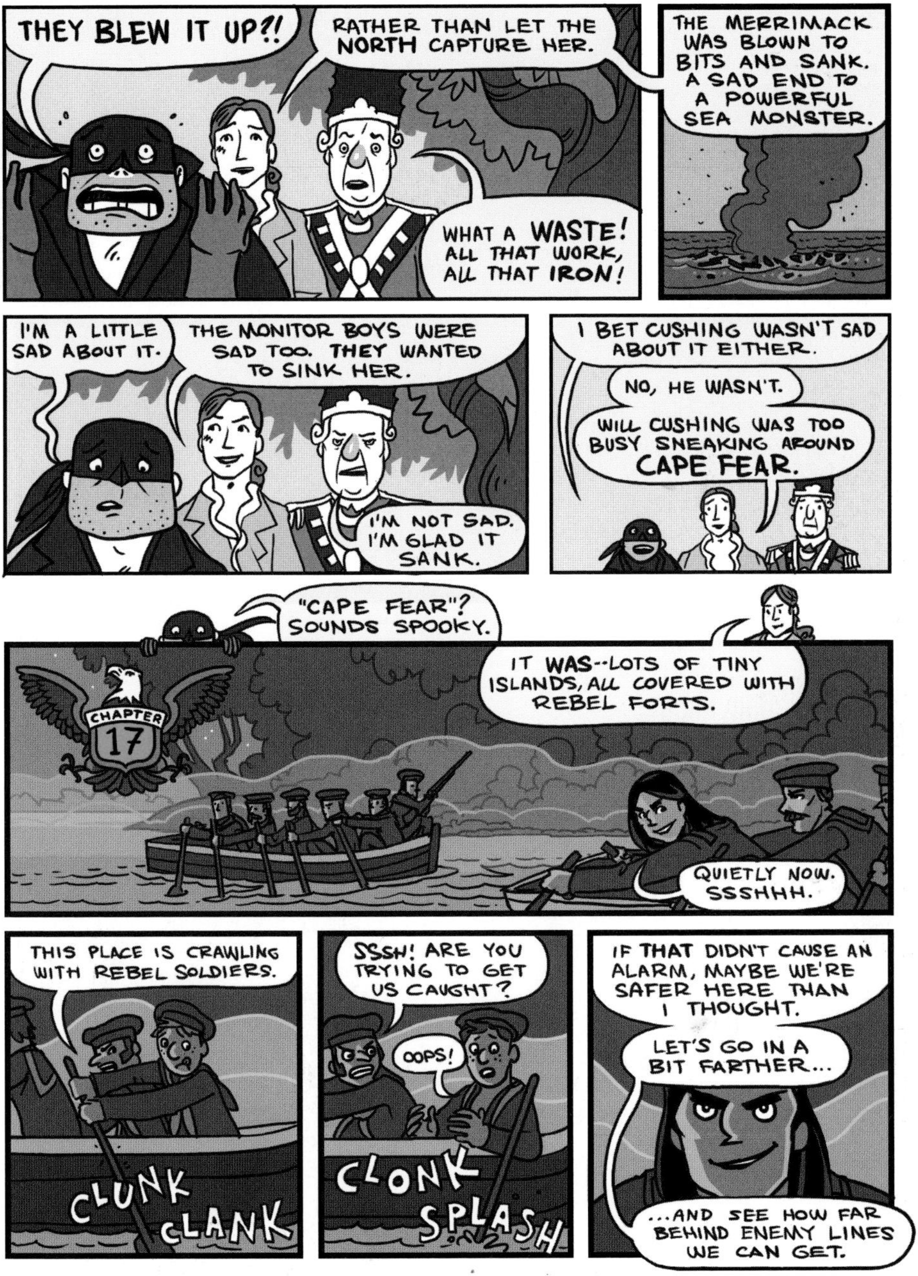
THEY BLEW IT UP?!
RATHER THAN LET THE NORTH CAPTURE HER.
WHAT A WASTE! ALL THAT WORK, ALL THAT IRON!
THE MERRIMACK WAS BLOWN TO BITS AND SANK. A SAD END TO A POWERFUL SEA MONSTER.
I'M A LITTLE SAD ABOUT IT.
THE MONITOR BOYS WERE SAD TOO. THEY WANTED TO SINK HER.
I'M NOT SAD. I'M GLAD IT SANK.
I BET CUSHING WASN'T SAD ABOUT IT EITHER.
NO, HE WASN'T.
WILL CUSHING WAS TOO BUSY SNEAKING AROUND CAPE FEAR.
"CAPE FEAR"? SOUNDS SPOOKY.
IT WAS--LOTS OF TINY ISLANDS, ALL COVERED WITH REBEL FORTS.
CHAPTER 17
QUIETLY NOW. SSSHHH.
THIS PLACE IS CRAWLING WITH REBEL SOLDIERS.
CLUNK
CLANK
SSSH! ARE YOU TRYING TO GET US CAUGHT?
OOPS!
CLONK
SPLASH
IF THAT DIDN'T CAUSE AN ALARM, MAYBE WE'RE SAFER HERE THAN I THOUGHT.
LET'S GO IN A BIT FARTHER...
...AND SEE HOW FAR BEHIND ENEMY LINES WE CAN GET.

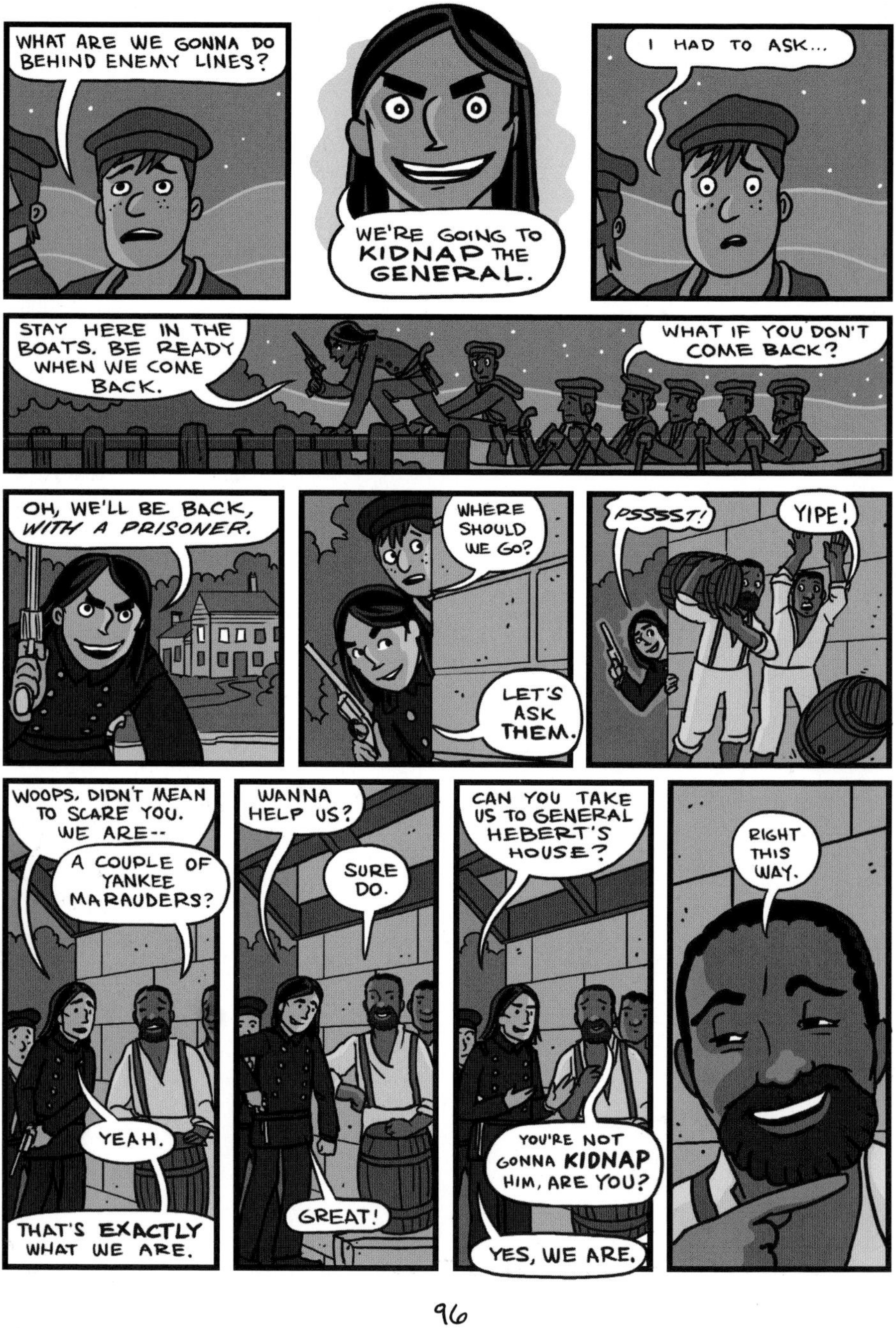
WHAT ARE WE GONNA DO BEHIND ENEMY LINES?
WE'RE GOING TO KIDNAP THE GENERAL.
I HAD TO ASK...
STAY HERE IN THE BOATS. BE READY WHEN WE COME BACK.
WHAT IF YOU DON'T COME BACK?
OH, WE'LL BE BACK, WITH A PRISONER.
WHERE SHOULD WE GO?
LET'S ASK THEM.
PSSSST!
YIPE!
WOOPS, DIDN'T MEAN TO SCARE YOU. WE ARE--
A COUPLE OF YANKEE MARAUDERS?
YEAH.
THAT'S EXACTLY WHAT WE ARE.
WANNA HELP US?
SURE DO.
GREAT!
CAN YOU TAKE US TO GENERAL HEBERT'S HOUSE?
YOU'RE NOT GONNA KIDNAP HIM, ARE YOU?
YES, WE ARE.
RIGHT THIS WAY.

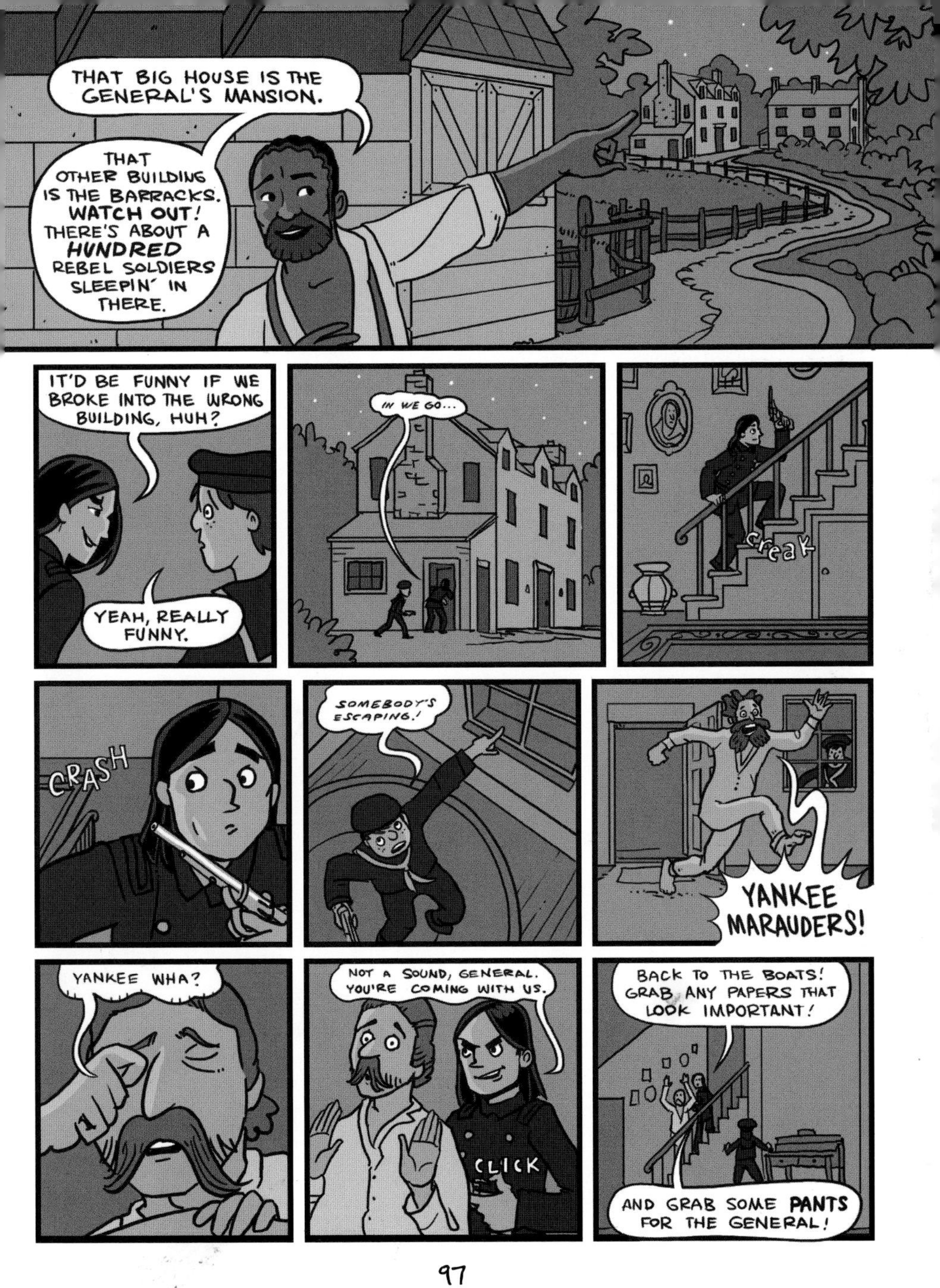
THAT BIG HOUSE IS THE GENERAL'S MANSION.
THAT OTHER BUILDING IS THE BARRACKS. WATCH OUT! THERE'S ABOUT A HUNDRED REBEL SOLDIERS SLEEPIN' IN THERE.
IT'D BE FUNNY IF WE BROKE INTO THE WRONG BUILDING, HUH?
YEAH, REALLY FUNNY.
IN WE GO...
CREAK
CRASH
SOMEBODY'S ESCAPING!
YANKEE MARAUDERS!
YANKEE WHA?
NOT A SOUND, GENERAL. YOU'RE COMING WITH US.
CLICK
BACK TO THE BOATS! GRAB ANY PAPERS THAT LOOK IMPORTANT!
AND GRAB SOME PANTS FOR THE GENERAL!

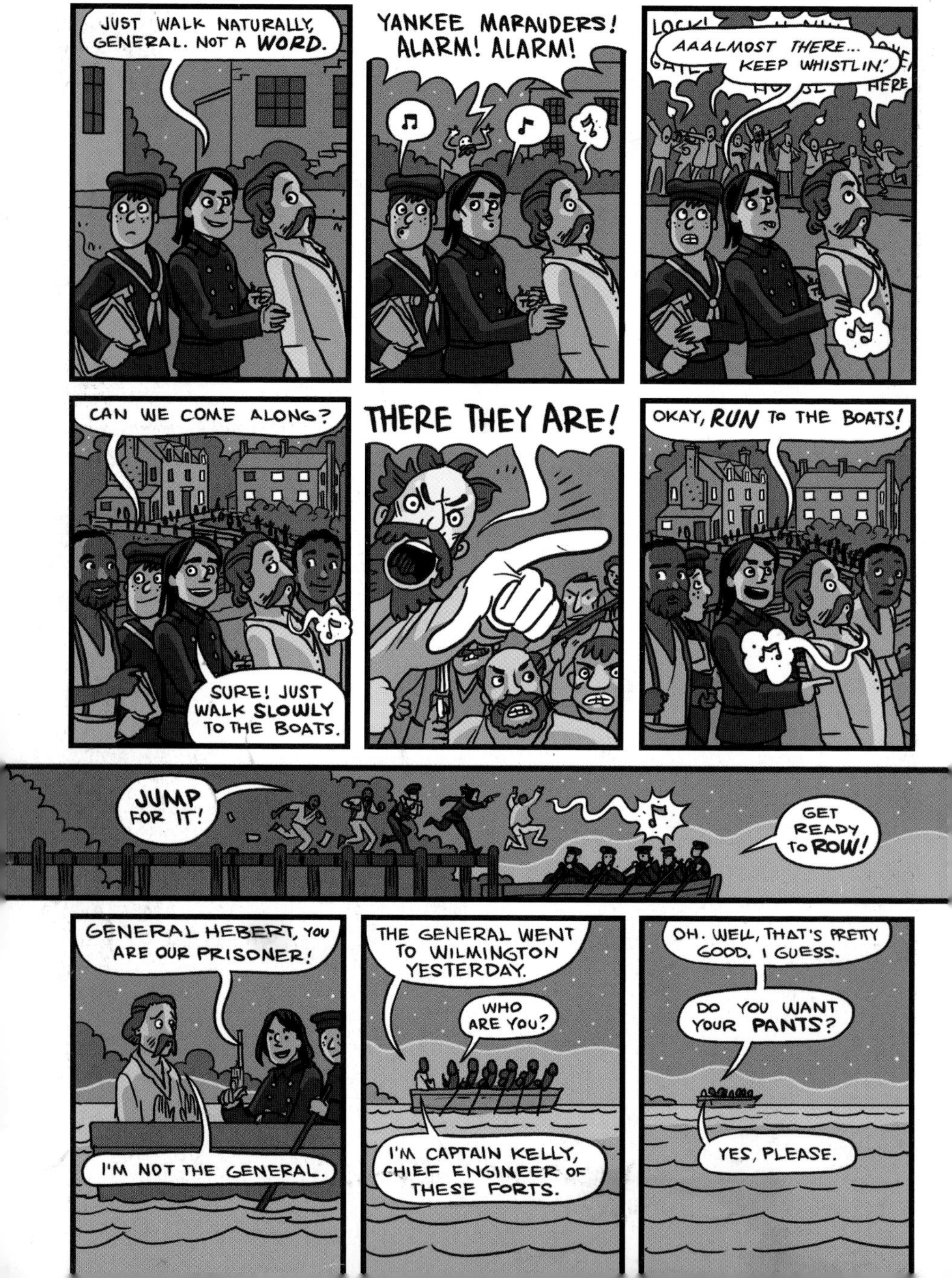

JUST WALK NATURALLY, GENERAL. NOT A WORD.
YANKEE MARAUDERS! ALARM! ALARM!
AAALMOST THERE... KEEP WHISTLIN.'
CAN WE COME ALONG?
SURE! JUST WALK SLOWLY TO THE BOATS.
THERE THEY ARE!
OKAY, RUN TO THE BOATS!
JUMP FOR IT!
GET READY TO ROW!
GENERAL HEBERT, YOU ARE OUR PRISONER!
I'M NOT THE GENERAL.
THE GENERAL WENT TO WILMINGTON YESTERDAY.
WHO ARE YOU?
I'M CAPTAIN KELLY, CHIEF ENGINEER OF THESE FORTS.
OH. WELL, THAT'S PRETTY GOOD, I GUESS.
DO YOU WANT YOUR PANTS?
YES, PLEASE.

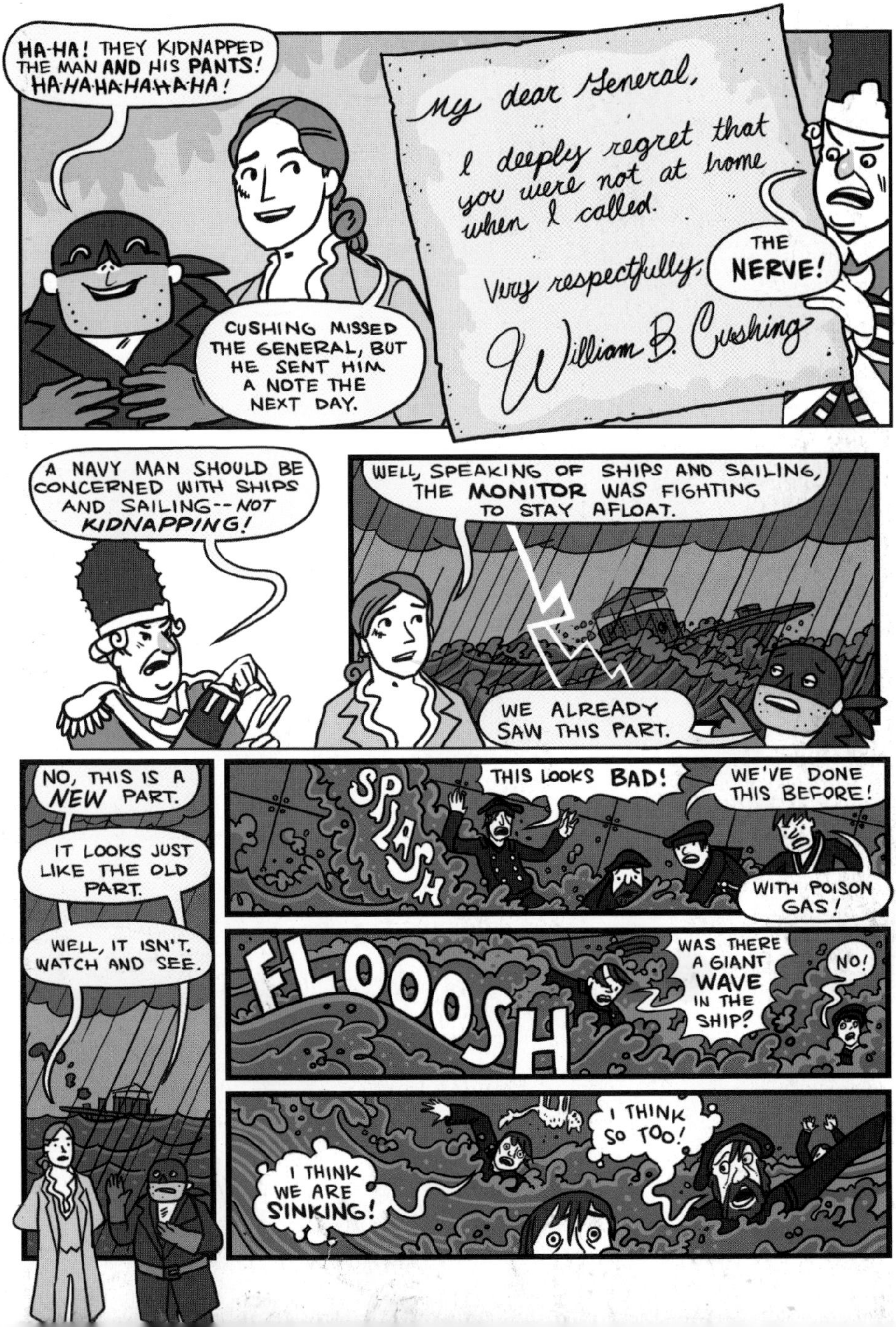
HA-HA! THEY KIDNAPPED THE MAN AND HIS PANTS! HA-HA-HA-HA-HA-HA!
My dear General,
I deeply regret that you were not at home when I called.
Very respectfully,
William B. Cushing
THE NERVE!
CUSHING MISSED THE GENERAL, BUT HE SENT HIM A NOTE THE NEXT DAY.
A NAVY MAN SHOULD BE CONCERNED WITH SHIPS AND SAILING--NOT KIDNAPPING!
WELL, SPEAKING OF SHIPS AND SAILING, THE MONITOR WAS FIGHTING TO STAY AFLOAT.
WE ALREADY SAW THIS PART.
NO, THIS IS A NEW PART.
IT LOOKS JUST LIKE THE OLD PART.
WELL, IT ISN'T. WATCH AND SEE.
SPLASH
THIS LOOKS BAD!
WE'VE DONE THIS BEFORE!
WITH POISON GAS!
FLOOOSH
WAS THERE A GIANT WAVE IN THE SHIP?
NO!
I THINK WE ARE SINKING!
I THINK SO TOO!

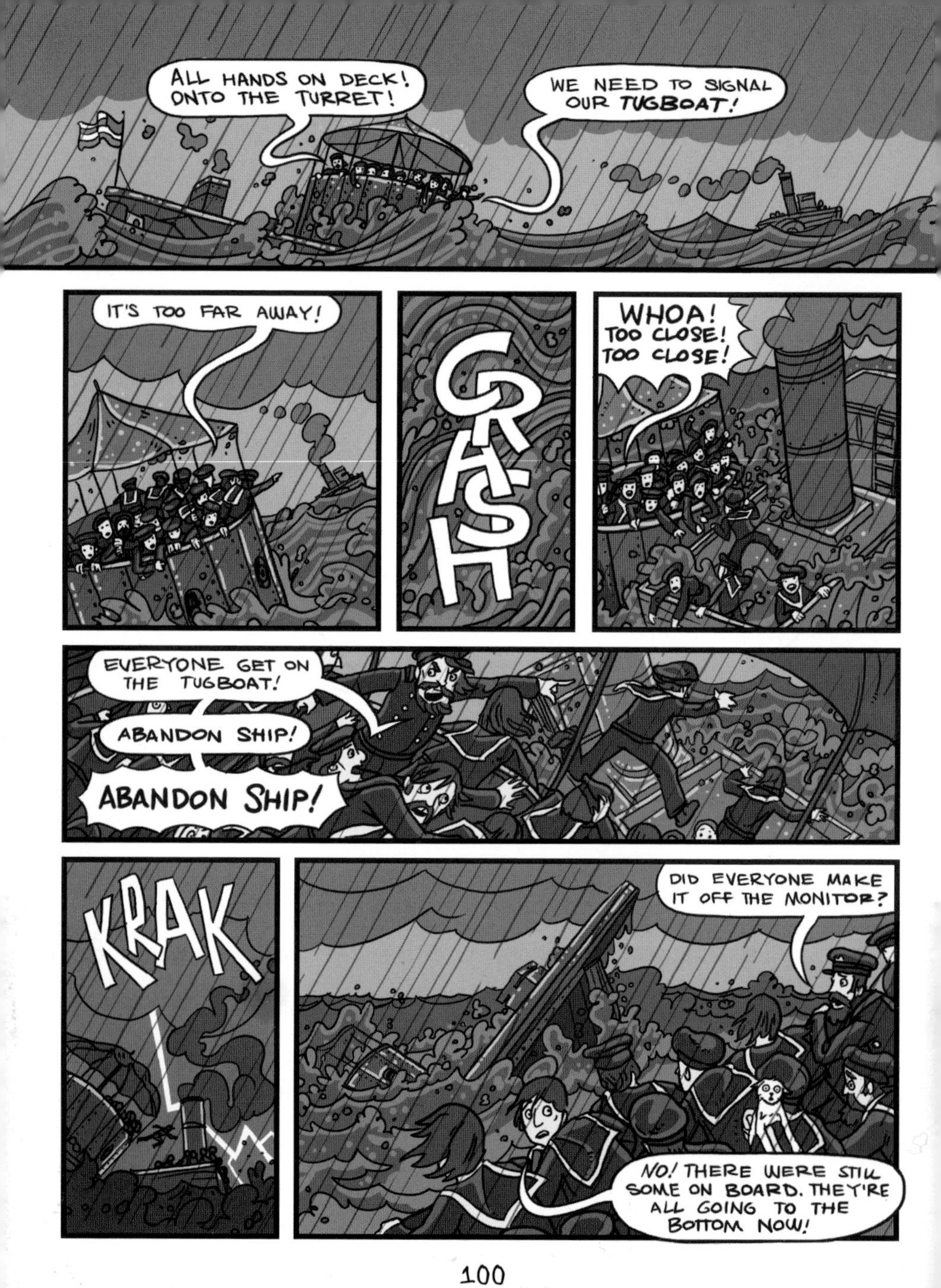
ALL HANDS ON DECK! ONTO THE TURRET!
WE NEED TO SIGNAL OUR TUGBOAT!
IT'S TOO FAR AWAY!
CRASH
WHOA! TOO CLOSE! TOO CLOSE!
EVERYONE GET ON THE TUGBOAT!
ABANDON SHIP!
ABANDON SHIP!
KRAK
DID EVERYONE MAKE IT OFF THE MONITOR?
NO! THERE WERE STILL SOME ON BOARD. THEY'RE ALL GOING TO THE BOTTOM NOW!

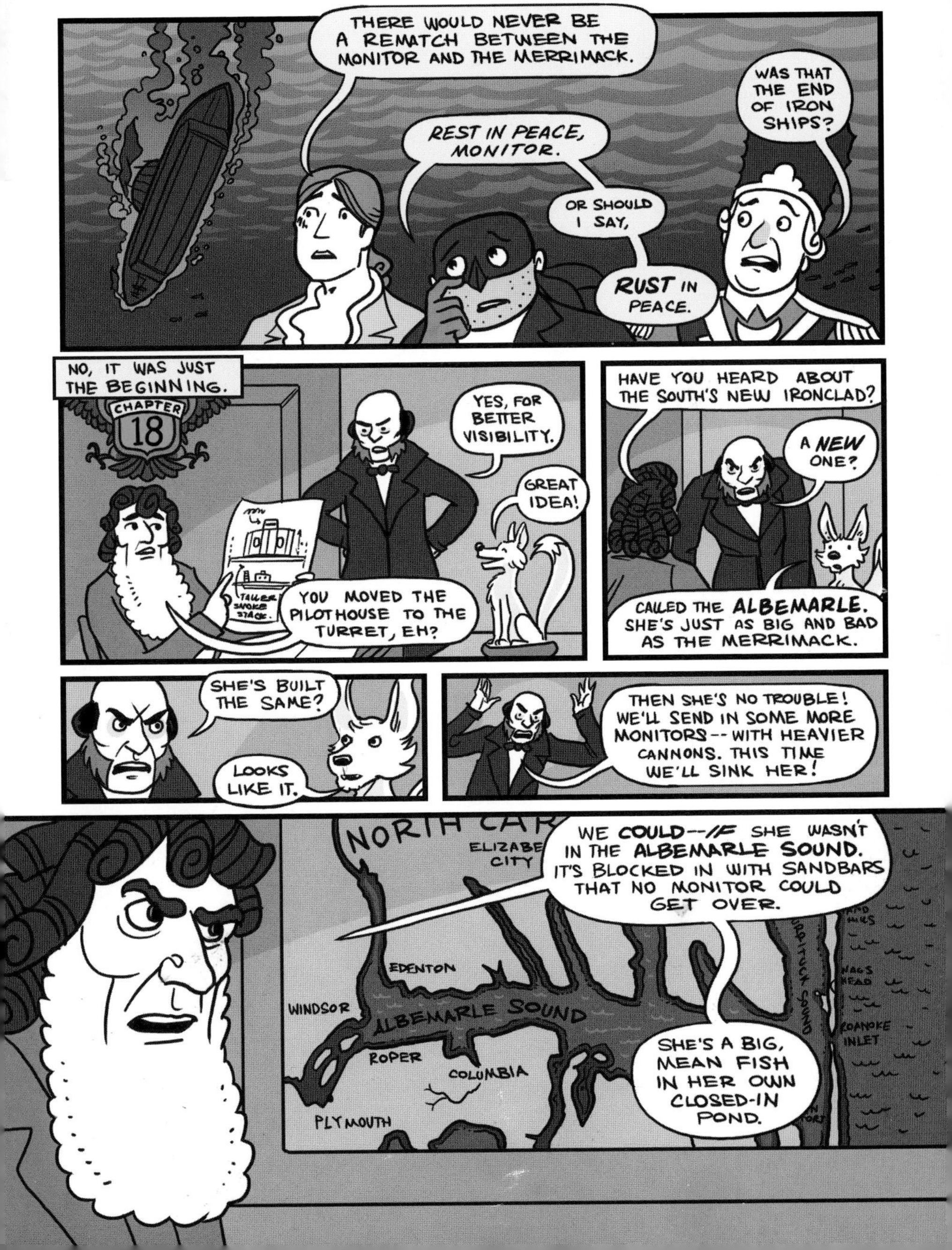

THERE WOULD NEVER BE A REMATCH BETWEEN THE MONITOR AND THE MERRIMACK.
REST IN PEACE, MONITOR.
OR SHOULD I SAY,
RUST IN PEACE.
WAS THAT THE END OF IRON SHIPS?
NO, IT WAS JUST THE BEGINNING.
CHAPTER 18
TALLER SMOKE STACK.
YOU MOVED THE PILOTHOUSE TO THE TURRET, EH?
YES, FOR BETTER VISIBILITY.
GREAT IDEA!
HAVE YOU HEARD ABOUT THE SOUTH'S NEW IRONCLAD?
A NEW ONE?
CALLED THE ALBEMARLE. SHE'S JUST AS BIG AND BAD AS THE MERRIMACK.
SHE'S BUILT THE SAME?
LOOKS LIKE IT.
THEN SHE'S NO TROUBLE! WE'LL SEND IN SOME MORE MONITORS--WITH HEAVIER CANNONS. THIS TIME WE'LL SINK HER!
NORTH CA
ELIZABE CITY
EDENTON
WINDSOR
ALBEMARLE SOUND
ROPER
COLUMBIA
PLYMOUTH
NAGS HEAD
ROANOKE INLET
WE COULD--IF SHE WASN'T IN THE ALBEMARLE SOUND. IT'S BLOCKED IN WITH SANDBARS THAT NO MONITOR COULD GET OVER.
SHE'S A BIG, MEAN FISH IN HER OWN CLOSED-IN POND.

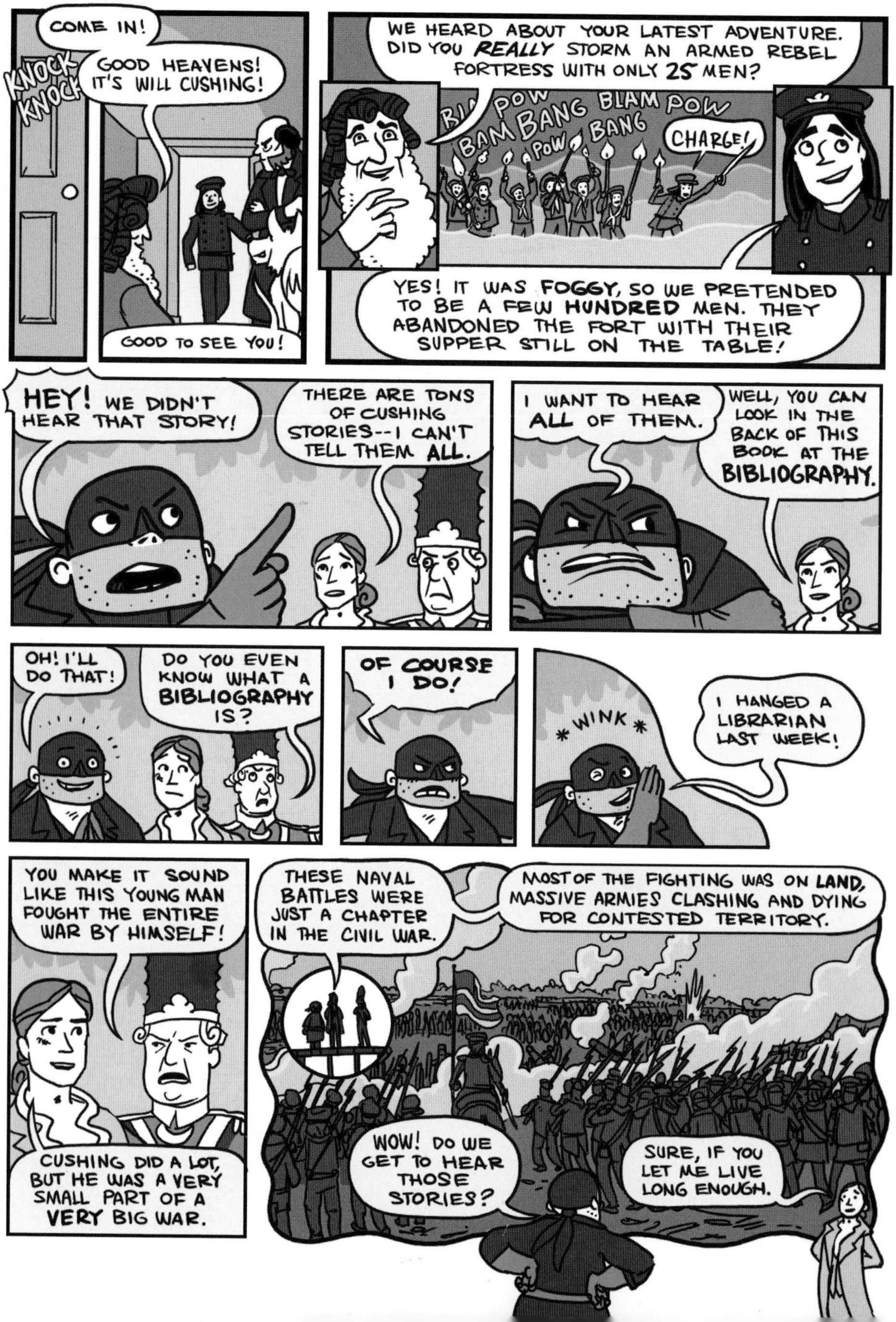
KNOCK KNOCK
COME IN!
GOOD HEAVENS! IT'S WILL CUSHING!
GOOD TO SEE YOU!
WE HEARD ABOUT YOUR LATEST ADVENTURE. DID YOU REALLY STORM AN ARMED REBEL FORTRESS WITH ONLY 25 MEN?
POW BAM BANG BLAM POW POW BANG
CHARGE!
YES! IT WAS FOGGY, SO WE PRETENDED TO BE A FEW HUNDRED MEN. THEY ABANDONED THE FORT WITH THEIR SUPPER STILL ON THE TABLE!
HEY! WE DIDN'T HEAR THAT STORY!
THERE ARE TONS OF CUSHING STORIES--I CAN'T TELL THEM ALL.
I WANT TO HEAR ALL OF THEM.
WELL, YOU CAN LOOK IN THE BACK OF THIS BOOK AT THE BIBLIOGRAPHY.
OH! I'LL DO THAT!
DO YOU EVEN KNOW WHAT A BIBLIOGRAPHY IS?
OF COURSE I DO!
WINK
I HANGED A LIBRARIAN LAST WEEK!
YOU MAKE IT SOUND LIKE THIS YOUNG MAN FOUGHT THE ENTIRE WAR BY HIMSELF!
CUSHING DID A LOT, BUT HE WAS A VERY SMALL PART OF A VERY BIG WAR.
THESE NAVAL BATTLES WERE JUST A CHAPTER IN THE CIVIL WAR.
MOST OF THE FIGHTING WAS ON LAND, MASSIVE ARMIES CLASHING AND DYING FOR CONTESTED TERRITORY.
WOW! DO WE GET TO HEAR THOSE STORIES?
SURE, IF YOU LET ME LIVE LONG ENOUGH.

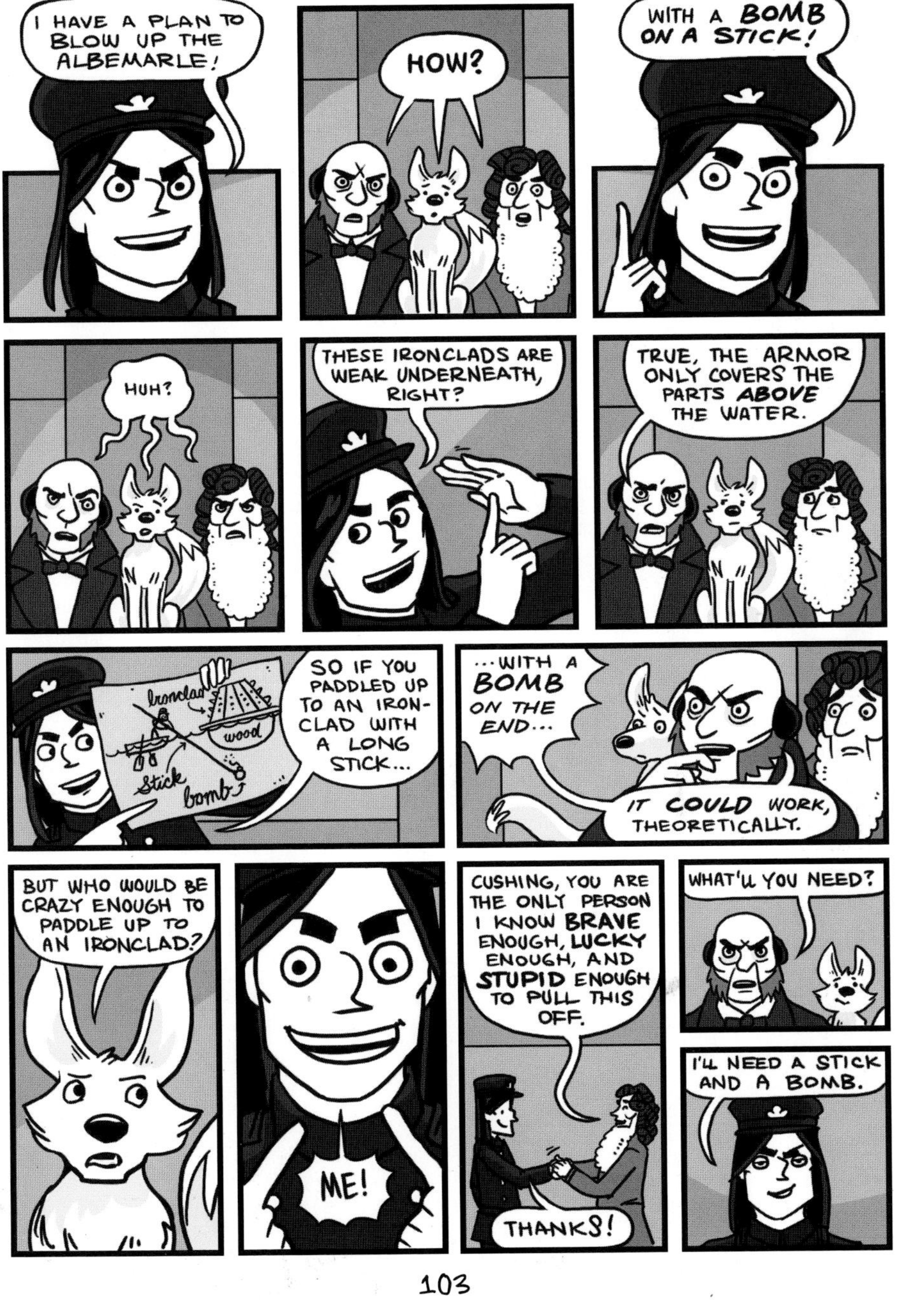
I HAVE A PLAN TO BLOW UP THE ALBEMARLE!
HOW?
WITH A BOMB ON A STICK!
HUH?
THESE IRONCLADS ARE WEAK UNDERNEATH, RIGHT?
TRUE, THE ARMOR ONLY COVERS THE PARTS ABOVE THE WATER.
ironclad
wood
stick
bomb
SO IF YOU PADDLED UP TO AN IRON-CLAD WITH A LONG STICK...
...WITH A BOMB ON THE END...
IT COULD WORK, THEORETICALLY.
BUT WHO WOULD BE CRAZY ENOUGH TO PADDLE UP TO AN IRONCLAD?
ME!
CUSHING, YOU ARE THE ONLY PERSON I KNOW BRAVE ENOUGH, LUCKY ENOUGH, AND STUPID ENOUGH TO PULL THIS OFF.
THANKS!
WHAT'LL YOU NEED?
I'LL NEED A STICK AND A BOMB.

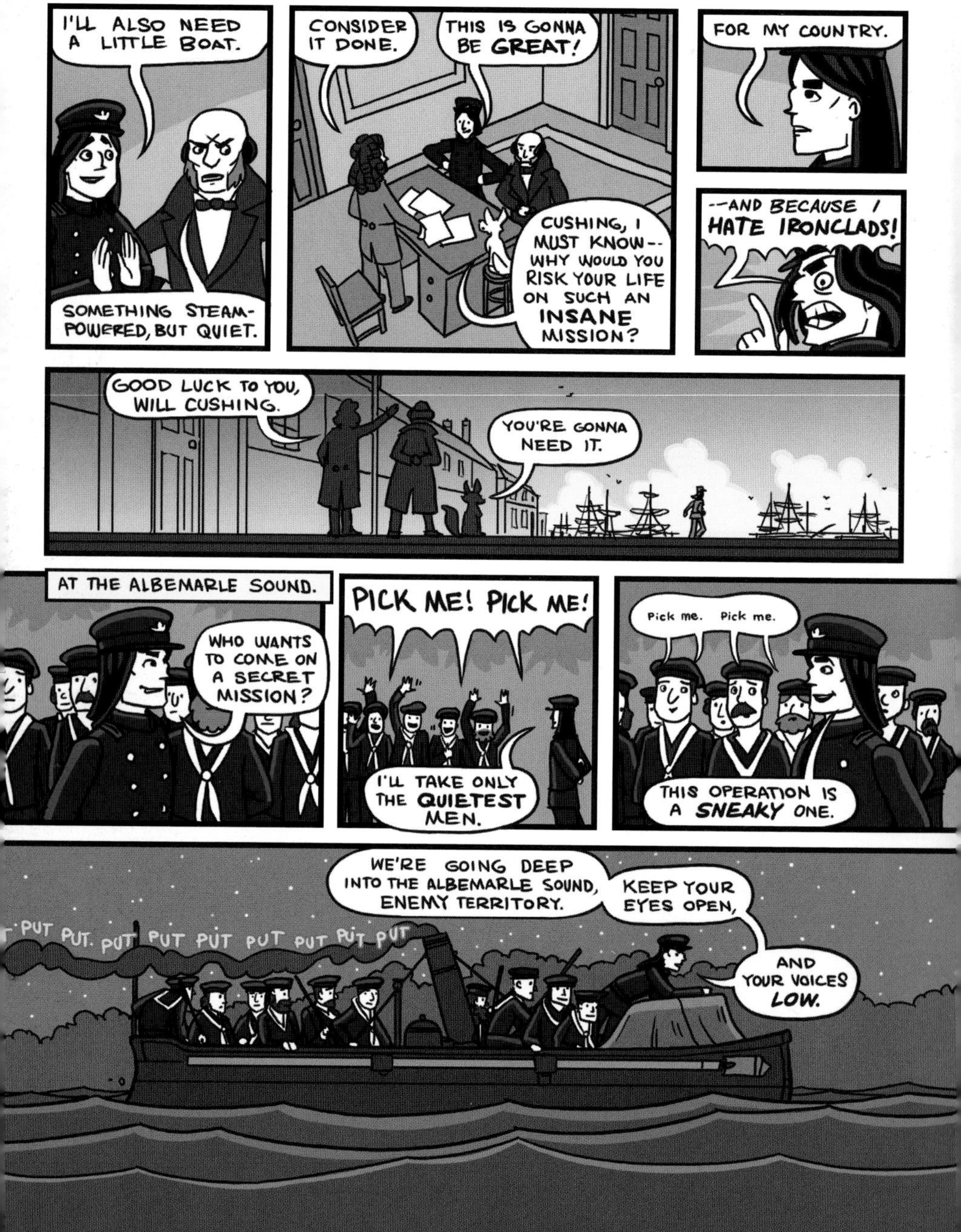
I'LL ALSO NEED A LITTLE BOAT.
SOMETHING STEAM-POWERED, BUT QUIET.
CONSIDER IT DONE.
THIS IS GONNA BE GREAT!
CUSHING, I MUST KNOW-- WHY WOULD YOU RISK YOUR LIFE ON SUCH AN INSANE MISSION?
FOR MY COUNTRY.
--AND BECAUSE I HATE IRONCLADS!
GOOD LUCK TO YOU, WILL CUSHING.
YOU'RE GONNA NEED IT.
AT THE ALBEMARLE SOUND.
WHO WANTS TO COME ON A SECRET MISSION?
PICK ME! PICK ME!
I'LL TAKE ONLY THE QUIETEST MEN.
Pick me. Pick me.
THIS OPERATION IS A SNEAKY ONE.
WE'RE GOING DEEP INTO THE ALBEMARLE SOUND, ENEMY TERRITORY.
KEEP YOUR EYES OPEN,
AND YOUR VOICES LOW.
PUT PUT. PUT PUT PUT PUT PUT PUT PUT

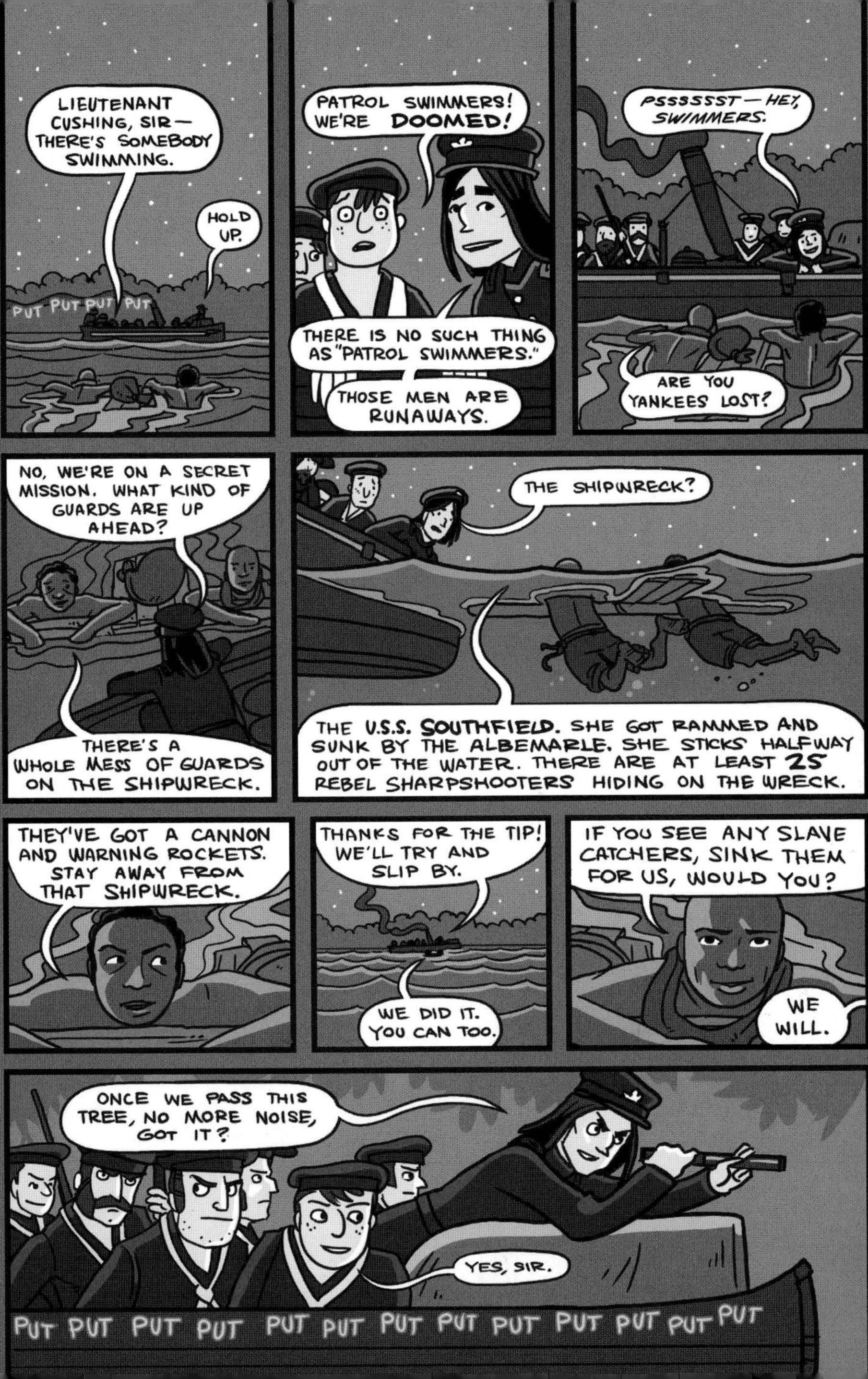
LIEUTENANT CUSHING, SIR— THERE'S SOMEBODY SWIMMING.
HOLD UP.
PUT PUT PUT PUT
PATROL SWIMMERS! WE'RE DOOMED!
THERE IS NO SUCH THING AS "PATROL SWIMMERS."
THOSE MEN ARE RUNAWAYS.
PSSSSSST—HEY, SWIMMERS.
ARE YOU YANKEES LOST?
NO, WE'RE ON A SECRET MISSION. WHAT KIND OF GUARDS ARE UP AHEAD?
THERE'S A WHOLE MESS OF GUARDS ON THE SHIPWRECK.
THE SHIPWRECK?
THE U.S.S. SOUTHFIELD. SHE GOT RAMMED AND SUNK BY THE ALBEMARLE. SHE STICKS HALFWAY OUT OF THE WATER. THERE ARE AT LEAST 25 REBEL SHARPSHOOTERS HIDING ON THE WRECK.
THEY'VE GOT A CANNON AND WARNING ROCKETS. STAY AWAY FROM THAT SHIPWRECK.
THANKS FOR THE TIP! WE'LL TRY AND SLIP BY.
WE DID IT. YOU CAN TOO.
IF YOU SEE ANY SLAVE CATCHERS, SINK THEM FOR US, WOULD YOU?
WE WILL.
ONCE WE PASS THIS TREE, NO MORE NOISE, GOT IT?
YES, SIR.
PUT PUT PUT PUT PUT PUT PUT PUT PUT PUT PUT PUT PUT

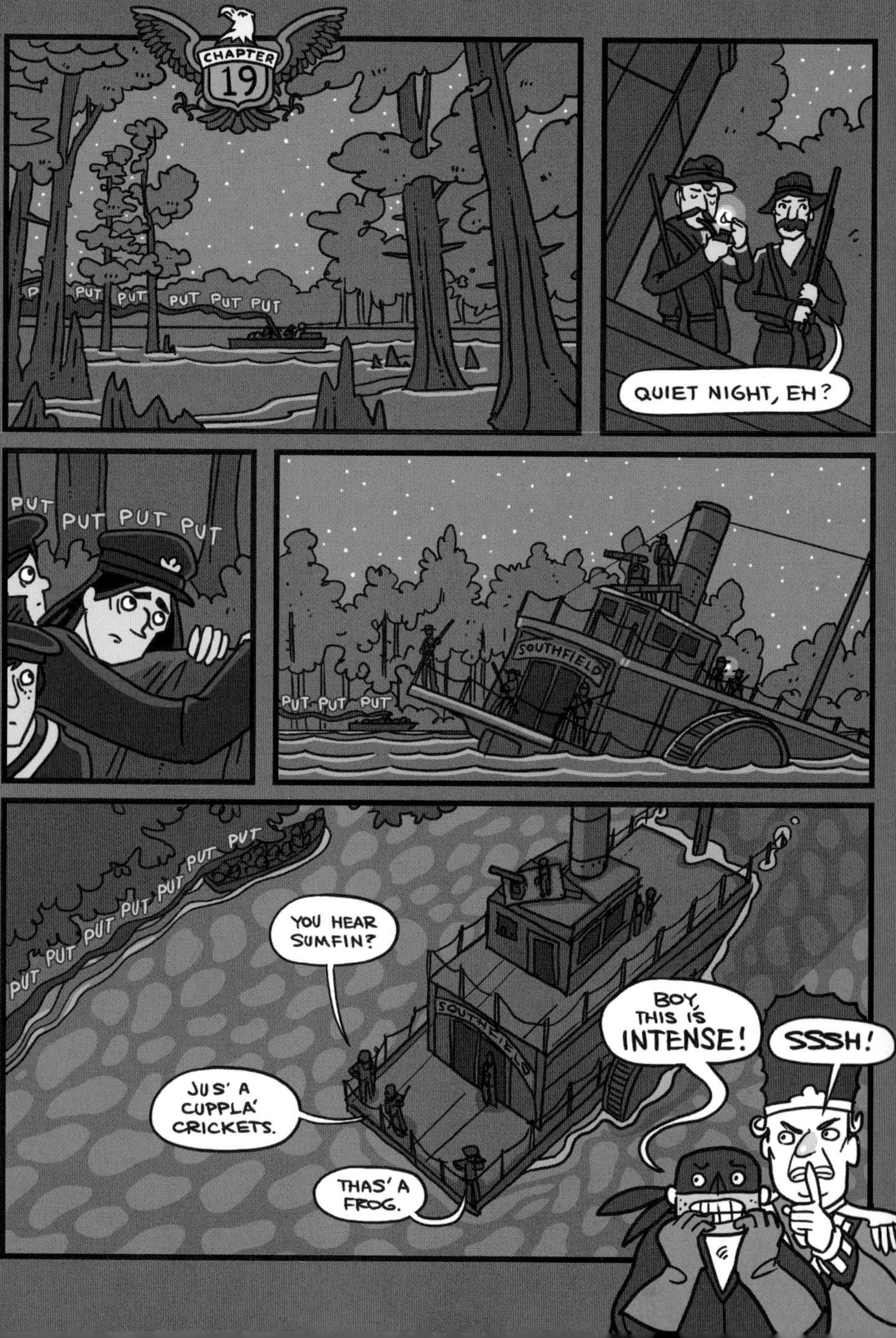
CHAPTER
19
P PUT PUT PUT PUT PUT
QUIET NIGHT, EH?
PUT PUT PUT PUT
PUT PUT PUT
PUT PUT PUT PUT PUT PUT PUT
SOUTHFIELD
YOU HEAR SUMFIN?
JUS' A CUPPLA' CRICKETS.
THAS' A FROG.
BOY, THIS IS INTENSE!
SSSH!

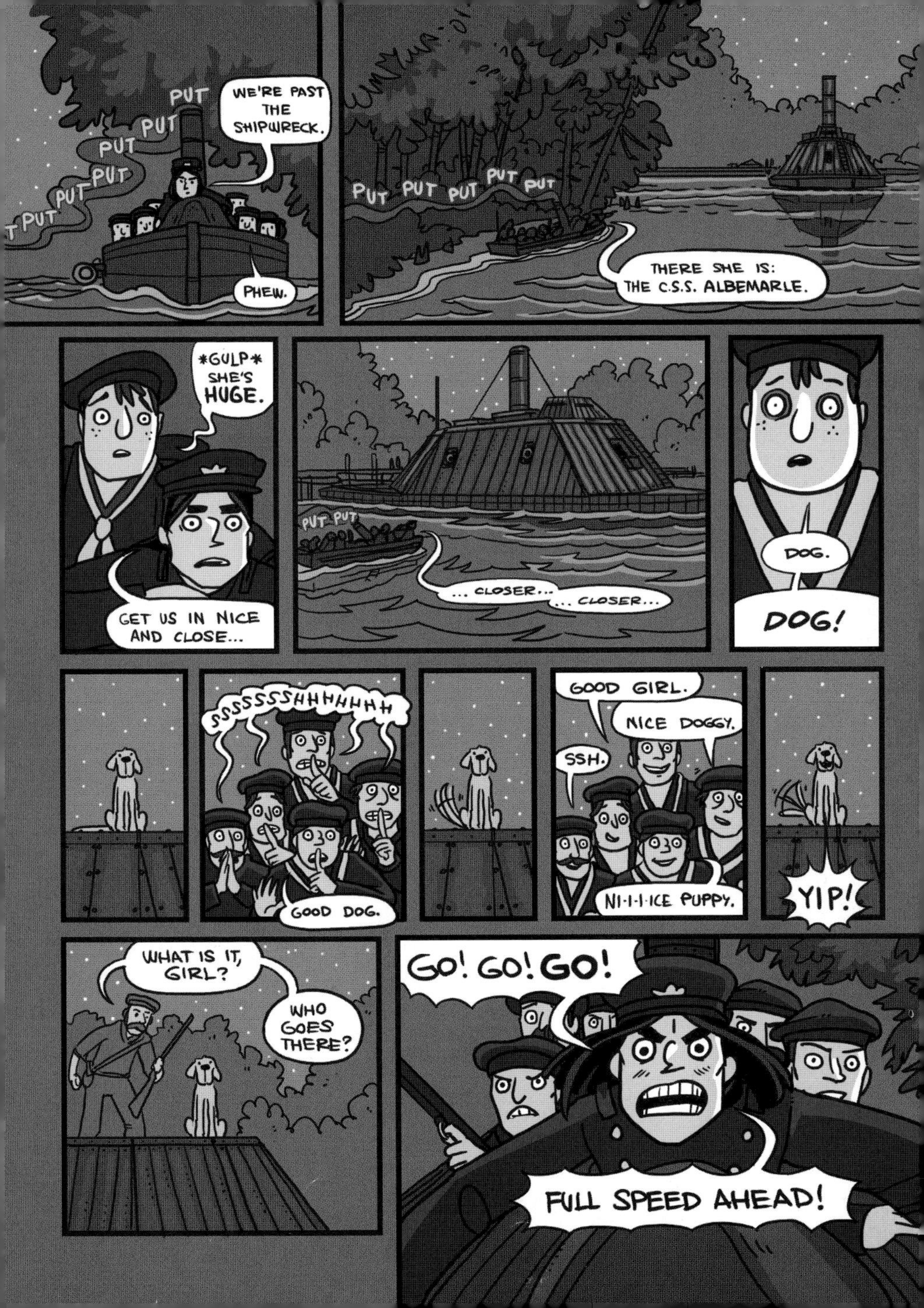
T PUT PUT PUT PUT PUT PUT
WE'RE PAST THE SHIPWRECK.
PHEW.
PUT PUT PUT PUT PUT
THERE SHE IS: THE C.S.S. ALBEMARLE.
GULP SHE'S HUGE.
GET US IN NICE AND CLOSE...
PUT PUT
... CLOSER...
... CLOSER...
DOG.
DOG!
SSSSSSSHHHHHHH
GOOD DOG.
GOOD GIRL.
NICE DOGGY.
SSH.
NI-I-I-ICE PUPPY.
YIP!
WHAT IS IT, GIRL?
WHO GOES THERE?
GO! GO! GO!
FULL SPEED AHEAD!

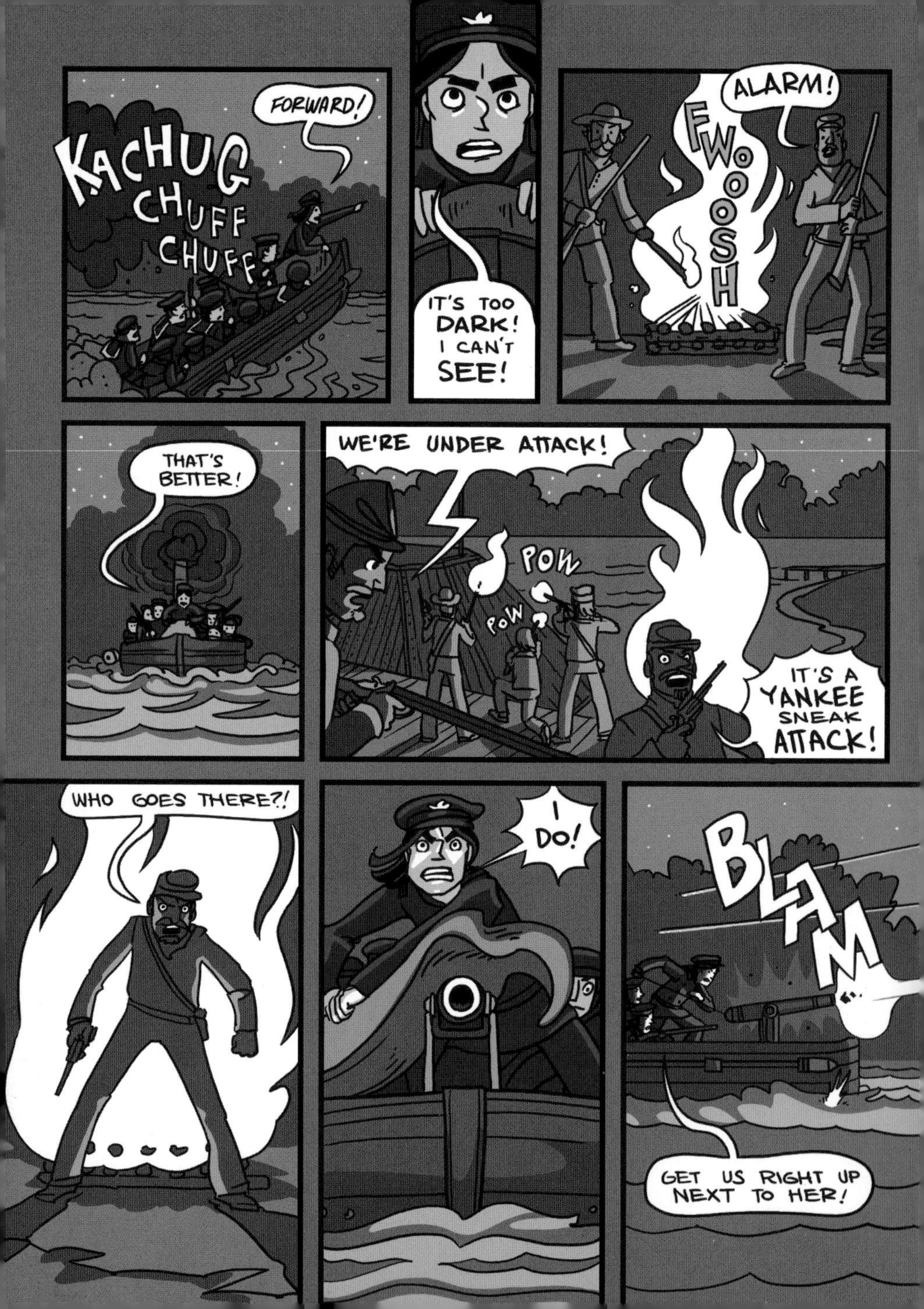
FORWARD!
KACHUG CHUFF CHUFF
IT'S TOO DARK! I CAN'T SEE!
ALARM!
FWOOOSH
THAT'S BETTER!
WE'RE UNDER ATTACK!
POW
POW
IT'S A YANKEE SNEAK ATTACK!
WHO GOES THERE?!
I DO!
BLAM
GET US RIGHT UP NEXT TO HER!

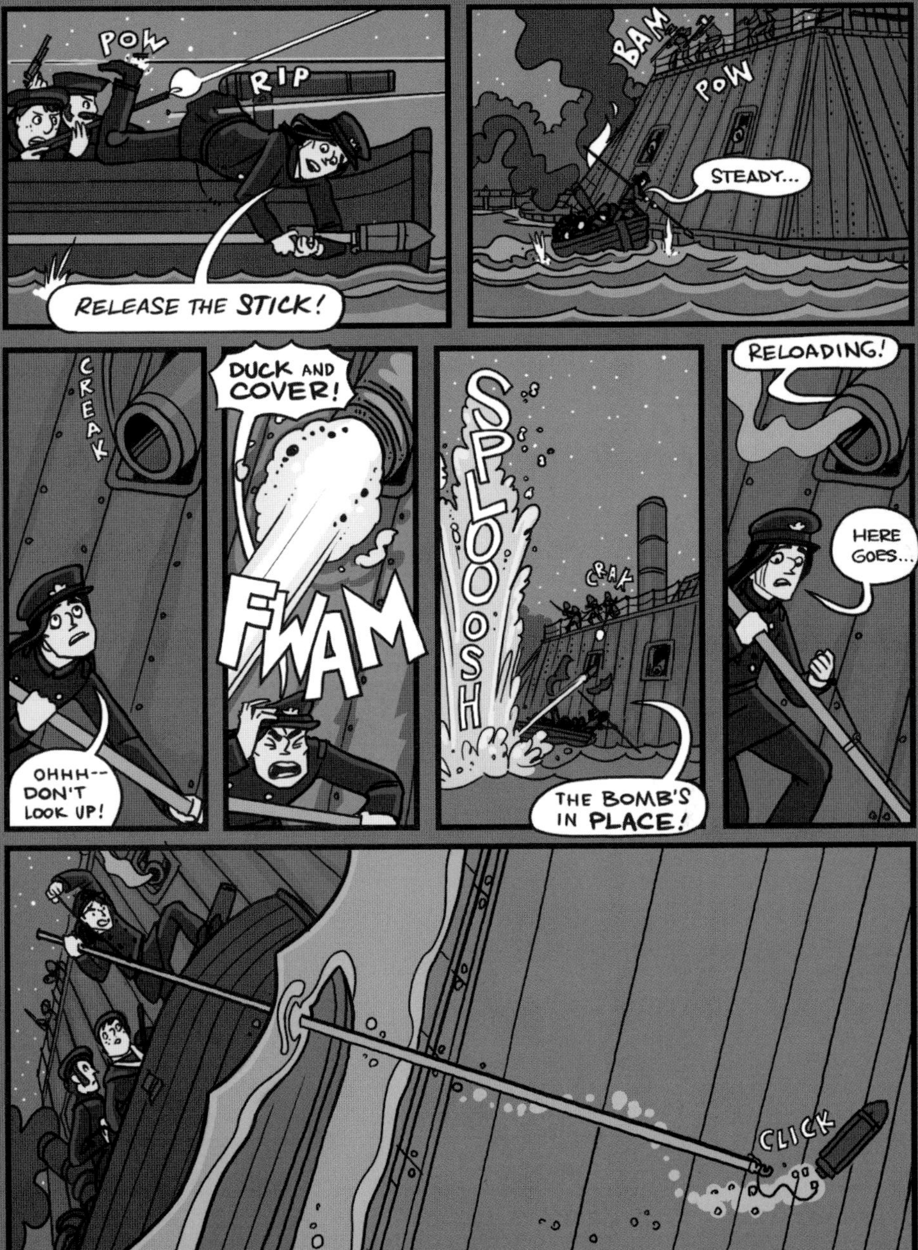

POW
RIP
RELEASE THE STICK!
BAM
POW
STEADY...
CREAK
OHHH-- DON'T LOOK UP!
DUCK AND COVER!
FWAM
SPLOOOOSH
CRAK
THE BOMB'S IN PLACE!
RELOADING!
HERE GOES...
CLICK

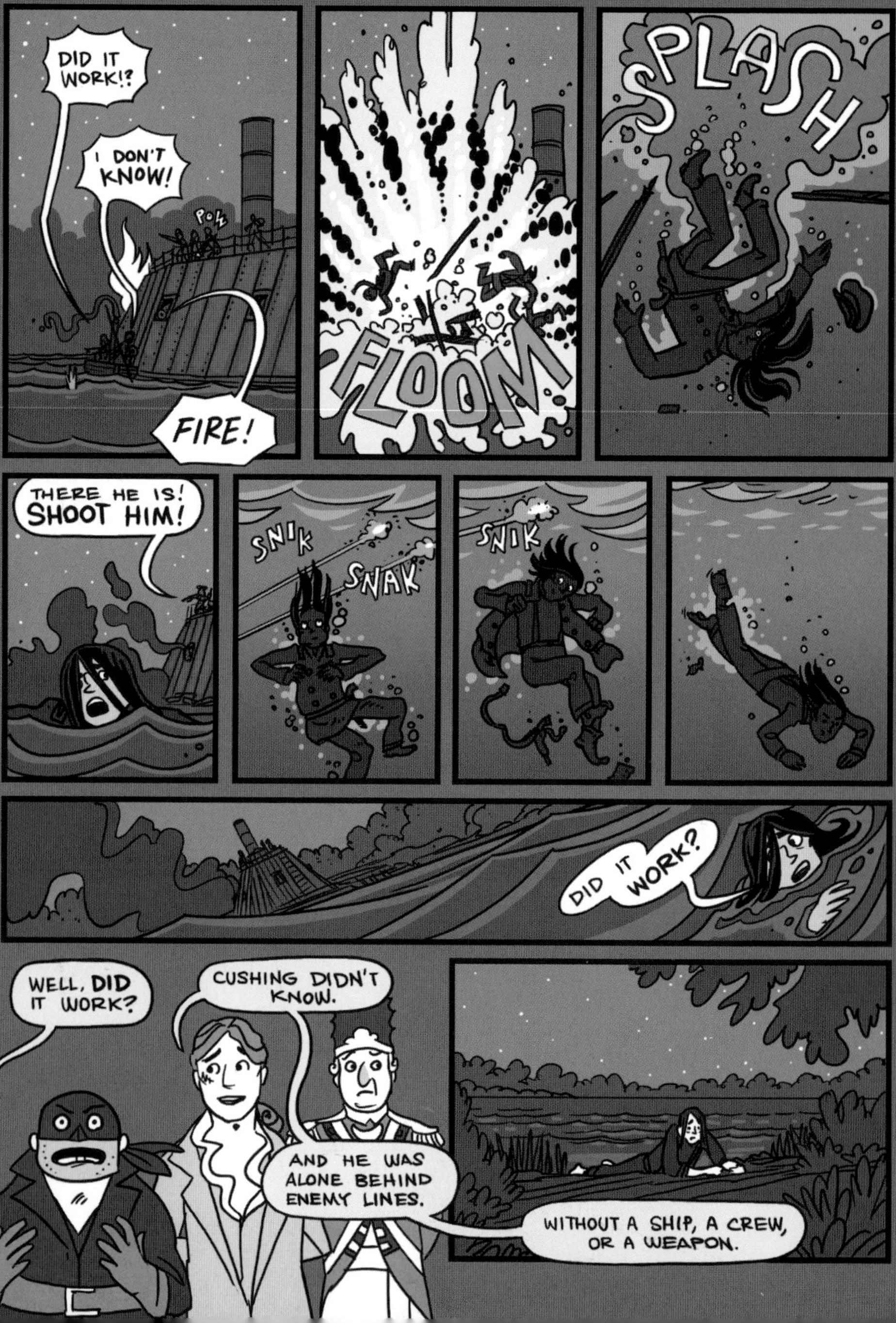
DID IT WORK!?
I DON'T KNOW!
FIRE!
FLOOM
SPLASH
THERE HE IS! SHOOT HIM!
SNIK
SNAK
SNIK
DID IT WORK?
WELL, DID IT WORK?
CUSHING DIDN'T KNOW.
AND HE WAS ALONE BEHIND ENEMY LINES.
WITHOUT A SHIP, A CREW, OR A WEAPON.

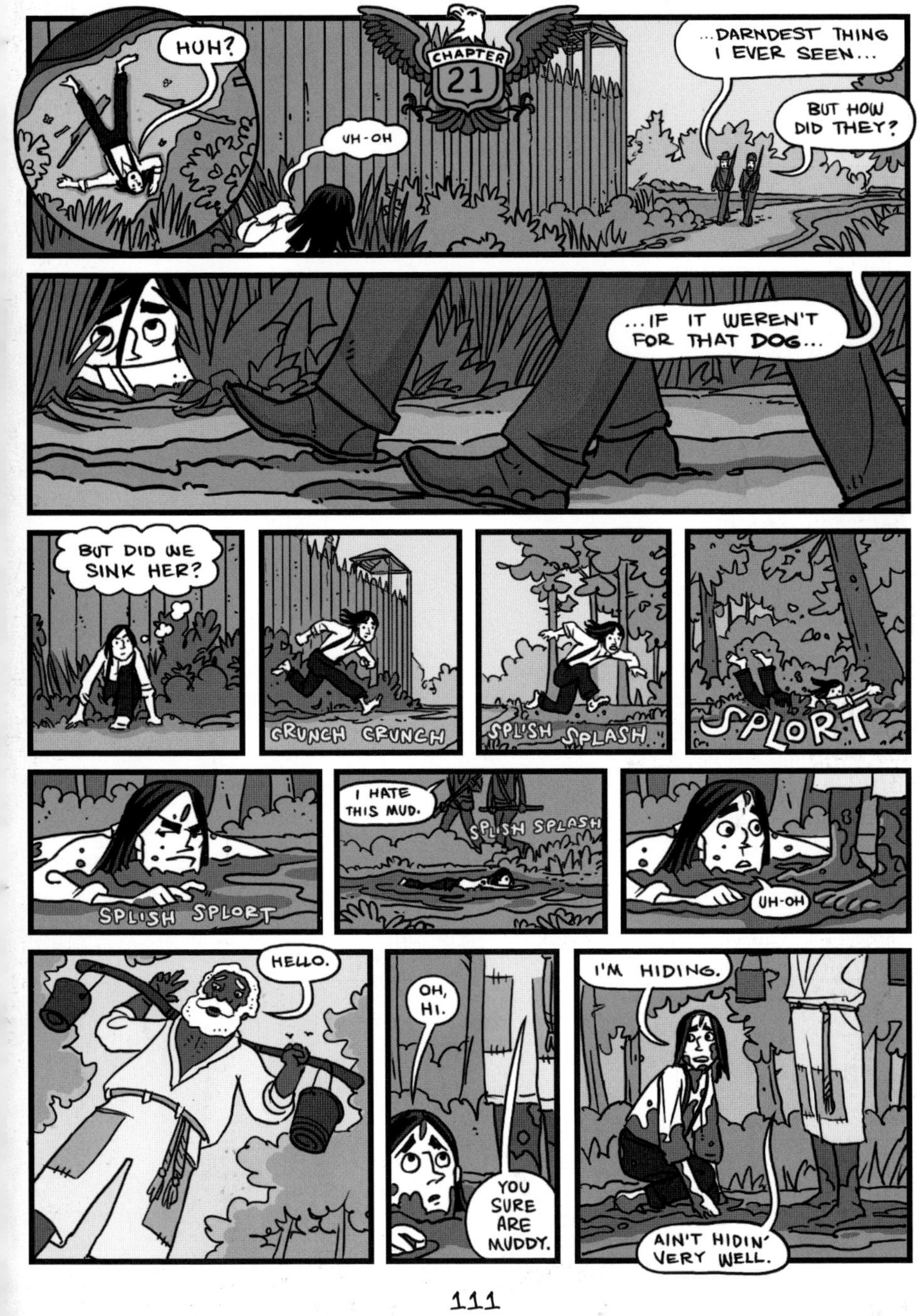
CHAPTER
21
HUH?
UH-OH
...DARNDEST THING I EVER SEEN...
BUT HOW DID THEY?
...IF IT WEREN'T FOR THAT DOG...
BUT DID WE SINK HER?
CRUNCH CRUNCH
SPLISH SPLASH
SPLORT
SPLISH SPLORT
I HATE THIS MUD.
SPLISH SPLASH
UH-OH
HELLO.
OH, HI.
YOU SURE ARE MUDDY.
I'M HIDING.
AIN'T HIDIN' VERY WELL.

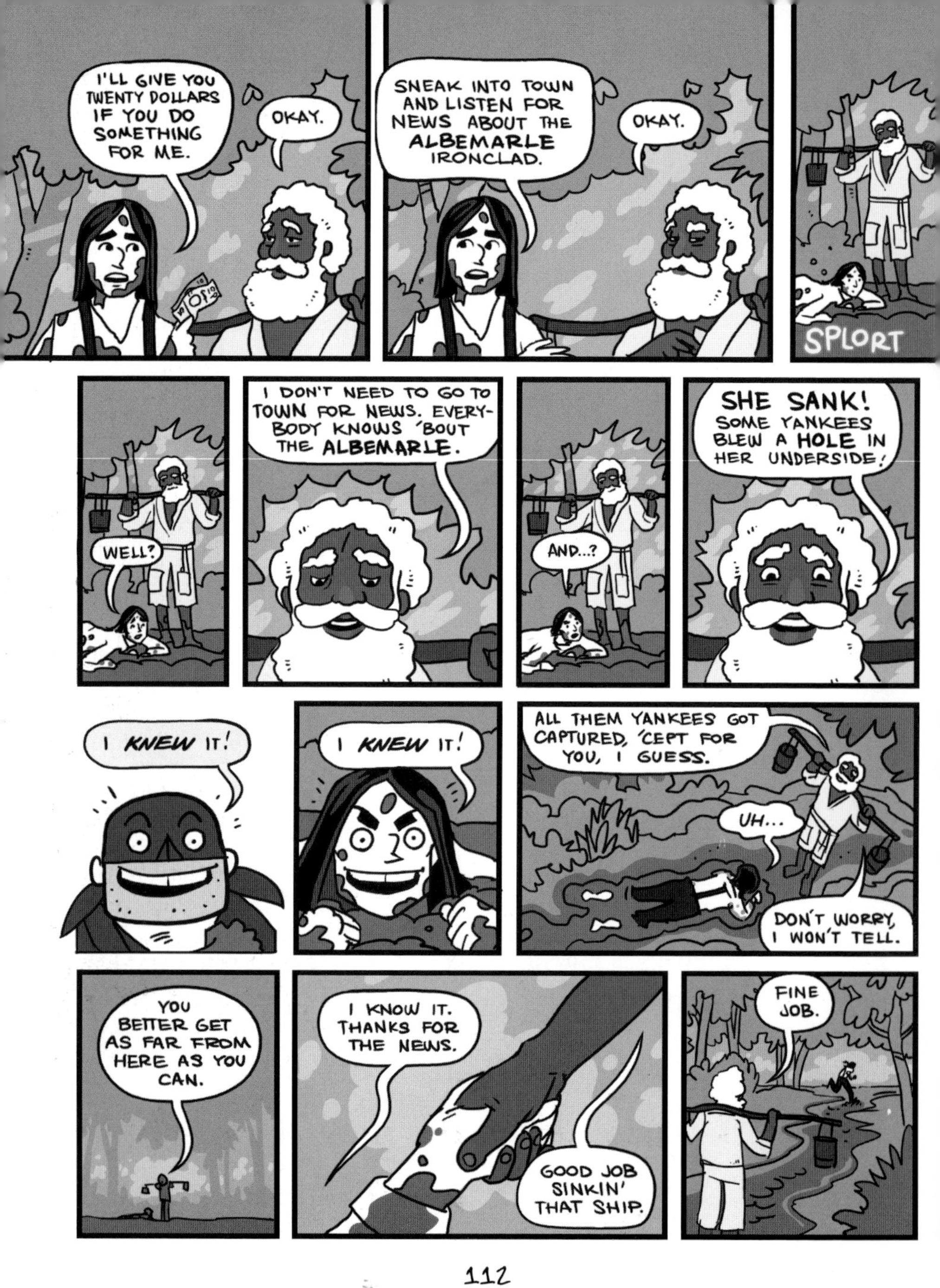
I'LL GIVE YOU TWENTY DOLLARS IF YOU DO SOMETHING FOR ME.
OKAY.
SNEAK INTO TOWN AND LISTEN FOR NEWS ABOUT THE ALBEMARLE IRONCLAD.
OKAY.
SPLORT
WELL?
I DON'T NEED TO GO TO TOWN FOR NEWS. EVERYBODY KNOWS 'BOUT THE ALBEMARLE.
AND...?
SHE SANK! SOME YANKEES BLEW A HOLE IN HER UNDERSIDE!
I KNEW IT!
I KNEW IT!
ALL THEM YANKEES GOT CAPTURED, 'CEPT FOR YOU, I GUESS.
UH...
DON'T WORRY, I WON'T TELL.
YOU BETTER GET AS FAR FROM HERE AS YOU CAN.
I KNOW IT. THANKS FOR THE NEWS.
GOOD JOB SINKIN' THAT SHIP.
FINE JOB.

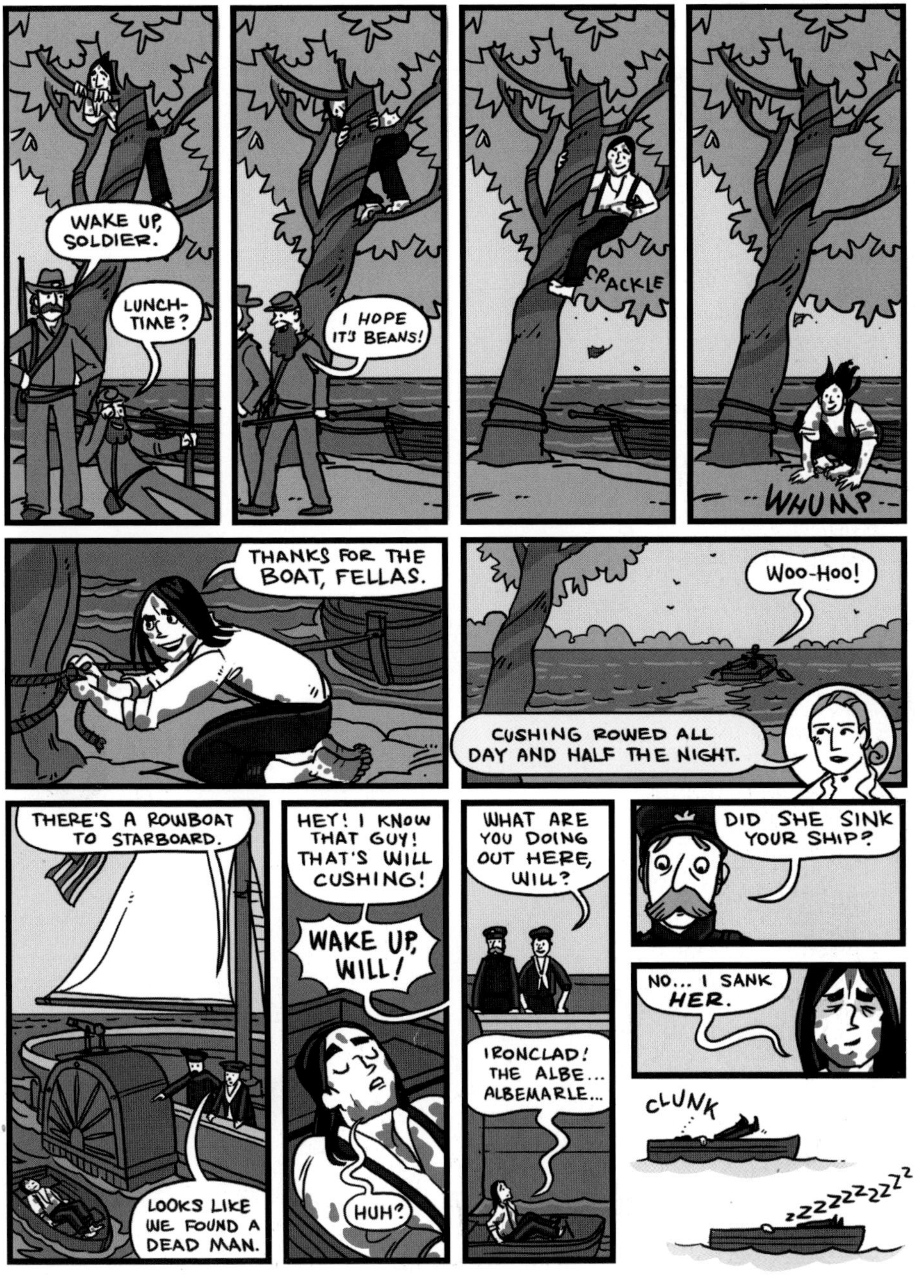

WAKE UP, SOLDIER.
LUNCH-TIME?
I HOPE IT'S BEANS!
CRACKLE
WHUMP
THANKS FOR THE BOAT, FELLAS.
WOO-HOO!
CUSHING ROWED ALL DAY AND HALF THE NIGHT.
THERE'S A ROWBOAT TO STARBOARD.
LOOKS LIKE WE FOUND A DEAD MAN.
HEY! I KNOW THAT GUY! THAT'S WILL CUSHING!
WAKE UP, WILL!
HUH?
WHAT ARE YOU DOING OUT HERE, WILL?
IRONCLAD! THE ALBE... ALBEMARLE...
DID SHE SINK YOUR SHIP?
NO... I SANK HER.
CLUNK
ZZZZZZZZZZZ

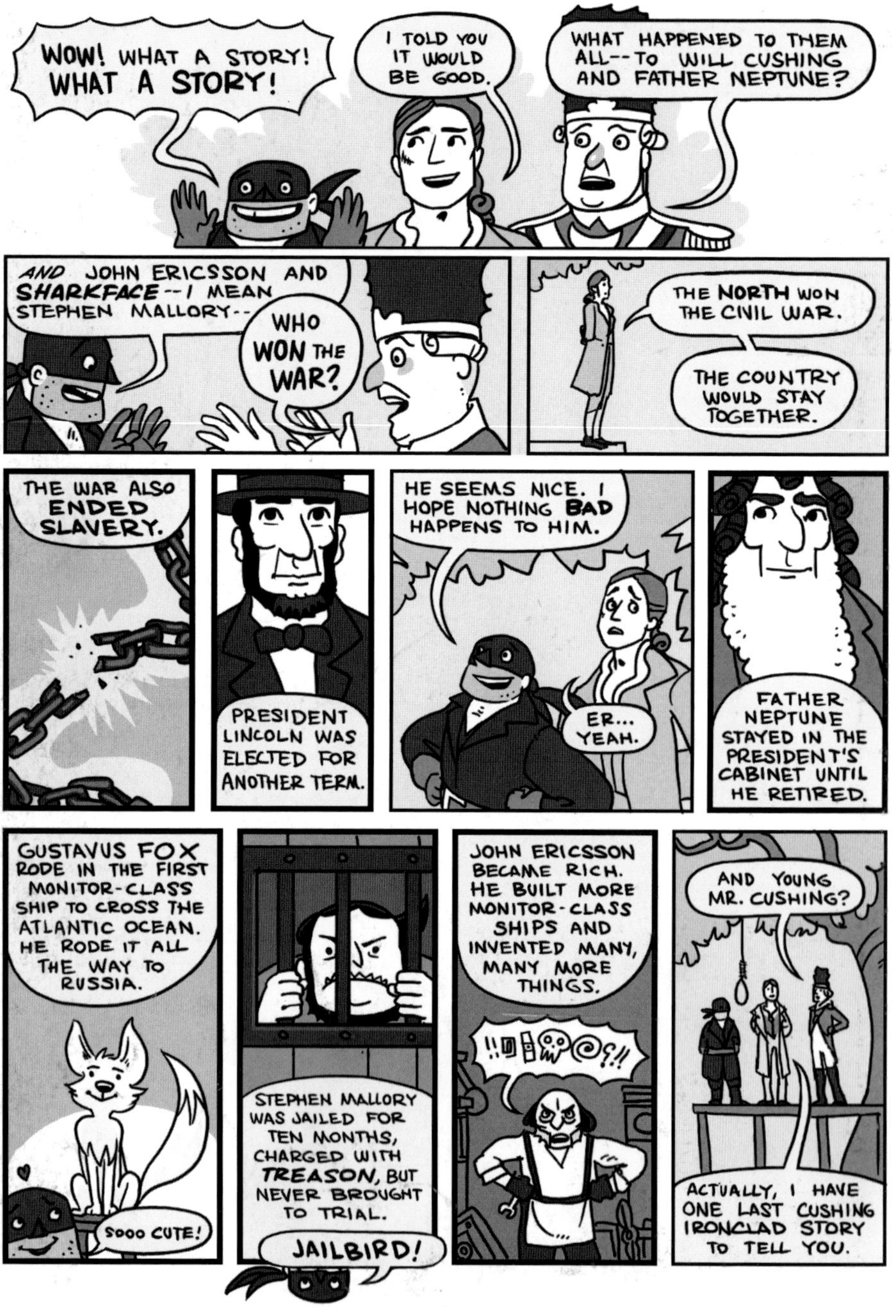
WOW! WHAT A STORY! WHAT A STORY!
I TOLD YOU IT WOULD BE GOOD.
WHAT HAPPENED TO THEM ALL--TO WILL CUSHING AND FATHER NEPTUNE?
AND JOHN ERICSSON AND SHARKFACE--I MEAN STEPHEN MALLORY--
WHO WON THE WAR?
THE NORTH WON THE CIVIL WAR.
THE COUNTRY WOULD STAY TOGETHER.
THE WAR ALSO ENDED SLAVERY.
PRESIDENT LINCOLN WAS ELECTED FOR ANOTHER TERM.
HE SEEMS NICE. I HOPE NOTHING BAD HAPPENS TO HIM.
ER... YEAH.
FATHER NEPTUNE STAYED IN THE PRESIDENT'S CABINET UNTIL HE RETIRED.
GUSTAVUS FOX RODE IN THE FIRST MONITOR-CLASS SHIP TO CROSS THE ATLANTIC OCEAN. HE RODE IT ALL THE WAY TO RUSSIA.
SOOO CUTE!
STEPHEN MALLORY WAS JAILED FOR TEN MONTHS, CHARGED WITH TREASON, BUT NEVER BROUGHT TO TRIAL.
JAILBIRD!
JOHN ERICSSON BECAME RICH. HE BUILT MORE MONITOR-CLASS SHIPS AND INVENTED MANY, MANY MORE THINGS.
AND YOUNG MR. CUSHING?
ACTUALLY, I HAVE ONE LAST CUSHING IRONCLAD STORY TO TELL YOU.

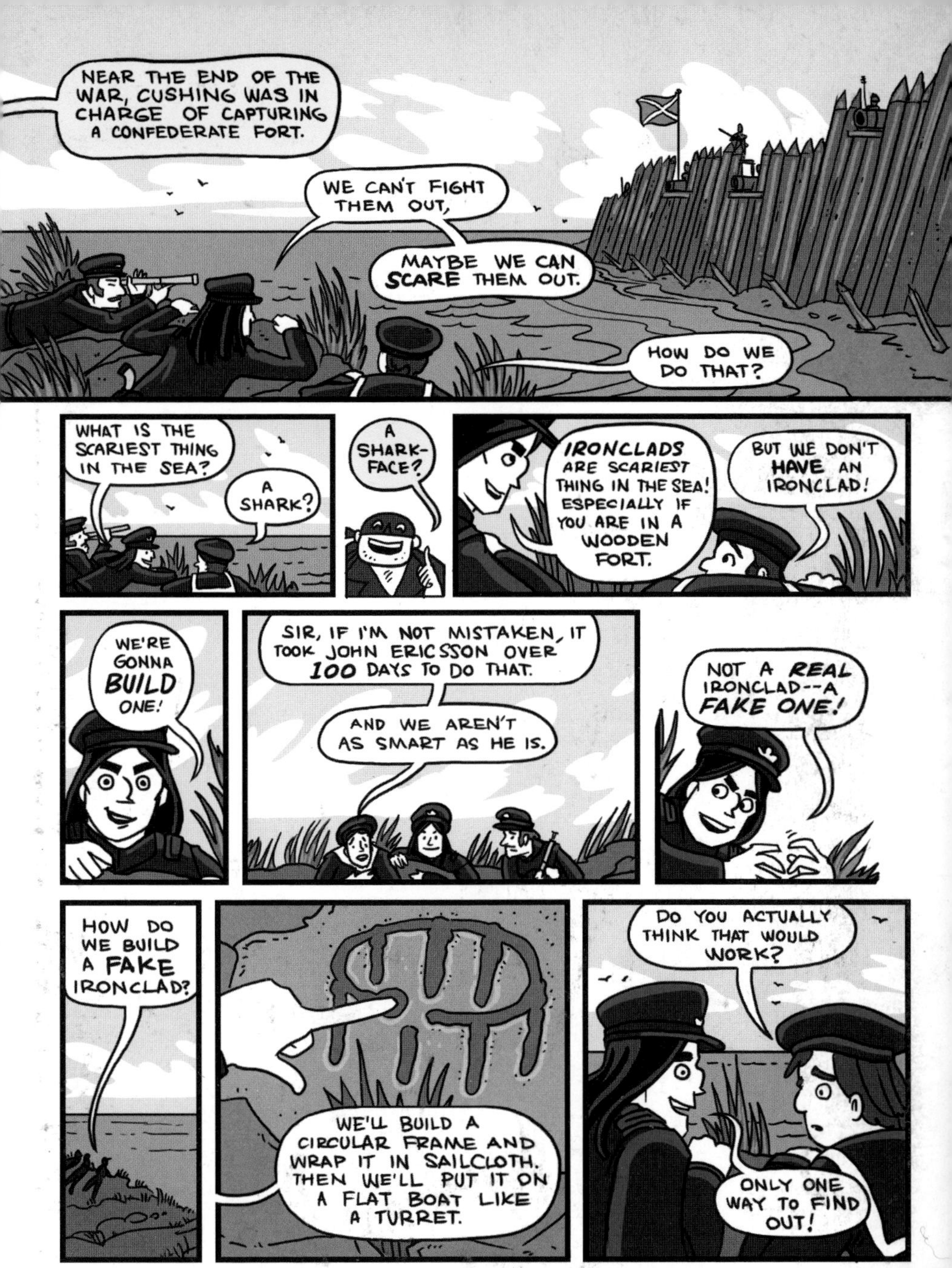
NEAR THE END OF THE WAR, CUSHING WAS IN CHARGE OF CAPTURING A CONFEDERATE FORT.
WE CAN'T FIGHT THEM OUT,
MAYBE WE CAN SCARE THEM OUT.
HOW DO WE DO THAT?
WHAT IS THE SCARIEST THING IN THE SEA?
A SHARK?
A SHARK-FACE?
IRONCLADS ARE SCARIEST THING IN THE SEA! ESPECIALLY IF YOU ARE IN A WOODEN FORT.
BUT WE DON'T HAVE AN IRONCLAD!
WE'RE GONNA BUILD ONE!
SIR, IF I'M NOT MISTAKEN, IT TOOK JOHN ERICSSON OVER 100 DAYS TO DO THAT.
AND WE AREN'T AS SMART AS HE IS.
NOT A REAL IRONCLAD--A FAKE ONE!
HOW DO WE BUILD A FAKE IRONCLAD?
WE'LL BUILD A CIRCULAR FRAME AND WRAP IT IN SAILCLOTH. THEN WE'LL PUT IT ON A FLAT BOAT LIKE A TURRET.
DO YOU ACTUALLY THINK THAT WOULD WORK?
ONLY ONE WAY TO FIND OUT!

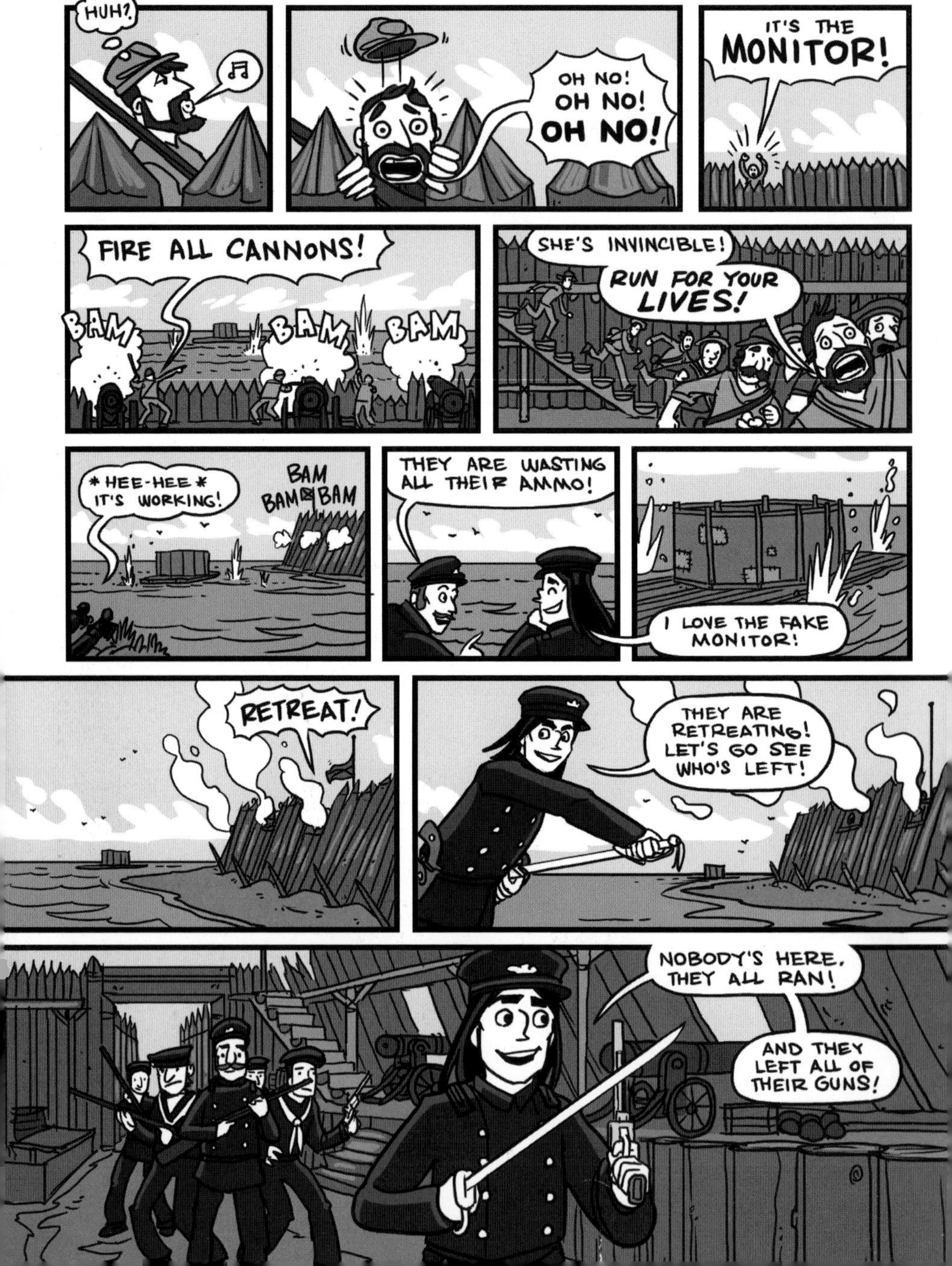
HUH?
OH NO!
OH NO!
OH NO!
IT'S THE MONITOR!
FIRE ALL CANNONS!
BAM
BAM
BAM
SHE'S INVINCIBLE!
RUN FOR YOUR LIVES!
HEE-HEE IT'S WORKING!
BAM
BAM BAM
THEY ARE WASTING ALL THEIR AMMO!
I LOVE THE FAKE MONITOR!
RETREAT!
THEY ARE RETREATING! LET'S GO SEE WHO'S LEFT!
NOBODY'S HERE, THEY ALL RAN!
AND THEY LEFT ALL OF THEIR GUNS!

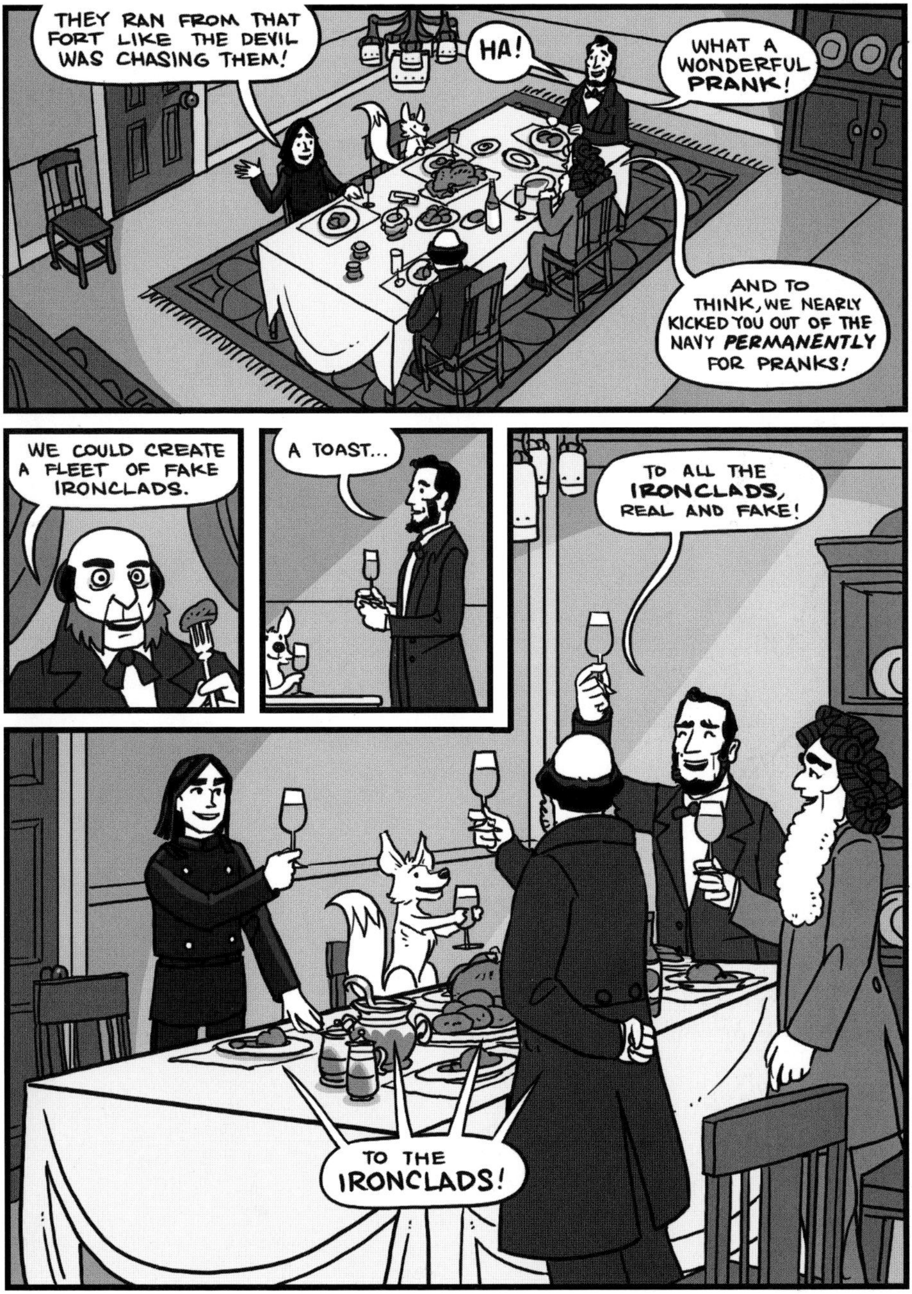
THEY RAN FROM THAT FORT LIKE THE DEVIL WAS CHASING THEM!
HA!
WHAT A WONDERFUL PRANK!
AND TO THINK, WE NEARLY KICKED YOU OUT OF THE NAVY PERMANENTLY FOR PRANKS!
WE COULD CREATE A FLEET OF FAKE IRONCLADS.
A TOAST...
TO ALL THE IRONCLADS, REAL AND FAKE!
TO THE IRONCLADS!

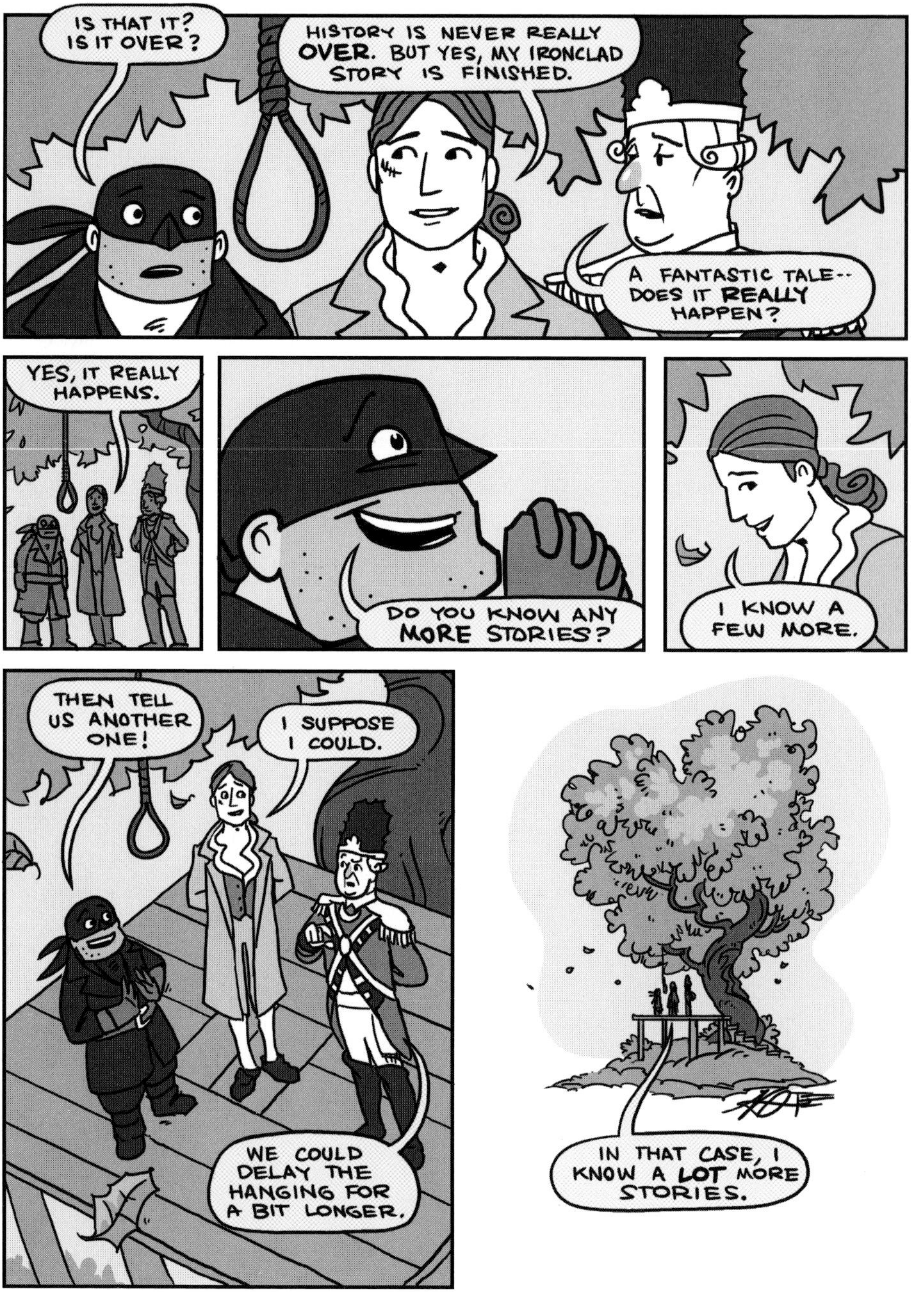
IS THAT IT? IS IT OVER?
HISTORY IS NEVER REALLY OVER. BUT YES, MY IRONCLAD STORY IS FINISHED.
A FANTASTIC TALE-- DOES IT REALLY HAPPEN?
YES, IT REALLY HAPPENS.
DO YOU KNOW ANY MORE STORIES?
I KNOW A FEW MORE.
THEN TELL US ANOTHER ONE!
I SUPPOSE I COULD.
WE COULD DELAY THE HANGING FOR A BIT LONGER.
IN THAT CASE, I KNOW A LOT MORE STORIES.

NATHAN HALE'S HAZARDOUS TALES

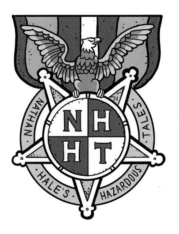

WILLIAM BARKER CUSHING (1842-1874)
WAS BORN IN A FRONTIER CABIN IN WISCONSIN. AT THE AGE OF FOUR, ON NEW YEAR'S DAY, HE WAS KICKED IN THE FACE BY AN UNBROKEN COLT. ALL OF HIS FRONT TEETH WERE KNOCKED OUT AND HE CRIED, **"NOW WILLIE CAN'T EAT TATO AND TURKEY!"**

IN 1847 DR. MILTON CUSHING, WILL'S FATHER, DIED OF PNEUMONIA. SO WILL'S FAMILY MOVED TO FREDONIA, NEW YORK. WILL WAS THE YOUNGEST; HE HAD FOUR BROTHERS AND A SISTER. WILL'S OLDER BROTHER ALONZO ALSO FOUGHT IN THE CIVIL WAR. HE DIED AT THE BATTLE OF GETTYSBURG DURING PICKETT'S CHARGE. ANOTHER BROTHER, HOWARD, DIED IN 1871 FIGHTING THE APACHES.

WILL'S NAVAL ADVENTURES MADE HIM FAMOUS. HE WAS A NATIONAL HERO. LINCOLN AWARDED HIM WITH THE "THANKS OF CONGRESS," WHICH, AT THAT TIME, HAD A HIGHER DISTINCTION THAN THE MEDAL OF HONOR.

WILL MARRIED KATHERINE FORBES IN 1870 AND FATHERED TWO DAUGHTERS.

IN 1872, WILL WAS GIVEN THE RANK OF COMMANDER. AT AGE 29, HE WAS THE YOUNGEST COMMANDER THE U.S. NAVY HAD EVER HAD.

WILL CUSHING DIED ON DECEMBER 17, 1874, POSSIBLY AS A RESULT OF RUPTURED DISCS AND AN INFLAMED SCIATIC NERVE, INJURIES HE SUSTAINED ON THE ALBEMARLE MISSION.

WILL CUSHING HAS BEEN CALLED "*LINCOLN'S COMMANDO*," AND WAS A FORERUNNER OF THE MODERN NAVY *SEAL*, FIGHTING AND RAIDING ON LAND AND SEA.

JOHN ERICSSON (1803-1889)
WAS ONE OF THE GREAT ENGINEERS OF THE STEAM AGE. HE WAS BORN IN VARMLAND, SWEDEN. AS A YOUNG MAN, HE SERVED AS AN OFFICER IN THE SWEDISH ARMY. THROUGHOUT HIS LIFE, HE PREFERRED TO BE ADDRESSED BY HIS MILITARY RANK, *CAPTAIN* ERICSSON.

IN 1826, HE MOVED TO ENGLAND WHERE HE BEGAN WORKING ON STEAM ENGINES. HE DESIGNED A STEAM-POWERED LOCOMOTIVE CALLED *NOVELTY.*

IT WAS LIGHT AND VERY FAST (IT COULD GO **28** MILES PER HOUR!). HE ENTERED IT INTO A CONTEST CALLED THE *RAINHILL TRIALS.* IT WAS THE FASTEST LOCOMOTIVE IN THE RACE. UNFORTUNATELY, *NOVELTY* HAD TO DROP OUT, DUE TO BOILER PROBLEMS.

IN 1839 JOHN LEFT ENGLAND AND MOVED TO NEW YORK, WHERE HE BEGAN WORKING WITH THE NAVY ON SCREW PROPELLERS. IT WAS THERE THAT THE FAMOUS ACCIDENT WITH THE *PEACEMAKER* HAPPENED. IT WOULD BE MANY YEARS BEFORE JOHN WORKED WITH THE U.S. NAVY AGAIN. LUCKILY HE DID, AND BUILT THE *U.S.S. MONITOR* IN **118** DAYS.

HE INVENTED MANY OTHER WARSHIPS, INCLUDING THE FIRST *DESTROYER.* HE EVEN EXPERIMENTED WITH SOLAR POWER!

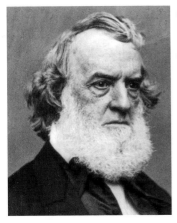

GIDEON WELLES (1802-1878), AKA *"FATHER NEPTUNE,"*
WORKED AS A LAWYER, A NEWSPAPER EDITOR, A POSTMASTER, AN ACCOUNTANT, AND A MEMBER OF THE CONNECTICUT LEGISLATURE BEFORE BECOMING LINCOLN'S SECRETARY OF THE NAVY. HIS BLOCKADE CHOKED SOUTHERN TRADE ROUTES AND HELPED WIN THE WAR.

FATHER NEPTUNE HATED SLAVERY AND GAVE HIS OFFICERS STANDING ORDERS TO OFFER PROTECTION TO RUNAWAY SLAVES.

HE RETIRED FROM THE CABINET IN 1869. HE DIED AT AGE 75.

AND, YES, THAT *IS* A WIG.

STEPHEN RUSSELL MALLORY (1812-1873)
AKA "SHARKFACE" AKA "BINGO FISHPUNCHER-- HUH? WHILE "FATHER NEPTUNE" WAS A NICKNAME REPORTEDLY GIVEN BY PRESIDENT LINCOLN TO GIDEON WELLES, "SHARKFACE" HAS NO CLAIMS ON HISTORICAL ACCURACY. THAT NICKNAME WAS MADE UP BY THE AUTHOR OF THIS BOOK. SO WAS "BINGO FISHPUNCHER," WHICH DOESN'T EVEN APPEAR IN THE STORY. BUT IT'S FUN TO SAY. TRY IT.

STEPHEN MALLORY WAS BORN IN BRITISH TRINIDAD. HE MOVED TO FLORIDA, WHERE HE BECAME A STATE SENATOR. HE JOINED THE COMMITTEE ON NAVAL AFFAIRS, WHERE HE LOBBIED CONGRESS FOR A RETURN TO *FLOGGING* (WHIPPING DISOBEDIENT SAILORS). HE LOST. HIS ENTHUSIASM FOR IRONCLAD SHIPS PUSHED TECHNOLOGY FORWARD AND USHERED IN THE AGE OF IRON WARSHIPS.

HE WAS ARRESTED AFTER THE WAR AND CHARGED WITH TREASON. HE WAS JAILED FOR TEN MONTHS BUT NEVER BROUGHT TO TRIAL.

HE WAS MARRIED TO ANGELA MORENO AND WAS THE FATHER OF NINE CHILDREN (ONE WAS NAMED *ATTILA* -- REALLY!).

THE U.S.S. MONITOR
THE MONITOR SANK IN A STORM NEAR CAPE HATTERAS, NORTH CAROLINA, IN 1862 (ON NEW YEAR'S EVE). SIXTEEN CREW MEMBERS WENT DOWN WITH HER.

IN THE SUMMER OF 2002, THE MONITOR'S TURRET WAS RECOVERED! THE ROTATING GUN TOWER REMAINED INTACT UNDER 250 FEET OF WATER. IT WAS RAISED AND CARRIED TO THE **MARINERS' MUSEUM** IN VIRGINIA. THE MUSEUM HOPES TO PUT THE TURRET ON DISPLAY IN 2026, AFTER THEY SCRAPE OFF ALL OF THE BARNACLES AND STORE IT IN A FRESH-WATER TANK FOR 15 YEARS.

JOHN LORIMER WORDEN (1818-1897)

CAPTAIN OF THE *MONITOR,* AKA "THE GUY WHO GOT SHELLED IN THE FACE DURING THE DUEL OF THE IRONCLADS."

JOHN WORDEN RECOVERED FROM HIS CANNON BLAST WOUNDS AND WENT ON TO CAPTAIN THE MONITOR CLASS *U.S.S. MONTAUK.* HE SANK THE *RATTLESNAKE,* A REBEL PRIVATEER. HE ALSO TOOK PART IN THE ATTACK ON CHARLESTON, SOUTH CAROLINA.

JOHN WORDEN RECEIVED THE **"THANKS OF CONGRESS."** HE AND WILL CUSHING WERE THE ONLY NAVAL OFFICERS OF THE CIVIL WAR TO RECEIVE THE HONOR.

GUSTAVUS FOX (1821-1883)

ASSISTANT SECRETARY OF THE NAVY, AKA "THAT CUTE LI'L FOX!"

GUSTAVUS FOX WAS GIDEON WELLES' RIGHT-HAND MAMMAL (ER, *MAN*), AND HELPED BUILD THE UNION'S BLOCKADE. AS A YOUNG FOX, HE SERVED IN THE MEXICAN-AMERICAN WAR AS A MIDSHIPMAN. AFTER THE CIVIL WAR, HE CROSSED THE ATLANTIC IN A MONITOR CLASS SHIP, THE *U.S.S. MIANTONOMOH.*

WINFIELD SCOTT (1786-1866)

GENERAL-IN-CHIEF OF THE UNION ARMY, AKA "THE GRAND OLD MAN OF THE ARMY" AKA "OLD FUSS AND FEATHERS" (YES, THESE *ARE* HISTORICAL NICKNAMES) AKA "THE GUY WHO KEPT SHOUTING **ANACONDA!**"

WINFIELD SCOTT WAS A HERO OF THE MEXICAN-AMERICAN WAR. BEFORE THAT HE FOUGHT IN THE BLACK HAWK WAR, THE SECOND SEMINOLE WAR, THE CREEK WAR AND THE WAR OF 1812. IN FACT, WINFIELD SCOTT SERVED UNDER EVERY PRESIDENT FROM THOMAS JEFFERSON TO ABRAHAM LINCOLN-- THAT'S **FOURTEEN** PRESIDENTS! HE EVEN RAN FOR PRESIDENT IN 1852. HE HOLDS THE RECORD FOR *LONGEST-SERVING AMERICAN GENERAL EVER.*

HE WAS 6'5" TALL. AT THE START OF THE CIVIL WAR, AT AGE 74, HE WEIGHED OVER 300 LBS. HIS HEALTH DIDN'T ALLOW HIM TO STAY IN COMMAND THROUGH THE WAR. HE RETIRED AND GENERAL GEORGE B. McCLELLAN TOOK OVER. BUT SCOTT DID LIVE TO SEE THE UNION WIN THE WAR (WITH THE HELP OF HIS ANACONDA PLAN).

FRANKLIN BUCHANAN (1800-1874)

CAPTAIN OF THE *C.S.S. VIRGINIA*, AKA "THE GUY WHO GOT SHOT IN THE LEG WHEN HE WENT OUT OF THE HATCH."

FRANKLIN BUCHANAN RECOVERED FROM HIS WOUND AND WAS PROMOTED TO ADMIRAL. HE WAS CAPTURED WHILE ON BOARD THE IRONCLAD *C.S.S. TENNESSEE* DURING THE BATTLE OF MOBILE BAY AND HELD PRISONER UNTIL THE END OF THE WAR.

CATESBY AP ROGER JONES (1821-1877)

LIEUTENANT ON THE *C.S.S. VIRGINIA*, AKA "THE GUY WHO TOOK OVER AFTER CAPTAIN BUCHANAN WAS SHOT IN THE LEG."

WHILE BUCHANAN WAS RESPONSIBLE FOR SINKING THE *U.S.S. CUMBERLAND* AND THE *U.S.S. CONGRESS*, CATESBY AP ROGER JONES WAS IN COMMAND FOR THE FAMOUS DUEL OF THE IRONCLADS.

AND THAT'S NOT A TYPO, HIS NAME REALLY WAS **CATESBY AP ROGER JONES.** "AP," IT'S A WELSH THING.

ABRAHAM LINCOLN (1809-1865)

HE WAS ABRAHAM LINCOLN. YOU SHOULD ALREADY KNOW ABOUT HIM!

SO THIS IS WHAT FOX REALLY LOOKED LIKE?
HE'S STILL SORT OF CUTE AND CUDDLY.
GUSTAVUS FOX

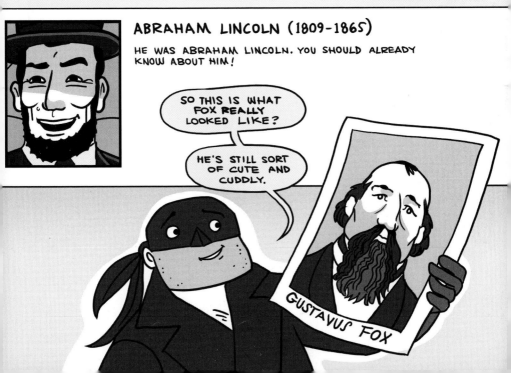

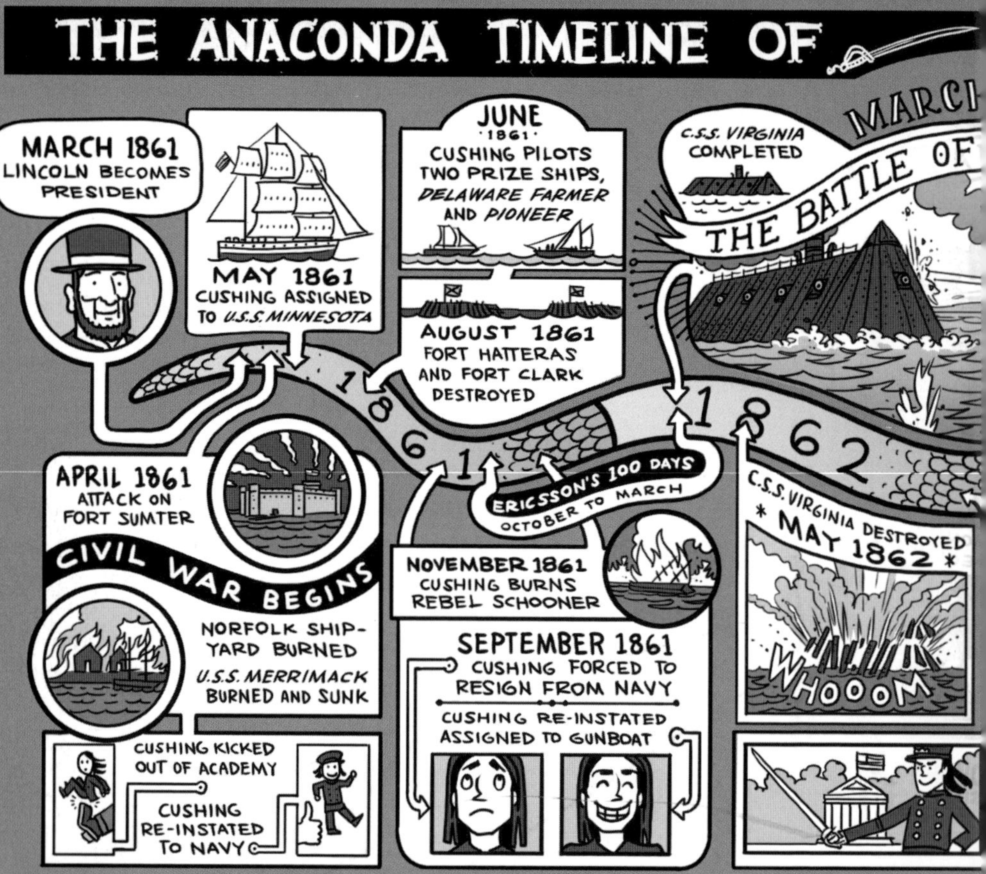
THE ANACONDA TIMELINE OF
MARCH 1861
LINCOLN BECOMES PRESIDENT
MAY 1861
CUSHING ASSIGNED TO U.S.S. MINNESOTA
JUNE 1861
CUSHING PILOTS TWO PRIZE SHIPS, DELAWARE FARMER AND PIONEER
AUGUST 1861
FORT HATTERAS AND FORT CLARK DESTROYED
C.S.S. VIRGINIA COMPLETED
THE BATTLE OF
1861
1862
APRIL 1861
ATTACK ON FORT SUMTER
CIVIL WAR BEGINS
NORFOLK SHIP-YARD BURNED
U.S.S. MERRIMACK BURNED AND SUNK
CUSHING KICKED OUT OF ACADEMY
CUSHING RE-INSTATED TO NAVY
ERICSSON'S 100 DAYS
OCTOBER TO MARCH
NOVEMBER 1861
CUSHING BURNS REBEL SCHOONER
SEPTEMBER 1861
CUSHING FORCED TO RESIGN FROM NAVY
CUSHING RE-INSTATED ASSIGNED TO GUNBOAT
C.S.S. VIRGINIA DESTROYED
* MAY 1862 *
WHOOOM

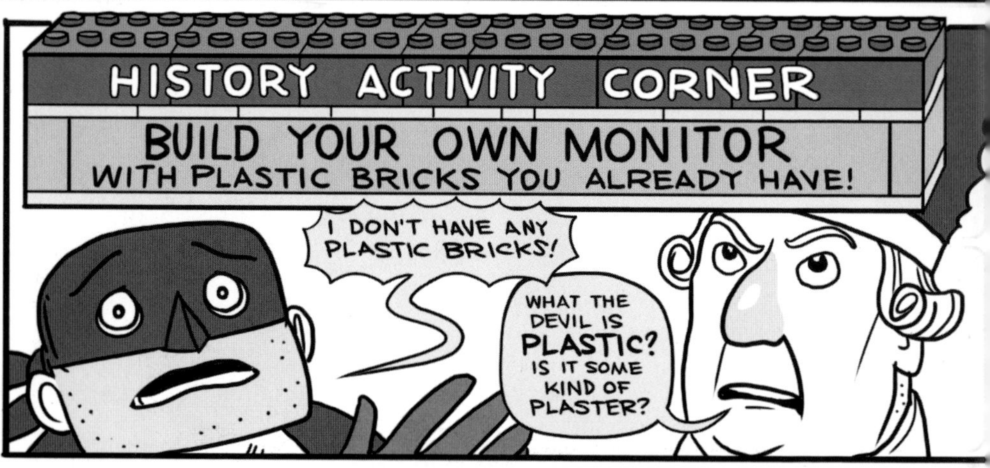
HISTORY ACTIVITY CORNER
BUILD YOUR OWN MONITOR
WITH PLASTIC BRICKS YOU ALREADY HAVE!
I DON'T HAVE ANY PLASTIC BRICKS!
WHAT THE DEVIL IS PLASTIC? IS IT SOME KIND OF PLASTER?

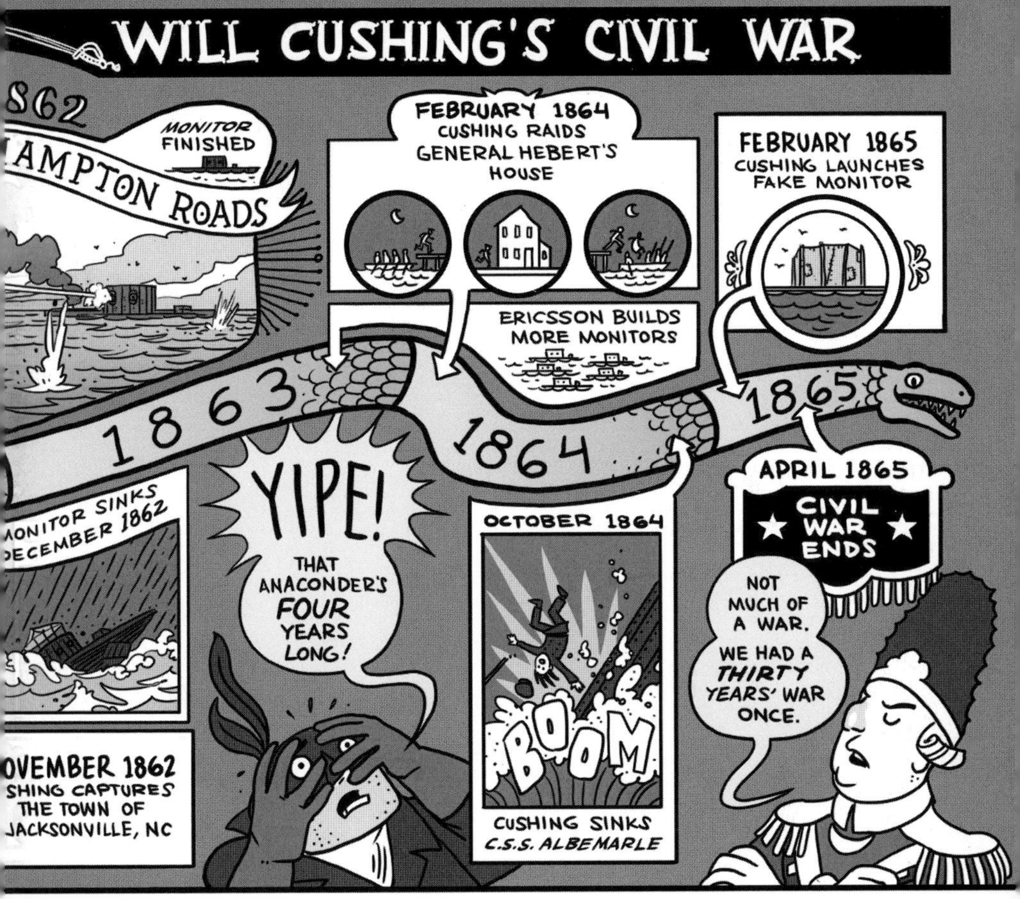

WILL CUSHING'S CIVIL WAR
862
MONITOR FINISHED
AMPTON ROADS
FEBRUARY 1864 CUSHING RAIDS GENERAL HEBERT'S HOUSE
ERICSSON BUILDS MORE MONITORS
FEBRUARY 1865 CUSHING LAUNCHES FAKE MONITOR
1863
1864
1865
MONITOR SINKS DECEMBER 1862
YIPE!
THAT ANACONDER'S FOUR YEARS LONG!
OCTOBER 1864
BOOM
CUSHING SINKS C.S.S. ALBEMARLE
APRIL 1865
CIVIL WAR ENDS
NOT MUCH OF A WAR.
WE HAD A THIRTY YEARS' WAR ONCE.
OVEMBER 1862 SHING CAPTURES THE TOWN OF JACKSONVILLE, NC

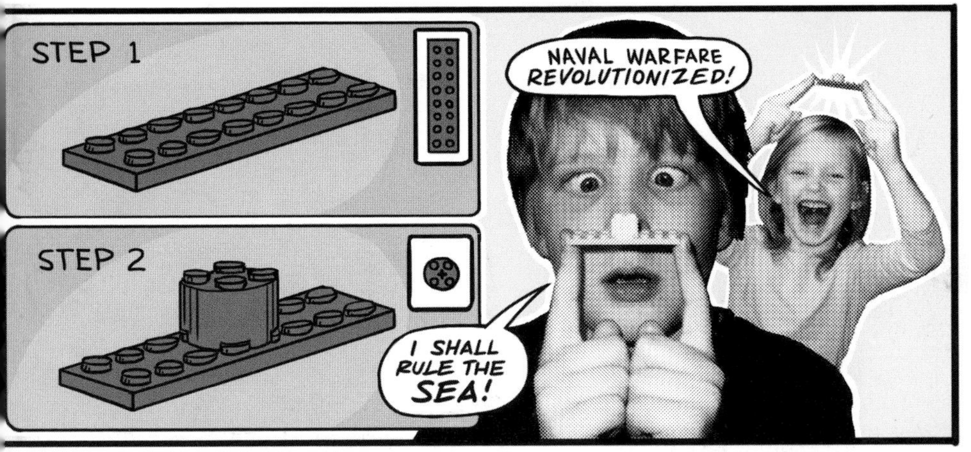

STEP 1
STEP 2
NAVAL WARFARE REVOLUTIONIZED!
I SHALL RULE THE SEA!

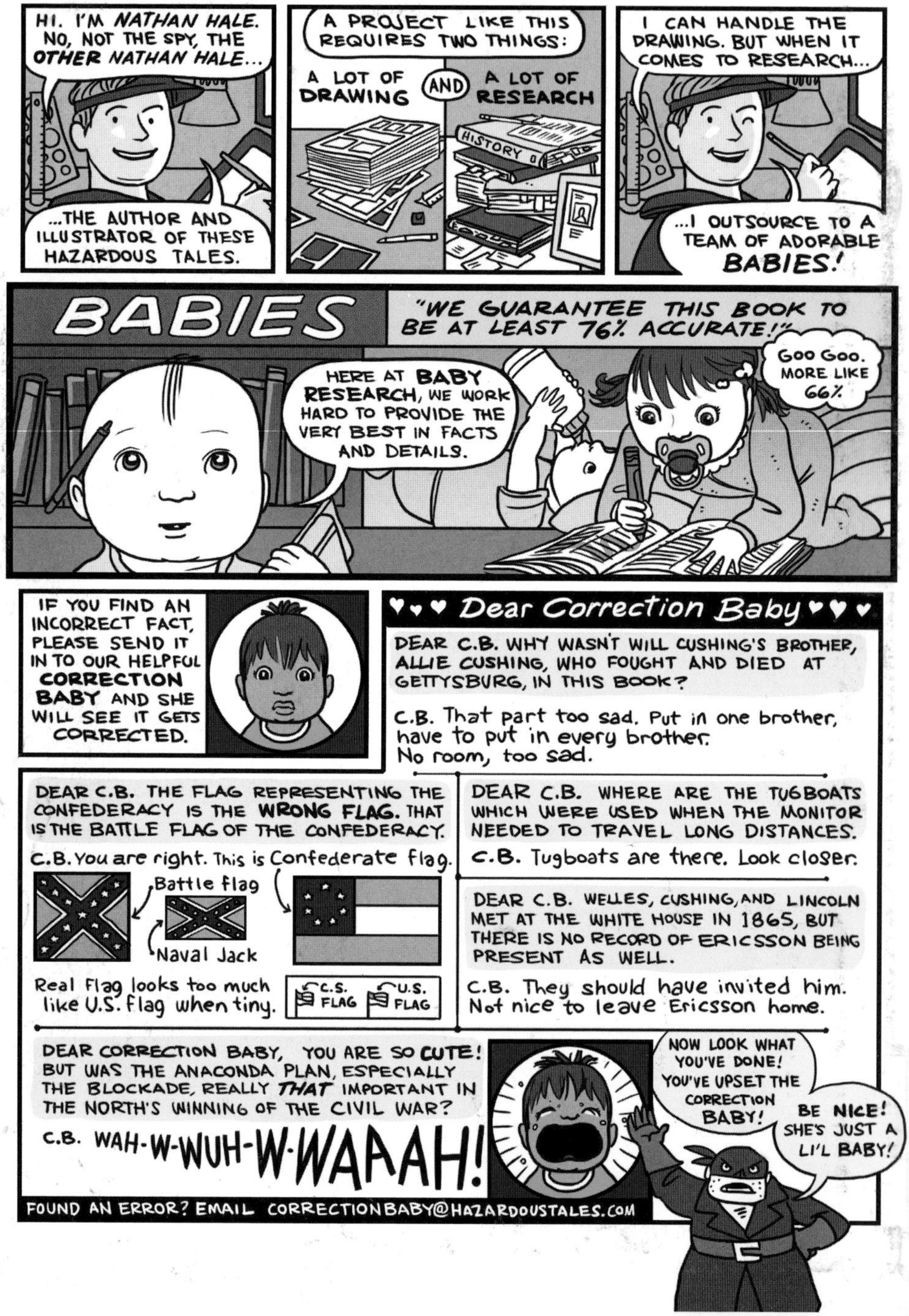

HI. I'M NATHAN HALE. NO, NOT THE SPY, THE OTHER NATHAN HALE...
...THE AUTHOR AND ILLUSTRATOR OF THESE HAZARDOUS TALES.
A PROJECT LIKE THIS REQUIRES TWO THINGS:
A LOT OF DRAWING
AND
A LOT OF RESEARCH
HISTORY
I CAN HANDLE THE DRAWING. BUT WHEN IT COMES TO RESEARCH...
...I OUTSOURCE TO A TEAM OF ADORABLE BABIES!
BABIES
"WE GUARANTEE THIS BOOK TO BE AT LEAST 76% ACCURATE!"
HERE AT BABY RESEARCH, WE WORK HARD TO PROVIDE THE VERY BEST IN FACTS AND DETAILS.
GOO GOO. MORE LIKE 66%
IF YOU FIND AN INCORRECT FACT, PLEASE SEND IT IN TO OUR HELPFUL CORRECTION BABY AND SHE WILL SEE IT GETS CORRECTED.
Dear Correction Baby
DEAR C.B. WHY WASN'T WILL CUSHING'S BROTHER, ALLIE CUSHING, WHO FOUGHT AND DIED AT GETTYSBURG, IN THIS BOOK?
C.B. That part too sad. Put in one brother, have to put in every brother. No room, too sad.
DEAR C.B. THE FLAG REPRESENTING THE CONFEDERACY IS THE WRONG FLAG. THAT IS THE BATTLE FLAG OF THE CONFEDERACY.
C.B. You are right. This is Confederate flag.
Battle flag
Naval Jack
Real flag looks too much like U.S. flag when tiny.
C.S. FLAG
U.S. FLAG
DEAR C.B. WHERE ARE THE TUGBOATS WHICH WERE USED WHEN THE MONITOR NEEDED TO TRAVEL LONG DISTANCES.
C.B. Tugboats are there. Look closer.
DEAR C.B. WELLES, CUSHING, AND LINCOLN MET AT THE WHITE HOUSE IN 1865, BUT THERE IS NO RECORD OF ERICSSON BEING PRESENT AS WELL.
C.B. They should have invited him. Not nice to leave Ericsson home.
DEAR CORRECTION BABY, YOU ARE SO CUTE! BUT WAS THE ANACONDA PLAN, ESPECIALLY THE BLOCKADE, REALLY THAT IMPORTANT IN THE NORTH'S WINNING OF THE CIVIL WAR?
C.B. WAH-W-WUH-W-WAAAH!
NOW LOOK WHAT YOU'VE DONE! YOU'VE UPSET THE CORRECTION BABY!
BE NICE! SHE'S JUST A LI'L BABY!
FOUND AN ERROR? EMAIL CORRECTIONBABY@HAZARDOUSTALES.COM

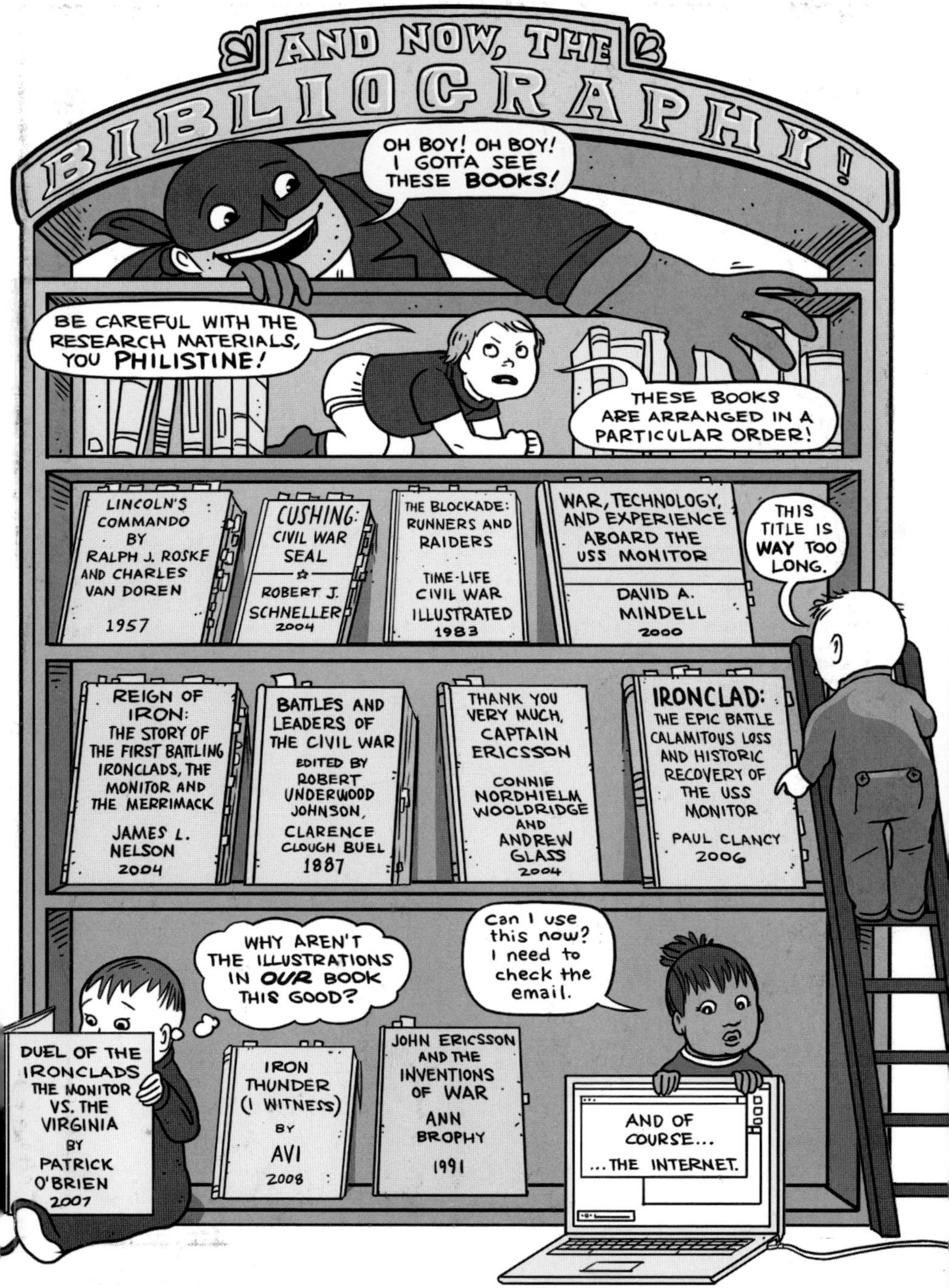

AND NOW, THE BIBLIOGRAPHY!
OH BOY! OH BOY! I GOTTA SEE THESE BOOKS!
BE CAREFUL WITH THE RESEARCH MATERIALS, YOU PHILISTINE!
THESE BOOKS ARE ARRANGED IN A PARTICULAR ORDER!
LINCOLN'S COMMANDO BY RALPH J. ROSKE AND CHARLES VAN DOREN 1957
CUSHING: CIVIL WAR SEAL ROBERT J. SCHNELLER 2004
THE BLOCKADE: RUNNERS AND RAIDERS TIME-LIFE CIVIL WAR ILLUSTRATED 1983
WAR, TECHNOLOGY, AND EXPERIENCE ABOARD THE USS MONITOR DAVID A. MINDELL 2000
THIS TITLE IS WAY TOO LONG.
REIGN OF IRON: THE STORY OF THE FIRST BATTLING IRONCLADS, THE MONITOR AND THE MERRIMACK JAMES L. NELSON 2004
BATTLES AND LEADERS OF THE CIVIL WAR EDITED BY ROBERT UNDERWOOD JOHNSON, CLARENCE CLOUGH BUEL 1887
THANK YOU VERY MUCH, CAPTAIN ERICSSON CONNIE NORDHIELM WOOLDRIDGE AND ANDREW GLASS 2004
IRONCLAD: THE EPIC BATTLE CALAMITOUS LOSS AND HISTORIC RECOVERY OF THE USS MONITOR PAUL CLANCY 2006
WHY AREN'T THE ILLUSTRATIONS IN OUR BOOK THIS GOOD?
Can I use this now? I need to check the email.
DUEL OF THE IRONCLADS THE MONITOR VS. THE VIRGINIA BY PATRICK O'BRIEN 2007
IRON THUNDER (I WITNESS) BY AVI 2008
JOHN ERICSSON AND THE INVENTIONS OF WAR ANN BROPHY 1991
AND OF COURSE... ...THE INTERNET.

THE SPY NATHAN HALE
WAS EXECUTED IN 1776.

THE ***AUTHOR*** NATHAN HALE
WAS **BORN** IN 1976.

THIS IS THE **THIRD** GRAPHIC NOVEL NATHAN HALE HAS ILLUSTRATED. THE FIRST WAS EISNER-NOMINATED **RAPUNZEL'S REVENGE,** BY SHANNON AND DEAN HALE, FOLLOWED BY ITS SEQUEL, **CALAMITY JACK.** THE FOURTH WAS **ONE DEAD SPY.**

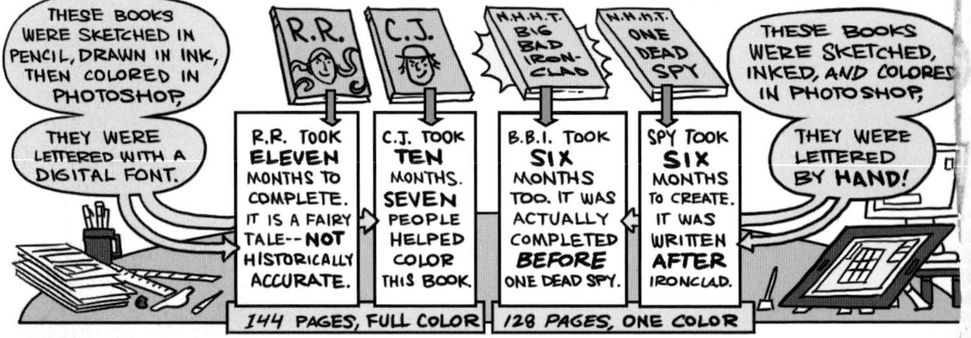

THESE BOOKS WERE SKETCHED IN PENCIL, DRAWN IN INK, THEN COLORED IN PHOTOSHOP,
THEY WERE LETTERED WITH A DIGITAL FONT.
R.R.
C.J.
N.H.H.T. BIG BAD IRON-CLAD
N.H.H.T. ONE DEAD SPY
R.R. TOOK ELEVEN MONTHS TO COMPLETE. IT IS A FAIRY TALE--NOT HISTORICALLY ACCURATE.
C.J. TOOK TEN MONTHS. SEVEN PEOPLE HELPED COLOR THIS BOOK.
B.B.I. TOOK SIX MONTHS TOO. IT WAS ACTUALLY COMPLETED BEFORE ONE DEAD SPY.
SPY TOOK SIX MONTHS TO CREATE. IT WAS WRITTEN AFTER IRONCLAD.
THESE BOOKS WERE SKETCHED, INKED, AND COLORED IN PHOTOSHOP,
THEY WERE LETTERED BY HAND!
144 PAGES, FULL COLOR
128 PAGES, ONE COLOR

FUN FACT: MOST OF THIS BOOK WAS CREATED *LATE* AT NIGHT. THE AUTHOR WAS EXPERIMENTING WITH A **REVERSE CIRCADIAN** NIGHT CYCLE (SLEEPING DURING THE DAY, WORKING AT NIGHT.)

THE PRIMARY **SNACK** CONSUMED DURING THIS PROJECT WAS THE **CRACKED PEPPER SUNFLOWER SEED.**

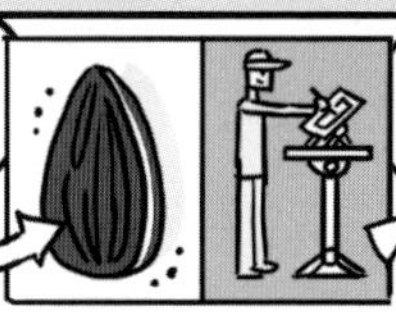

THIS BOOK WAS DRAWN ENTIRELY IN THE **STANDING** POSITION, WITH HELP FROM A **VERY TALL DESK.**

THE AUTHOR WOULD LIKE TO THANK HIS FAMILY FOR SUPPORTING HIS BIZARRE LATE-NIGHT WORK HABITS.

NATHAN LIVES IN THE MOUNTAINS OF **UTAH** WITH HIS WIFE AND TWO CHILDREN. HE POSTS WEEKDAY COMICS ON HIS WEBSITE:
WWW.SPACESTATIONNATHAN.COM

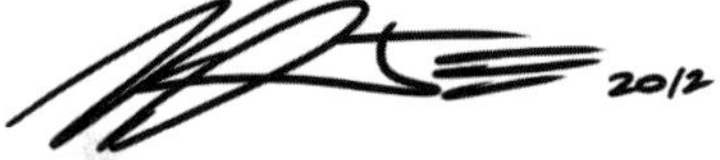

2012